General Rowland Hill

General Rowland Hill
Wellington's Trusted Commander of Brigade, Division & Corps.

Rev. Edwin Sidney

With a Short Biography of Lord Hill by Alexander Innes Shand

General Rowland Hill
Wellington's Trusted Commander of Brigade, Division & Corps.
by Rev. Edwin Sidney edited by the Leonaur Editors
With a Short Biography of Lord Hill by Alexander Innes Shand

FIRST EDITION

Leonaur is an imprint of Oakpast Ltd
Copyright in this form © 2014 Oakpast Ltd

ISBN: 978-1-78282-391-9 (hardcover)
ISBN: 978-1-78282-392-6 (softcover)

http://www.leonaur.com

Publisher's Notes

The views expressed in this book are not necessarily those of the publisher.

Contents

The Hill Family	7
Change in Colonel Hill's Plans	26
Colonel Hill Arrives in England, April 1, 1802	40
General Hill Brings Home Troops to Plymouth	52
General Hill Takes the Command	71
Abrantes	98
General Hill's Return to the Army	127
Sir Rowland Marches to Join Lord Wellington	157
Battle of Vittoria	179
Abdication of Bonaparte	208
Lord Hill Arrives in London	229
Lord Hill: A Short Biography	251

LORD HILL'S COLUMN AT SHREWSBURY

CHAPTER 1

The Hill Family

The patriotism and benevolence so admirably blended together in the character of the late Lord Hill, were the fruits of a rare union of firmness and kindness which has distinguished other eminent members of the same family, and may be said to be a property of their race. It obtained for Richard "the Great Hill" the confidence of his sovereigns, respect in courtly circles, success in his diplomatic undertakings, influence with the army, attention from the legislature of his native realm, and the esteem of all classes of society. The same excellence raised the first Sir Rowland Hill—a column to whose memory adorns the romantic park at Hawkstone—to the enviable honour of being the first Protestant Lord Mayor of the city of London. He was truly designated "a grave and worthy father of the citye," for by his munificence he added to its approaches, and by his charities enriched its hospitals.

When sheriff, he was committed to the Tower for a defence of what he believed to be its privileges, against the power of Parliament; but his high reputation quickly moved the Speaker and the Commons to give him his release. He embellished his native county with religious and useful erections, and made the homes of his tenants happy by his liberality as a landlord. The exemplary and illustrious nobleman whose life will form the subject of these pages was the inheritor of his name, and of his virtues, with a wider scope for their development. In my biographies of two eminent members of his family, the Rev. Rowland Hill, and Sir Richard Hill, M.P, for Shropshire, I have shown the antiquity of his descent, and exhibited the claims of his ancestors and cotemporary relatives, to the respect of the nation and the gratitude of their own county. I shall therefore proceed at once to trace that brilliant and modest career, which terminated in his elevation to the command in chief of the forces of Great Britain, and led to the rank of Viscount in the peerage, with descent to the representative of the elder branch of the house of Hawkstone.

The retired village of Prees, in Shropshire, has the honour of being the birth-place of this amiable and brave man, where his father, Mr. John Hill, who succeeded to the title and estates of his brother Sir Richard Hill, occupied the Hall, till the decease of the latter placed him in possession of the mansion of his family. He married Mary, the youngest daughter of John Chambre, Esquire, of Petton, in the county of Salop, and was the father of no less than sixteen children. Their names and order of birth are as follow:—John, Mary, Jane, Rowland, the subject of this memoir, Richard, Elizabeth Hannah, who died in infancy, Elizabeth, Harriet, Robert Chambre, Francis Brian, Emma, Clement, Charles, who died an infant, Thomas Noel, William Henry, who died while yet a child, and Edward.

Such was the numerous progeny of the parents of the late Lord Hill, five of whom the aged father was permitted to see survivors of the great conflict of Waterloo, while he himself was welcomed at court by George the Fourth, then Prince Regent, with the gratifying salutation, "I am glad, indeed, to see the father of so many brave sons." It appears, from the list just given, that Lord Hill was the second son and fourth child of his attached parents. He was born at the Hall, in the village before mentioned, about three miles from Hawkstone, and in the same county, on the 11th of August, 1772, and was nearly three years junior to his brother John, whose birthday was the 10th of October, 1769. The characteristic qualities of their minds were extremely similar, and both commenced life with the choice of the profession of a soldier.

Mr. John Hill entered the Royal Horse Guards, Blue, and was engaged on foreign service in Flanders, under the command of His Late Royal Highness the Duke of York. His brother Rowland said of him that "he was sure if Jack had *fair play*, he would manage half a dozen Frenchmen;" and that those in office entertained the same opinion, is demonstrated by the fact of his being promoted to the rank of field officer in the 25th Light Dragoons. On his marriage to Elizabeth Rodes, daughter of Philip Cornish, Esquire, of Exeter, he yielded to the earnest solicitations of his relatives, and quitted the army, but employed his military knowledge in raising and organising an effective regiment of Volunteer Cavalry in his native county.

At the same time he discharged the various duties of a country gentleman, in a manner that won him the respect of all classes, exhibited in gratifying testimonials while he lived, and in unequivocal marks of universal regret when it pleased God to remove him. This unhappy event happened in the month of January, 1814; and his loss was most sincerely lamented. He left a widow with five sons, the eldest of whom is the present Viscount Hill, and two daughters. Their bereaved mother, a person of much energy and true piety, found comfort, while she displayed consummate judgment, in daily vigilance over her children. I shall reserve further particulars of the interesting group now presented to the notice of the reader, until the appropriate periods pass under review in the course of this narrative, and at once resume the history of the opening day of Lord Hill.

The charm of biography is in making the subject of it speak as much as possible for himself; and fortunately Lord Hill, in the quietude of peace, drew up a memorial of his early life, from which I shall frequently have the advantage of quoting. It is dated March 25, 1822, and is entitled *Memorandum from Authentic Papers and Recollections*. He commenced it thus:

> I was born August 11th, 1772. At the age of seven or eight I was sent to Ightfield School, where I remained about one year. From thence I was sent to Mr. Vanburgh's and Mr. Winfield's[1] schools at Chester, where I continued till I was seventeen.

Both at Ightfield, which is a village in Shropshire, where he was under the instruction of a clergyman named Edwards, and at Chester, for a time, he had the advantage of numbering his brother John amongst his schoolfellows. Young Rowland manifested at this stage of life those attractive qualities of heart and manner, which caused him to be the object of such extensive esteem both in private and public during his long and arduous career. He was a great favourite with Mr. and Mrs. Winfield, and his straightforward disposition gained him the confidence of the whole school. Major Cotton of Chester, who was one of the boys there with him, says,

> He was extremely good-natured and amiable, ever ready to assist a lad out of a scrape, and never tumbled into one himself.

He also pleasantly describes him as "toiling through the week's work, without ever coming in contact with *Doctor Birch* or his partner *Supple Jack*."

---

1. Mr. Winfield was a clergyman, and second master to the Rev. Robert Vanburgh. When Mr. Winfield married in 1783, the two Hills, John and Rowland, with some other boys, were removed and placed under his care.

The Dean of Bangor, who was also at school with him at Chester, of which place his father was Dean, testifies, "He was a boy of gentle, unaffected manners, beloved by all the younger boys, and ever the friend of the oppressed." He was naturally diffident and reserved, but always willing to join in school sports, and to contribute to the amusement of others, cheerfully assisting his juniors in any little objects they had in hand. This diffidence was not the result of timidity, but was only part of that gentleness of nature which rendered the contrast of his heroism the more brilliant, just as the simplest setting displays to most advantage the beauty of some precious jewel.

It was not fear, but keen sensibility, in regarding the troubles of others; and being coupled with a delicate constitution, it caused his friends some solicitude. He required many little indulgences, which brought him under the constant notice of Mrs. Winfield, whose almost maternal kindness he never forgot as long as he lived. She was spared to see him in the high situation of Commander-in-Chief; and his attentions to her at that time will be mentioned when we arrive at the proper place for their introduction. Miss Winfield, in an interesting communication of what she had heard her parents relate of him, says:

> He was remarkable for the mildness and equanimity of his temper, and his kindness and sensibility to the feelings of others were evident upon all occasions. His delicate health frequently prevented him joining in the athletic exercises of his more robust companions; but his little garden, and his numerous pet animals, testified his systematic care and attention, by their succeeding better than those of his schoolfellows. My mother used to say, 'Everything that Rowland Hill undertook prospered.'

With regard to his fondness for his garden, and his love of animals, if Miss Winfield had written the account of his rural pleasures in later life, she could not have hit upon subjects more characteristic of him. His garden at Hardwick was the most productive for its size I have ever seen, and he constantly won the best prizes at the Salop Horticultural shows; while his fondness for tame animals of all descriptions, and his delight in exhibiting them and watching them, are notorious to his friends. With respect to the tenderness of his spirit, Miss Winfield further observes:

> His sensibility was almost feminine. One of the boys happened to cut his finger, and was brought by Rowland Hill to my mother to have it dressed; but her attention was soon drawn

from the wound to Rowland, who had fainted.

Mrs. Winfield, happening to see him on a visit to Chester—for he invariably sought her out at every opportunity—after one of his achievements in the war, brought this fact to his recollection, remarking that she wondered how he could have acted with such coolness and vigour in the midst of the dreadful scenes of carnage surrounding him. He replied:

> I have still the same feelings; but in the excitement of battle all individual sensation is lost sight of.

Just before he joined his regiment for the first time, he sickened at the sight of a human heart preserved in spirits, shown him by his medical attendant; and after he had entered on his military duties he was unable to look at a prize-fight between Humphries and Mendoza, near the windows of his lodging, and was taken out fainting from the room. No common observer would have imagined for an instant that the army could have been his choice; yet as every one knows that bully and coward may be almost placed in the list of synonyms, so gentleness and bravery, sensibility and courage, and we may add humility and piety, are capable of a similar classification.

In the spring of the year 1790 his parents suggested to him the choice of some profession, and seemed desirous that he should adopt that of the law. His reply still remains in the original letter he addressed to his mother from Chester, on the 6th of March in that year. An extract from it will exhibit his own view. He wrote:

> Last Wednesday I received your very kind letter, in which you desired I would let you know what profession I should really like best. I know it is yours and Papa's wish that I should be in the law, but I hope you will forgive me if I say I should not like that line of life; for, indeed, I have a dislike to the law, and am sure I should neither be happy nor make any figure, as a lawyer. The profession which I should like best, and I hope you and Papa will not object to, is the army.

To this letter, which was transmitted to his father, that kind-hearted and affectionate parent replied in the following terms:—

> My dear Rowland,
> Your mother sent me the letter you wrote her, whereby. I find you wish to decline following the line of life we had chalked

out for you, and expressing a wish to go into the army. Now, my dear lad, do not think me in the least angry with you for coming to this resolution, but rather glad that you have declared your sentiments, though I wish they had been for what was struck out for you, as I think your prospect of comfort and happiness, and perhaps cutting a figure in life, would have been much greater in the former than in the latter line. You know my situation, and that I can do very little more for my numerous family than putting them in a way to get their living, and giving them the best advice in my power.

Immediately on seeing your letter, I consulted those whom I thought most likely to inform me on the best plan for a young man to pursue who went into the army. What is most recommended is to go to a foreign academy for about two years, where strict attention to the several studies necessary to cut any figure in the profession must be attended to. By great favour, a commission may be purchased before you go abroad, with leave of absence, whereby you may stand a chance of creeping a little forward towards rank, the same as if you was with the regiment. This, to be sure, is a more expensive plan than I can well afford; but as I have not a doubt but you will make every proper return, I will exert myself to put it, or something of the sort, into execution (provided you continue in your present resolution); for I much dread the idea of a young man starting in any line of life without his being determined to use his utmost endeavours to advance in it, which I am well assured no one can in the military line, any more than any other, without a proper previous education.

It is true, a commission may be purchased for a few hundreds: but what a miserable situation for a young man of spirit, with scarce any thing but three and sixpence per day, to saunter about from town to town, unless he has a good prospect of advancing from it. I returned from London last night, but shall go back again in the Easter week, when some plan for you must be determined on. In the meanwhile seriously reflect upon what I have said above, and believe me to be

  Your sincere friend, as well as
   Your most affectionate father,
               J. H.

I think I will ask Mr. Winfield to let you come over to Prees for a very few days at Easter. It is, at all events, probable you will not leave him before Midsummer. Do attend as much as possible to your French.

After this judicious statement of his views, Mr. Hill speedily obtained the desired commission for his son. It is stated in Lord Hill's own memoranda:

> I got an ensigncy in the 38th Regiment, and obtained leave of absence to go to Strasburg, where I remained till the 24th of January, 1791, on which day my commission as Lieutenant in Captain Broughton's Independent Company is dated. During the time I was in this company I was quartered with it at Wrotham in Kent. On the 16th of March, 1791, I was appointed Lieutenant in the 53rd, or Shropshire Regiment of Foot. On receiving this appointment I obtained leave to return to Strasburg, and had not been there many weeks when Sir Richard Hill, Reverend Brian Hill, and my brother John came to Strasburg on their return to England from Italy. France at this time was much disturbed, and it was thought advisable that I should accompany Sir Richard to England, which I did, by a pleasant tour down the Rhine through Holland, Flanders, and the Netherlands. We arrived at Hawkstone the end of the summer.

The 38th Regiment, in which Lord Hill commenced the duties of a soldier, was commanded by Sir Robert Pigot: and he was exceedingly esteemed by all his brother officers. His worthy uncle and godfather, Sir Richard Hill, placed him in a military academy at Strasburg, with a view to his improvement in the knowledge of the profession which he had now embraced; and it was for this purpose, and not for any object of ease or pleasure, that his leave of absence was procured. As he advanced, it was not by favour but by service, for he added twelve men to Captain Broughton's Independent Company before he was promoted to a lieutenancy under that officer.[2]

At this time the relations alluded to by Lord Hill were on an extensive continental tour, and had left him engaged with his military studies, and gone to Venice.

Before they parted they were all put into high spirits by an amusing accident to Mr. Brian Hill. Their landlady, to do them honour,

---

2. Since Sir J. D. Broughton, Baronet.

insisted on bringing forth a bottle of special Champagne Mousseux from her own vineyard. Mr. Brian Hill happened to be close against the mouth of the bottle at the instant the cork was unloosed, and out it flew with the fury of a pistol-shot, and half the contents spirted over him. He looked as most men would, completely wetted, with no change of clothes unpacked, while the landlady, instead of making apologies, laughed vociferously, and cried out with evident delight, "*Monsieur, comment vous trouvez-vous?*" The good-natured sufferer then said, "I have the advantage of you all now, for I can boast of wearing a dress that has been washed in champagne." This cheerful party had scarcely reached Venice, before the subject of this incident wrote to his sister to mention that directions had been given to young Rowland to return home. His words are:

> The same post that brought yours brought one from Prees with information of Rowly's preferment. It was sent immediately to Strasburg with directions for him to return to England, where I presume he will go directly, unless he receives a letter from his father in the mean time to forbid him.

He did return to England, and, as he has stated, was quartered in Kent.

On his removal into the 53rd Regiment, at that time commanded by Major Mathews, his return to Strasburg was permitted for the sake of perfecting himself in military knowledge, until he was taken home, as he has recorded, by his relatives. His own account proceeds—

> I remained in Shropshire till the January following, and joined my regiment (the 53rd), on the 18th of that month, in Edinburgh Castle. We marched from thence about Midsummer to Ayr, where I was stationed about two months, and was then sent on detachment with a command of eighteen men to Ballantrae, where I remained till the end of 1792.

During this time of service in the North the amiable young officer won the regard of the whole regiment, and gave many indications of those meritorious qualities which shone forth so conspicuously as his star of fortune rose to a higher elevation.

A letter from Major Mathews to Sir Richard Hill has been preserved, which gives testimony to the truth of this assertion. It is as follows:—

Ayr, 12th Sept. 1792.

Sir,

Tempted by the opportunity, and encouraged to embrace it by the assurance of Lord Balgonie that it would not be disagreeable to you to hear from me, though I have not the honour of being known to you, I presume to take this liberty in justice to your nephew, Mr. Hill, of the 53rd Regiment, whom I have had under my particular observation and direction since he joined the regiment at Edinburgh, and who, desirous of paying his duty to you, accompanies Captain Houghton, of the 53rd, who will have the honour to deliver this to you, to Buxton. You, sir, are sufficiently acquainted with the many good qualities of this excellent young man, not to be under any apprehensions for his conduct when at a distance from you.

I nevertheless think it will be satisfactory to you, and to Mr. Hill, his father, to learn from me that, as an officer, his talents, disposition, and assiduity are of the most promising nature; and that his amiable manners, sweetness of temper, and uncommon propriety of conduct, have not only endeared him to the regiment, but procured him the most flattering attentions from an extensive circle of the first fashion in this country. And with regard to the regiment and myself, in a selfish point of view, it is with much regret that I look forward to the probability of our losing him ere very long; for, with the advantages which he possesses, it is scarcely to be expected that he will wait the common course of promotion in any one regiment. Whenever this shall happen, it will be very much lamented by us all, and by no one more than him who requests your forgiveness for the liberty he has taken, and who has the honour to subscribe himself, sir,

Your most obedient and most humble Servant,

R. Mathews, Maj. 53rd Regt.

It has rarely happened to anyone to be endowed with an equal firmness of purpose in pursuit of his own designs, combined with the same forgetfulness of self, which marked the conduct of him to whom such a tribute of regard was paid by his commanding officer. Throughout life his attention to others was as remarkable as his vigilance over his own interests. When invited, as a boy at school, to the deanery at Chester, his chief object was to divert the children of the family, who were younger than himself; and, though manly for his age, he would pass his afternoons in helping them to swim their little ships in a cistern on their father's premises, and in raising mimic storms for their enjoyment, evidently best pleased when he could most amuse others. Hence his presence always afforded gratification, and his departure was viewed with regret; while all reflecting persons who regarded his talents, marked him out in their opinions as one born to rise to eminence, and adorn it.

The prognostication of Major Mathews was soon verified. Determined to advance himself, Lieutenant Hill made a successful effort to raise his rank in the army. His own account continues—

> In the beginning of 1793 I raised an independent company, and on the 23rd of March in that year I got my commission as captain.
>
> The men were raised chiefly in Shropshire: they were approved of by General Fox, at Chatham.
>
> On the 12th of April I embarked with this company in the *Aurora* transport; arrived at Cork in the course of one week; marched from Cork, by orders from Sir David Dundas, about the end of April, to Belfast, where I delivered the men of my company over to the 38th Regiment, and returned to Shropshire about June.

During the short time he was in Ireland, where he was much noticed, he paid a visit to an eminent literary gentleman, well known as one of the most brilliant sons of Erin. I remember his telling me, that, on going to his house to pass a night, he was shown to his room before dinner, and being about to dress, he looked round for the usual washing apparatus, but could see nothing of the sort. Just as he was on the point of making an effort to obtain these requisites of the toilet, he heard to his great surprise and amusement a creaking in the floor, and a trapdoor gradually opened, through which ascended, by a steady invisible movement, wash-hand-stand, basin, towels, hot-water, and all other due accompaniments. He used to say he never met with a parallel to this, except in the house of a gentleman who had a railroad made from his kitchen to his dining-room, to send in the dishes quick and hot.

Among other invitations in Ireland, he received one to a wedding of a Protestant gentleman to a Roman Catholic lady. It happened to be a Popish fast-day, but the bridegroom, not thinking it necessary to keep it, permitted the Protestant guests to help him to a variety of good things on the table; but as soon as the bride perceived that any of them contained animal food, she desired a servant to take his plate away from him. The company were highly excited by this commencement of a wedded life; and at last one of them proposed a resolution, that if Papists and Protestants chose to wed, their friends in that neighbourhood at least should protest against its being on fast-days. Lord Hill used to tell this story with great humour. The lady herself only gave a specimen of what her mother church would do in higher matters, if the half-Romanist movements of the age should induce any alliance with her. Soon after he left Ireland, not being attached to any corps. Captain Hill accompanied Mr. Drake to Genoa, he says:

> Thence I proceeded to Toulon, and was employed as *aide-de-camp* to Lord Mulgrave, General O'Hara, and Sir David Dundas.

The impression he made on these officers, while on the staff of each in succession, was of the most favourable kind; and General O'Hara emphatically predicted his future distinction in the service. One day as he quitted the room this general said to those present, "That young man will rise to be one of the first soldiers of the age." Captain Hill's first active services commenced at this period, and I give his own reminiscences of the proceedings in which he was engaged:—

> Lord Hood took possession of Toulon, August, 1793. On the 6th of September Lord Mulgrave arrived there. About a week afterwards I joined his Lordship, who, at my earnest request, appointed me his *aide-de-camp*—a situation I preferred much to being an assistant-secretary to Mr. Drake. On the 30th of September the enemy got possession of the important port of Faron. This information was brought to Lord Mulgrave by Mr. Graham.[3] His Lordship, with great quickness and decision, attacked and drove the enemy back amidst great difficulties. On this occasion I was *aide-de-camp*. On the 8th of October we destroyed the batteries in the Hauteur de Reinière. On the 9th a spirited sortie by our troops; on the 15th the enemy got possession of Cape le Brun.
>
> About this time General O'Hara arrived to take the command, Lord Mulgrave returned to England, and I remained with General O'Hara as his *aide-de-camp*. I remember General O'Hara being much displeased at the favourable report made by Lord

---

3. Afterwards Lord Lynedoch.

Mulgrave of the state of affairs at Toulon, the general adding that it was quite impossible to keep the place—that is, Toulon and the harbour—with so small a force. The French having erected a battery against the port of Malbourquet, General O'Hara, on the 30th of November, prepared to destroy it; for which purpose Sir David Dundas marched in, before daybreak, with two thousand men, composed of five nations, British, French Loyalists, Neapolitans, Spaniards, and Piedmontese.

Sir David succeeded in obtaining full possession of the height and battery; but the impetuosity of some of the troops led them to pursue the flying enemy, whilst others were occupied in plundering the enemy's camp. In this scattered and irregular state, the enemy, who had collected in great force, made an attack, and obliged us to relinquish the advantages we had gained. General O'Hara arrived at the redoubt as it was taken; and, perceiving the disorder of the troops, was extremely displeased at their having left the hill. He used every exertion to form the troops, and sent me to bring up the artillery-men, and order these to spike the guns, and destroy them as effectually as possible. This was the last time I saw General O'Hara[4]; for before I returned to the battery he received a wound, and was taken prisoner. During the time General O'Hara was prisoner, he was treated very ill. On our return to the town, which we did with great haste, Sir David Dundas assumed the command, and I was appointed one of his *aides-de-camp*.

The conduct of Captain Hill, modestly passed over by himself, was, on all these occasions, the subject of high encomium from those under whom he served. Lord Mulgrave wrote thus to Mr. Drake on the subject:—

> For the particulars of our action of the 1st of October, I must refer you to your relation and my friend and *aide-de-camp*. Captain Hill, who was in the midst of it, and whose intelligence, activity, and courage rendered him of great service to me.

He had a most providential escape just at the time when General O'Hara was taken prisoner. He was called down by that general from a tree, into which he had climbed to make observations, and Captain Snow, his brother *aide-de-camp*, having ascended to replace him, was

---

4. He means, on this occasion.

instantly killed. Captain Hill was, however, wounded slightly in the right hand, which he does not notice, nor the fact of his having had committed to him the direction of the retreat to Toulon, which he conducted in the most satisfactory manner. His talents gained confidence, and his unpretending demeanour won affection, so that no one seemed ever to regard him with jealousy. How his superior officers felt towards him, though still so young a man, will be easily collected from a letter of Lord Mulgrave, who had left him at Toulon:—

Harley Street, Nov. 28, 1793.

Dear Hill,
I have this morning seen Sir Richard Hill, who is very much delighted with your conduct at Toulon, and happy to hear that you are in General O'Hara's family. I enclosed your letter to your father, and wrote him an account of you. I shall be happy to hear from you when you have any good news to send me from Toulon. Pray speak to Barailly about the drawing of Mount Faron, which Michel, of the Marine Engineer corps, was to make for me, and send it by the first favourable opportunity, and let me know if there is any thing I can send Monsieur Michel from England, in return for his trouble, that may be useful to him, and which is not to be got at Toulon. Pray remember me to Rudswell. Smith, &c.

Yours sincerely,

Mulgrave.

On the 13th of December, 1793, Lord Hood and Sir David Dundas sent Captain Hill with despatches to England, where he arrived on the 13th of January, 1794. Sir David observed, in his despatch:

This will be delivered by Captain Hill, a very deserving young man, who has been *aide-de-camp* to Lord Mulgrave, Lieutenant-General O'Hara, and myself.

"These despatches," we learn from Lord Hill's own memoranda:

. . . .contained the difficulties of the situation of our navy and army. The evacuation of Toulon took place on the 18th and 19th December, 1793. On my return to England I saw the Duke of York at Ghent. His Royal Highness commanded the allied armies in Flanders at this time. I breakfasted with him and his secretary, and reported the accounts from Toulon."

Amongst those who witnessed the admirable conduct of Captain Hill at Toulon was the veteran Lord Lynedoch, then Thomas Graham, Esq., serving as a volunteer, and gaining great honour. His admiration of our young officer was such as to create in him a desire that he should serve in the same regiment with himself. Accordingly, Lord Hill has made the following entry of this circumstance in his own notes:

> In the early part of 1794 Mr. Graham raised a regiment of infantry, and offered me the majority of it on raising a certain quota of men.

With his usual simplicity and conciseness, he merely added to the record of the proposal, "This I did." This regiment was the brave 90th, in which he was destined to win so many honours, and to gather the laurels of the highest achievements. It was afterwards augmented to a thousand strong, when he became the lieutenant-colonel on the usual terms. The year in which this body of men was first formed, was an epoch of remarkable events on the face of afflicted Europe. It was the period of the Duke of York's operations near Cambray and Tournay, while the arrival of Lord Moira at Ostend preceded those in the Netherlands. France was agitated by the insurrection in La Vendée, and by Robespierre's brutal administration. That talentless monster—cunning without genius, and a tyrant without a single quality calculated for wholesome rule, as well as ferocious without a spark of courage —found his sole element in fiendish cruelty. Under his hands, the captive general suffered most unworthy hardships. Lord Hill alludes to the subject thus:—

> General O'Hara was treated with the utmost rigour and barbarity by him. The general has told me that he was placed in the common gaol, and was fed on artichoke leaves and bullock's liver.

The well-known occurrences of the time now occupying our attention, are thus briefly adverted to by Lord Hill; and as enlargement upon them would be foreign to the object before us, I shall merely give his own words:—

> The hard frost which marked the close of 1794 and beginning of 1795, enabled the French to cross the Waal. The Duke of York departed for England. On the 6th of January the British Army retired, or, more properly speaking, made a hasty retreat

through Holland, suffering extreme hardships. The *Stadtholder* and Prince of Orange came to England. The French took possession of Holland. In April the British troops returned to England.

While the *Stadtholder* was in this country, he was most splendidly entertained by Sir Richard Hill at Hawkstone, where that excellent baronet drew around him the most illustrious men of his age; while his charities succoured the poor, and his protection shielded the pious, who were forgotten or opposed in those extraordinary times.

The summer of 1795 was passed by the 90th regiment, and its young lieutenant-colonel, on foreign service. It was one of the regiments which, under General Doyle, took possession of Isle Dieu, where they remained unmolested by the French till the following December. Colonel Hill, who never could be inactive, and had always a keen enjoyment of field diversions, amused himself and brother officers by coursing, keeping greyhounds for that purpose. He and his senior and friend Lord Lynedoch were kindred spirits in this respect; and the veteran in one of his letters to Lord Hill, still preserved, commissioned him to procure pointers and setters from Shropshire for shooting—a pursuit he keenly relished throughout his very long and distinguished life. In December Colonel Hill gladly quitted Isle Dieu, where there was so little scope for the development of his military genius. His words are:

> I embarked from Isle Dieu in the *Artois*, Sir Edmund Nagle's frigate. At night we were on the rocks near Quiberon, and were in considerable danger. The ship, however, reached Portsmouth in safety about Christmas-Day. The regiment afterwards was quartered at Poole for some months.

The anxious spirit of Colonel Hill could not reconcile itself to the narrow bounds of a small island, while the whole continent of Europe was in a state of agitation at the progress of Napoleon, then in the vigour of his days, and the excitement of his amazing projects. At this time his aspiring energies were encaged in the Isle Dieu, and had scarcely any thing to occupy them but field-sports. In 1796 Bonaparte's Italian campaign was the wonder of the nations and the theme of every discourse, and quickened in the minds of the brave a desire for active employ. Colonel Hill, accordingly, gladly welcomed an opportunity of going abroad. He has recorded:

I went with the 90th to Gibraltar in the summer of 1796, where I found my old general, O'Hara, in command of the garrison. I had not seen him since the day he was taken prisoner. He received me most kindly, and gave me a house of his own as a quarter.

The terms on which Colonel Hill was with this veteran, will be perceptible from a laconic epistle to the former, who had sent his esteemed general a comfortable cloak or wrapper of some kind, as a mark of his gratitude. The letter, too, is quite that of the old soldier.

"Convent, 26th of July, 1796
My dear Hill,
I am much obliged by the very comfortable present you made me yesterday. I shall, however, put off being a swaddled old fellow as long as I can.
Yours ever, most sincerely and faithfully,
Chas. O'Hara.

General O'Hara's kind disposition towards Colonel Hill was founded upon a much firmer basis than a mere value of his attentions or pleasure in his society: he entirely confided in the clearness of his understanding and the soundness of his judgment; and, young as he was, he selected him for the discharge of a delicate duty. What this was, we learn from Lord Hill's own notes:

> In the beginning of October, 1796, General O'Hara entrusted me with a verbal communication to convey to the British ambassador at Lisbon. This communication was the expected war with Spain. It proved correct; for, before I could return, hostilities had commenced, and it was with difficulty I got back to the garrison of Gibraltar—not only from the declaration of war, but also in consequence of the illness occasioned by great exertion to accomplish the duty I was employed on for my respected general.

The same spirit which breathes in this sentence, animated its worthy writer through the performance of the infinite number of arduous trusts reposed in him as he rose in the army, and brought him into the same confidence with the Duke of Wellington, that he inspired in his superiors before he was called upon to serve with that illustrious leader. He knew not only how to command, but how to obey; and both by those to whom it was his province to give, and by those from whom it was his duty to receive orders, he was equally beloved.

On Colonel Hill's return to Gibraltar he found himself almost as much confined as he was in Isle Dieu, for the declaration of war between Spain and England prevented any communication with the country. Still it was the scene of much that was interesting, and the focus of tidings respecting the events of the day. In February, 1797, the news of Lord St. Vincent's victory over the Spanish fleet on the 14th reached the garrison to their great joy. Colonel Hill, who had a truly keen sense of the ludicrous, was extremely amused by the account given of one of the Spanish ships which was making her escape into Cadiz, and the way in which his old friend General O'Hara received it. The captain of a cutter came and told the general that he had come across her with his vessel as she was getting away. "She is wonderfully damaged," he exclaimed, "and has a hole in her side big enough to run my cutter-into."

"Then why on earth," replied the general, drily, "did you not do so?"

During this year England was threatened with the boasted French invasion, and what was much more to be dreaded, a mutiny in the navy; but the absence of Colonel Hill allowed him no acquaintance, except that of distant report, with these serious affairs. In July, 1798, the mission of Lord Malmesbury to Lisle, to negotiate a peace with the French, proved a failure; and Bonaparte took possession of Malta, and sought to make Egypt the scene of his conquests. The check he received from Nelson's victory at Aboukir is fresh in the recollections of a grateful nation. Colonel Hill, however, still remained with the 90th regiment. The events of that period are thus briefly summed up in his manuscript:—

> In August, 1798, the French landed at Killala, under the command of Humbert. This force did not exceed 844, officers and men. I remained in arms till the 8th September. I remained with the 90th regiment, which was under the command of Lieutenant-Colonel Moncrieff, the whole of this year.

He then mentions various circumstances which induced him to apply for leave of absence, "which," he adds, "was granted;" continuing:

> I came to England in 1799, and remained till the expedition sailed from Portsmouth, under Sir Ralph Abercromby. My leave, on this occasion, was prolonged in consequence of an accident, occasioned by Clement's setting fire to spirits of wine, which I

used for chilblains. The year 1799 exhibited a strange picture of the world turned upside down,—Turks, Mahometans, Roman Catholics, Protestants, all at war, and supporting each other. Bonaparte continued in possession of Egypt; various battles took place in that country between Mamelukes, Turks, and French. Sir Sidney Smith at Acre. In August, 1799, Sir R. Abercromby landed at the Helder. Lord Duncan commanded the fleet. The Duke of York afterwards took the command of the army.

This brief epitome of events requires no further expansion, as they are notorious matters of history, and contain no particulars illustrative of the career of Lord Hill beyond the reflex effects they had upon his movements. When he came to London he was much struck with the noble bearing and generous spirit of Sir Ralph Abercromby, and had the privilege of conversing with that gallant officer before he sailed. He used frequently to mention Sir Ralph's liberal feelings towards his sons, of whom he said:

> They ought, as soldiers, never to want money. I wish them to have what is handsome, which both causes them to spend less, and never to be embarrassed by appearing needy.

For himself, Colonel Hill had, notwithstanding his services, never received any remuneration from the government beyond his pay, at which several officers, who knew and appreciated his exertions and successes, were exceedingly surprised, and did not hesitate to say so. Still he was in no degree disheartened, and quietly determined to persevere in his efforts for advancement in his profession. For this purpose he was anxious to see the service of the troops on the Continent, and applied to the Duke of York for leave to accompany his friend Mr. Drake, who was about to depart on a diplomatic journey to Switzerland, and was willing to take him. Colonel Hill made application to the Horse Guards through the secretary of his Royal Highness, to whom he wrote the subjoined letter:—

> Sir,
> I shall be extremely obliged if you will lay the following request before his Royal Highness the Commander-in-Chief:
> Mr. Drake, who is going into Switzerland in a diplomatic line, has offered to take me with him; and as I am desirous of accompanying him to the Continent, with a view of seeing some more service with the Austrian and Russian armies, I shall esteem it a

very particular favour if the Duke of York will grant me permission to go with him. And if I find, after a short residence on the Continent, that my endeavours to serve with the armies are of no avail, I will in that case immediately proceed by way of Leghorn to join my regiment at Minorca. I beg to assure his Royal Highness that the sole motive of my making such a request is an ardent wish of improving myself in my profession.

I have the honour to be,
Your obedient servant,
R. Hill, Lt. Col. 90th Regt.

The leave sought in this letter was readily granted; and how near he was going out with Mr. Drake, will appear in a summons to prepare himself from that gentleman.

Wells, March 12, 1800.

My dear Sir,

Sir Richard informed you of my having received orders to prepare for my immediate departure for the Continent, and of the necessity of your being ready to come to town on the shortest notice. As my instructions could not be prepared until the arrival of the Hamburgh mails, which are now icebound in the Elbe, Lord Grenville permitted me to return hither upon condition that I should be ready to set out at forty-eight hours' notice; and as the thaw has now begun, it is probable that the mails will soon be released, and consequently that I shall very soon be called upon. I therefore beg to apprise you that it will be necessary for you to be prepared to set out for London, the moment you receive an intimation to that effect from Sir Richard. It might, perhaps, be advisable for you to forward immediately by the waggon to London, such things as you may wish to carry with you beyond what you may have daily occasion for. Francis is very well; and we all join in kind regards to your father, mother, and family.

Believe me to be,
Yours, very sincerely,
Francis Drake.

Thus it seems that Colonel Hill was on the very eve of departure for the continent of Europe: and if this intention had been carried into effect, the whole future current of his life would have probably been altered.

Chapter 2

Change in Colonel Hill's Plans

On the 1st of January, 1800, Lieutenant-Colonel Hill was made full Colonel; and the year itself was destined to be spent by him in very different scenes from those he had contemplated visiting under the auspices of Mr. Drake. Mr. Drake did not go out, and this was the cause of Colonel Hill's finding in Egypt such an arena of military glory. His own narrative is written with his usual simplicity, both in the memoranda quoted in the last chapter, and in a small pocket journal kept amidst the sands of the desert and on the banks of the Nile. The latter record commences thus:

> Having procured leave from the Duke of York to accompany Mr. Drake, and join my regiment by way of Italy, I waited in London some months; but finding it uncertain when he was to set out, and hearing the 90th Regiment was to be actively employed with Sir Ralph Abercromby, I determined to join my regiment as soon as possible; therefore on May the 15th set out with Admiral Holloway for Portsmouth.

This diary continues:

> Saturday the 24th May, embarked at Spithead on board the *Pegasus*, 28 guns, fitted up as a troop-ship, and having on board about 200 men and 30 officers, and I, being senior officer, gave out orders necessary to be observed on board—25th dropped down to St. Helen's—26th sailed, fine breeze—27th fine—28th placed the men at the guns according to the directions of Captain Pingelly.

Here all the officers seem to have looked up to Colonel Hill with the greatest deference. Amongst these were Lord Blaney and others, forming the personal staff of Sir Ralph Abercromby, who had become acquainted with Colonel Hill at Portsmouth, where they were all detained several days together, he says:

> During this time the pompous Lieutenant-Governor, General Whitelock, showed attention to all the officers except myself, which I could not account for, until his *aide-de-camp* told me the reason, which was, because I was not in uniform when I waited on him.

This individual was the only person in power, who ever appears to have slighted one whom all others concurred in valuing and commending both for efficiency and conduct.

Though Colonel Hill was gentle in the extreme, he never permitted any deviation from discipline. An instance of this occurred while he was in the *Pegasus*. An officer on board that ship was reported to him, on the 28th of May, as having been the previous night intoxicated. This charge being fully substantiated, he says:

> I assembled all the officers, and before them told ——— that his conduct had been highly improper, and that if he behaved in like manner again I should report him to the commander-in-chief. ——— promised to conduct himself in future as an officer; and by the approbation of all the officers he was re-admitted to their society.

After passing a few more days at sea, the party landed at Mevagissy, in Cornwall, and made an expedition to see a tin-mine, and then sailed again with a fair wind.

> Sunday the 1st of June off Scilly, fell in with the outward-bound East India fleet. The commander reported the French fleet to be at sea, and imagined Lord St. Vincent was between us and it. In the evening placed the men at their quarters, two to each gun.

He also arranged that three captains and six subalterns with sixty men should act as marines, and put every thing in the ship into the most complete order. On the 4th of June they fell in with Captain Legg, who also informed them that he had heard the French fleet was out; and the very next day they came across an enemy's vessel, which they chased and fired at for four hours, but could not come up to her. After the usual occurrences of a sea voyage, they made the Straits of Gibraltar on the 10th of June; but the gunboat not coming out to them as was expected, they did not go on shore till early the next morning. Colonel Hill found his old friend General O'Hara up and on parade, and went home to breakfast with him, when "a very satisfactory conversation" ensued. After this he "walked about the garrison, and saw the works at Landport," but "at one got under way, and with a fair wind and large convoy waited on Sir Ralph Abercromby."

In the evening a ship ran foul of the *Pegasus*, but nothing disastrous was the result. She does not seem to have been a good sailer, for on the 15th chase was given by her to four vessels, all of which escaped. During this time Colonel Hill was not negligent as to improving himself in his profession, and was paying studious attention to the theory of field fortification, reading diligently on that subject. The 24th found him near Cabrera, where they were much distressed for provisions. At this place he mentions that "a pair of boots were dressed, boiled, and roasted with lemon, for dinner in the gun-room;" but he does not state with what appetite they were eaten, nor the cause of this burlesque upon their scanty fare.

On arriving at Majorca, they were informed by "the commander that Genoa had surrendered, and was retaken by Bonaparte, and that Sir Ralph had sailed with 3000 men." They made the utmost expedition to join him off Leghorn, and were becalmed near Corsica, but reached that port on the 8th of July, when they found the place in a state of disturbance, and Sir Ralph gone to Malta. Lord Hill's remarks on Leghorn are very brief.—

> 10th, went on shore. Saw Lord Keith. The Queen of Naples, with Sir William and Lady Hamilton, on board the *Alexander*, Lord Nelson. Most of the shops and public places shut up.

It was on the 21st of July that he reached Minorca, where he remained till the 27th of August, when he embarked with Sir Ralph Abercromby and "an army of 12,000 men." A brief entry in his journal shows that though he had the satisfaction of joining his general, he was tried by indisposition:

> 11th September, I was taken very unwell, and so ill, not able to keep a memorandum. Got to Gibraltar. Day after dined with General O'Hara, but was so very ill at dinner, I was obliged to leave the room. Two days after I came on shore and lived with General Wemyss.

Sir James Pulteney at this time arrived at Gibraltar with 5000 men. Soon after, the whole fleet, with an army of 25,000 men, sailed for

Cadiz, off which place they remained three days.

The troops were ordered to land, and General Moore's division was embarked in the boats; but before they reached the shore, they were recalled and the landing abandoned. Signal made to return to Tetuan Bay. 10th October, much better. Off the Straits of Gibraltar.

These various manoeuvres were performed with the intention of deceiving the enemy; but General O'Hara, who was labouring under impaired health and spirits, and whose tactics were all of the straightforward order, became furiously enraged at the whole proceeding. "What is the meaning of all this pretence of landing at Cadiz, passing backwards and forwards, and all the rest of it?"

"It is a diversion, General," was the answer given to the brave and blunt veteran.

"*Diversion!*" he exclaimed. "'Tis a *diversion*, for all Europe is laughing at you. Why, your commander cannot see the length of his nose; and as for your fighting-cock Moore, he has trimmed his tail! Pretty doings!"

This ebullition of the worthy veteran was in allusion, in the first instance, to the well-known nearsightedness of Sir Ralph Abercromby; and certainly the general could not regard the rendezvous at Gibraltar with much personal satisfaction, since the price of provisions had been enormously augmented by it. Lord Hill used to mention, that being forbidden, on account of his illness at that time, to eat anything but fresh meat, he was obliged to give three pounds twelve shillings sterling for a turkey, and a guinea for a fowl. Of course General O'Hara could not think this increase in the expenses of his own very hospitable board, by any means a *diversion*. And then, in those days of all-prevailing powder and pomatum, Sir John Moore had actually dared the innovation of a crop, and appeared unfrizzled and unfloured upon parade. This was the source of the second remark of the harassed old soldier, who no doubt considered, as many of his years would have done, that, with the curls and the pigtail the age of chivalry was gone.[1]

---

1. Probably the authorities were of the same opinion, for it was not till the arrival of Sir John Moore from Stockholm in 1808, that an order reached his troops to cut off their *queues*. It was dated 24th July, and gave universal delight. The signal was made for all haircutters to proceed to headquarters: and Cadell tells us "As soon as they had finished on board the headquarter ship, the adjutant, Lieutenant Russell, proceeded with them and a pattern man to the other troop-ships. The tails were kept till all were docked, when, by signal, the whole (were hove over board with three cheers." (*Slashers* by Charles Cadell is also published by Leonaur.)

On the 10th of October Colonel Hill was so much better as to be able to proceed to Tetuan, he says:

> Stayed there till a violent gale of wind from the east obliged us to leave our anchor and come off Cape Spartel. The fleet very much scattered; all officers on salt provisions.
> Monday, October 20th, at anchor off Cape Spartel. 21st, Sir Ralph joined the fleet, after being separated in the last gale. Miserably bad; no provisions; all tired with being on board so long; very ill; returned to Gibraltar.

There seemed to be no end of this passing to and fro, while various untoward circumstances, and above all the illness which affected a constitution never robust, threatened a far different termination to those hopes of service and distinction which animated his heroic breast, than fortunately for himself and his country he was at last permitted to realise. But we will let him tell the brief tale of his own progress:—

> 27th, sailed from Gibraltar: contrary winds. Off Cape Gata till the 7th of November, when we made Minorca, and anchored. Still unwell. Remained at Minorca till the 16th of November; was on shore most of the time for the benefit of my health. Sailed 17th, fine wind, for Malta.

There they arrived on the 20th, after a quick passage, but "blowing a gale of wind," and "the regiment disembarked, and remained on shore till the 13th of December."

The 1st of January, 1801, presented to his admiring view the noble harbour of Marmora; and better health enabled him to hear with cheerful spirits, the sounds of preparation for the campaign in Egypt. His own note runs thus:—

> January 1st, 1801, Marmora; all well; wrote to Prees; preparing for our expedition against the French troops in Egypt.

Here they passed the whole month.

> February 1st, still at Marmora; dined with Lord Keith. Preparation for our departure.

On the 9th there arose a "tremendous storm, accompanied with most violent thunder and lightning, and hailstones the size of a pigeon's egg." They did not sail for some time after this, as appears from his own record:—

22nd, sailed from Marmora, or Marmorice, with a fleet of about 200 sail, some Turkish, some Greeks. 23rd, fine wind, steering for Egypt.

A more magnificent sight than the fleet under Lord Keith can scarcely be imagined; but these notes of Colonel Hill plainly prove that the noble admiral knew better than to venture its safety by bringing it out of Marmorice harbour in a gale of wind, as has been stated by some writers. At the same time, his determination to convey the army on board to the coast of Egypt, manifested the most cool and masterly seamanship; for it was taken in the face of the opinion of all the pilots, who designated the attempt no less than madness, and proclaimed the landing impossible till the equinox was past. The progress is thus shortly mentioned by Colonel Hill:—

March 1st, saw Alexandria; 2nd, anchored in Aboukir Bay; 8th March, the landing was gallantly made.

12th (March), moved on towards Alexandria; 13th March, attacked the French, defeated them, and gained a glorious victory. was wounded, and went on board the expedition.

This short extract is from his diary kept at the time; but the following quotation from the later memoranda will give fuller particulars:—

On the 2nd February, 1801, the expedition under Sir R. Abercromby and Lord Keith weighed. On the 27th it blew tremendously. On the 1st March we anchored in the celebrated bay of Aboukir. On the 8th we landed in Egypt. On the 12th the army advanced, skirmishing with the enemy till dusk. At night, the 90th, which I commanded, and the 92nd, were placed along the front of the army. On the morning of the 13th, at six, the British Army began to move, the 90th regiment as its advanced guard. At this moment a considerable body of cavalry made a spirited and impetuous charge on the 90th, who, as Walsh[2] says, with the coolness and intrepidity of veterans received them, unbroken, upon the points of their bayonets. The French were obliged to retreat. I was wounded by a musket-ball, which struck the peak

---

2. *The Cockade in the Sand,* the defeat of Napoleon's Egyptian Adventure & the Campaign of 1801, containing *Journal of the Late Campaign in Egypt* by Thomas Walsh and *The Expedition to Egypt* (Except) by Colonel W. W. Knollys is also published by Leonaur.

of the helmet, now at Hawkstone. After being wounded I was taken on board Lord Keith's ship, where I remained about three weeks, and then returned to the regiment.

Colonel Hill's escape was truly providential; and the helmet is still kept as a memorial of his danger and his merciful deliverance. In the general orders of Sir Ralph Abercromby, issued the next day, was contained this unequivocal praise of the conduct of the 90th:—

> He desires that Major-General Cradock will assure the officers and men of the 90th Regiment, that their meritorious conduct commands his admiration.

The description of the gallantry of the 90th by Sir Robert Wilson, plainly shows that this encomium was well deserved. He says;

> At the same time the cavalry, under the orders of General Bron, charged down a height on the 90th Regiment, forming the advanced guard of the right column. This regiment, undismayed, firmly maintained its ground, and, allowing the cavalry to approach, fired such a volley as completely altered their direction, and compelled them to retreat.

Though Colonel Hill was rendered insensible by the violence of the concussion from the ball, which his helmet was mercifully permitted to arrest, he speedily revived, and was much consoled by the friendly invitation of Lord Keith to come on board the *Foudroyant*.

16th M(arch), 1801.

Dear Hill,
I am happy to hear you are so well, and I think you will be more at ease here than where you are. I beg you will come, and I will do all I can to make the ship comfortable to you. I wish my poor friend Erskine were able to come also.

Yours ever,
Keith.

Col. Hill, 90th Regt., *Cyclops*.
Keith.

The day after the date of this invitation Colonel Hill removed to the *Foudroyant*. While there, still weak from the effect of his wound, he saw with grief his brave commander brought from the battlefield of the 21st of March, to die in the same cabin where he himself was gradually recovering. He says, in his diary:

Remained on board the *Foudroyant* till 14th April. The glorious 21st of March, poor Sir R. Abercromby was brought on board. He was in the same cabin with me, and lived one week: his lady sent to Malta in the *Flora*.

While Colonel Hill was confined in the *Foudroyant*, the Capitan Pacha, who came to that ship, presented him with a sabre, a gold box, and a handsome shawl, as a testimony of admiration of the gallant manner in which he had led the 90th Regiment on the 18th of March, and invited him to pay a visit to the Sultan Selim.

It was the misfortune of this brave army, which first taught Frenchmen under Bonaparte the surpassing skill and excellence both of our men and officers, to have lost Sir Ralph Abercromby, the admirer of Colonel Hill, and his companion in the cabin of the wounded, where the latter was obliged to remain till the 14th of April. But the conflict of the 13th, and the decisive victory of the 21st of March, had rendered it impossible for the French to maintain themselves for any great length of time in Egypt. Though many that were arrayed against the English had crossed the Alps with Napoleon, they confessed that they had never fought till now. And who gave the first repulse to their hitherto undaunted assaults and victorious movements? It was the 90th Regiment, commanded by Colonel Hill, on whom the opening onslaught was directed, and whose conduct became the first omen of victory, brilliantly achieved, and only clouded by the loss of Sir Ralph Abercromby, whom every soldier loved as a father, and confided in as a leader.

On the 19th of April Colonel Hill commanded the camp at Hamed, and on the 4th of May orders were given for the British and Turkish army to march forward. From Colonel Hill's Diary it appears that:

> The British Army consisted of Major-General Cradock's brigade, Brigadier-General Doyle's part of the reserve, four three-pounders, four six, two howitzers, and a few cavalry.

As the British advanced, the French receded before them, till, on the 10th of May, the former marched towards Ramanieh. He states:

> About four miles before we reached that place the enemy came out, and with cavalry and light troops skirmished with our advanced guards and light troops. Our loss was about thirty killed and wounded; that of the Turks more considerable; that of the French may be about sixty or seventy. The French at

night evacuated their position. I was on duty, and, from the noise I heard, I imagined they were moving off. I reported the same to General Cradock. On the 11th the fort of Ramanieh surrendered. The same day a party of dragoons, coming from Alexandria to Ramanieh, were taken, not knowing we were in possession of the place.

Ramanieh itself was by no means a strong fort, and the village was filthy, but the produce of the surrounding country in corn, was such as to cover the land like the years of plenty in the days of Joseph.

The army continued marching on without any encounter till the 17th, when, says Colonel Hill:

A convoy, consisting of 600 French, 400 camels, and 200 cavalry, &c., coming from Alexandria, were heard of in the desert. The whole army was under arms, and proceeded in different directions in three columns, and after a fatiguing march in the desert, General Doyle's brigade came up with the convoy, which surrendered. At night I had the command of the guard over them.

1st of June, the army changed its ground, and moved forward four miles. 2nd, Osman Bey, with his noble cavalry, came into our camp. 4th, the army moved forward, the band of the 90th playing 'God save the King.'

A few more changes occurred, and on the 16th the army "encamped before Grand Cairo;" and the next extract from the diary will inform us under what circumstances.—

During the march from Hamed to Grand Cairo the weather was extremely hot, and the fatigue the soldiers endured, I believe to be unparalleled. One day, about the 20th of June, the thermometer was at 120°; some say 128°: it was generally near 100°. The country we passed through was covered with corn, the finest possible. The villages were nearly the same, and all equally miserable. In general there was one mosque in each; the houses built of mud; the inhabitants naked, wretched, and savage. If the country had not been plundered by the French and Turks, we might have had plenty of provisions. Buffaloes in great abundance. On our march every preparation, though slow, was making to bring up the heavy artillery for the siege of Cairo.

The result of all these demonstrations is thus mentioned:—

> On the evening of the 21st I was colonel for the day. The next morning a French officer came out with a letter for the commander-in-chief, in consequence of which a conference took place, and ended in the French agreeing to evacuate Egypt, and surrender the citadel of Cairo in twelve days.
>
> July 6, the *grand vizier* came to the British camp. On the 15th of July the army began its march from Cairo, the Turks in front, then the British, and afterwards the French.

The march from Cairo to Hamed occupied fourteen days, when the French, who had left the former place, moved off by divisions and embarked for France, and the British encamped among the date-trees near Rosetta. From this place General Hope's brigade marched to Alexandria; and, on the 16th of August, Colonel Hill and the 90th were placed once more in the front of the line, and soon had the pleasure of seeing the last remnant of the enemy depart from Egypt. On the 8th of September General Hope inspected the 90th Regiment, and thus addressed Colonel Hill:—

> Sir, considering the service your regiment has gone through, it is impossible a regiment can be more complete than it is at present. I have minutely inspected every part of it, and it is with pleasure I tell you that the whole corps does you and the officers the greatest credit.

He also wrote in the most commendatory terms of their gallant conduct to General Hutchinson, who succeeded Sir Ralph Abercromby in the command of the British army in Egypt.

But Colonel Hill had the happiness of receiving congratulations on his escape and distinction, dearer to him than all besides. These were letters from his family and friends in England. One particularly from Sir Richard Hill, is eminently characteristic of that deservedly-popular and pious man.

London, May 12. 1801.

My very dear Rowland,

With the most inexpressible pleasure and satisfaction have I this day received your letter mentioning your truly providential escape on the 13th of March, for which we can never be sufficiently thankful to Him who *screened your head in the day of battle*. God knows that my prayer for you, my very dear lad, has been that you may return to your anxious friends and relatives, whole in body and renewed in soul; and that the many wonderful instances you have experienced of sparing mercy, may be crowned with that greatest of all mercies, converting, saving mercy.

As soon as I received the most welcome epistle, I made its contents known to many who had made frequent inquiries after you; and the account has rejoiced them. Maria will have told you that some of the newspapers had stated that you were killed. However, a letter which I got from kind Mr. Addington dispersed, or rather prevented, our apprehensions on that account, as it was the first which we had from any quarter, and, indeed, was written before any other accounts had transpired.

I believe that all the letters you have forwarded to England have been received. Yours written to me from Malta came duly to hand.

Maria has no doubt sent you what little domestic news may be stirring. However, that certainly is not much. The best piece of news you can send us in return, is that we may venture to entertain hopes of seeing you before long In England; and I hope you will not fail to bring with you the friendly helmet which first received the ball, and prevented the stroke from being fatal to the wearer.

Our stay in town will be very short; and indeed the country is now so delightful, that I care not how soon I visit the romantic scenes at Hawkstone.

As it is by no means certain when this may reach you, or, indeed, whether you will get it at all, I will add no more but that my best wishes and prayers follow you whithersoever you go, and that I remain, with love from all here, the Tudways, &c. &c.,

>My very dear Rowland,
>>Yours most affectionately and truly,
>>>R. H.

All the domestic news was sent to Colonel Hill in the way Sir Richard supposed, and that in a most engaging and talented style of writing. One piece of intelligence his sister made known to him was the determination of his servant, who had been ill at Hawkstone for some time, to set off at all hazards to attend him in Egypt, the instant he heard of his being wounded. She also communicated to him the deep concern of other humble individuals in the employment of the family, whose attachment his kind and condescending treatment had won. Nor did she forget to mention the state of his pheasants and his poultry, which were the subjects of his amusement when at home. Nothing was more remarkable in his rare and winning disposition, than the contrast exhibited in his indulgence to dependants, and fondness for tame animals, to the vigour of his military command, and the splendour of his victories. On the latter, as regarded the campaign now before our view, he was thus congratulated by the gallant founder of his regiment:—

London, May 23. 1801.

Dear Hill,
I rejoice to hear you are doing so well, and most sincerely congratulate you on the conduct of the regiment, which I never doubted would distinguish itself, though certainly the occasion was the most trying possible, and its behaviour has established its reputation for ever. I am extremely hurried, and have only time to request you will assure them all of the pride and satisfaction I have felt on this glorious occasion. With the best and sincerest wishes, I remain,

Ever most truly yours,

Thos. Graham.

Col. Hill, 90th Regt.

These letters reached Colonel Hill in the midst of his arduous duties; and the care with which he preserved them in after-life, best proves the comfort they conveyed to him amidst the sands and conflicts of Egypt. Notwithstanding his military occupations, he found time to visit every object of curiosity in Cairo, Alexandria, and the Pyramids. He quitted Egypt on the 23rd of September, carefully superintending the embarkation of his regiment, and on the 9th of October anchored at Malta. Here he lost the faithful servant, who had left the comforts of Hawkstone to attend his wounded master. His name was Joseph Willoughby, and he died on the 18th of October. The regiment stayed at Malta till the 28th of February, 1802; and this honourable testimony to its conduct still remains in the handwriting of its beloved colonel:—

On the regiment quitting Malta every one spoke highly of the corps, particularly General Valette, who expressed regret that it was leaving his garrison. No soldier of the 90th was punished on the public parade;—two tried, but both acquitted. Received great civilities from Lord Keith, General Fox, and all the general officers.

On the passage from Malta to Gibraltar they were twice in the most imminent danger, but had what Colonel Hill very appropriately calls, each time, "a most providential escape." On the 11th of March they encountered a tremendous storm. The sea "broke in upon the quarter-gallery of Colonel Hill's vessel, and nearly covered the cabin."

Observing the carpenter putting in the dead-lights, he inquired of him, in his usual quiet manner, "Any damage done. Carpenter?" "*No*," said he, coolly, "*only poor carpenter wet.*"

On the 12th the storm abated, and the rock of Gibraltar once more met his eyes. There he had hoped to see the countenance of his esteemed friend General O'Hara lighted up with joy as he recounted to him the adventures and conquests of Egypt. But this pleasure was not awarded to him; the first news he heard being that of the death of the excellent governor,—"his worthy, good, and ever-to-be-lamented friend." He has thus expressed his sentiments towards him:—

> His abilities as an officer, and his character as a man, never were surpassed. Some say he was passionate;—those who have deserved censure have received it strongly from him;—those who have not, *never*. He was charitable and generous to a degree, and none knew his generosity but the individuals who benefited by it.

No one would more cordially have rejoiced at the non-fulfilment of his prophetic forebodings as to the result of the expedition, than this respected old officer, whose eulogium was so justly pronounced by his grateful friend. His more deliberate impression as to the future eminence of that friend, as was likely, had its accomplishment, rendering this tribute to O'Hara's merits a memorial worthy of his name.

At the termination of this arduous service, the army of Egypt received the thanks of both Houses of Parliament, and of the Corporation of the City of London, which were communicated to each officer in command of a regiment by Sir John Doyle, in a circular couched in very flattering language. General Hutchinson received the order of the Bath, and the entire conduct of the army merited and won the admiration of all men. The achievements of the expedition were of extreme importance; the Arabs were astonished at deeds of arms, of which they had not the remotest conception, and still more at the deportment and integrity of the high-minded victors who obtained their confidence, and with it an ample supply of provisions. The glittering Mamelukes came again upon the scene, brilliant in costume and marvellous in their feats, and even the dull *fellahs* roused themselves into energy under the exciting influence of the soldiers of Great Britain.

The sleepy *grand vizier* also, and the Capitan Pacha advanced to meet our troops as friends. Though the army of India, under Major-General Baird, appeared at Jeddah, on the Red Sea, and was joined by a division of infantry and horse from the Cape of Good Hope, their aid was not required. The triumph had been won, and Egypt was cleared of the invaders, before any union took place between the first army and these forces; and the whole world was taught that Britons knew how to conquer, and how to win respect even from the vanquished, while the uncivilized spectators of their career reposed the utmost reliance on their honour, as on their strength and their sagacity. Nor were individuals overlooked by the observers of these movements; and it is no slight testimony to Colonel Hill that the presents of the Capitan Pacha, who expressed great regret that he had no worthier offering to make, were the result of the high reputation he had obtained, and the coolness and courage which so fairly won and preserved it.

CHAPTER 3

Colonel Hill Arrives in England, April 1, 1802

On the 1st of April, 1802, Colonel Hill, after a voyage in which he encountered several dangerous incidents, found himself comfortably anchored at Spithead, where he "received very pleasant letters from Sir Richard," breathing gratitude in all the writer's fervour for his rising nephew's preservation. They were not released from quarantine till the 6th, when he and his companions trod once more on their native land, an honour to its name. In Colonel Hill's diary, this event is thus marked:—

> 6th, released from quarantine; went on shore at Portsmouth.
> 'Well has thy bark o'er life's uncertain main
> 'Scaped the rough storm, and found the land of rest.'

The regiment was landed at Chatham on the 15th of April, and:

> Marched immediately to Chelmsford, where it remained a few months; then proceeded to Scotland, under the impression that it was to be reduced at Fort George, where every necessary arrangement was made for its being disbanded.

In the month of June, Colonel Hill visited his relatives in Shropshire, and was received at Hawkstone with the honours due to the high merit which reflected so much lustre on his family. Sir Richard Hill gave a splendid *fête* in the park, where the magnificent tent of Tippoo Saib, obtained by Colonel Hill in Egypt[1], was erected to receive the numerous guests assembled to welcome his return. When his health was given, and the helmet that had so providentially saved his

---
1. From the army returning by the Red Sea from India.

life was handed round. His genuine simplicity and urbanity are agreeably evidenced in a letter written to his tutor, Mr. Winfield, during this pleasurable sojourn at Hawkstone:—

Hawkstone, July 5th.

My dear Sir,
I cannot delay a moment returning you my sincere thanks for your kind and affectionate letter, which would have afforded me the greatest pleasure if it had not contained such an indifferent account of yourself; but I trust and hope you will soon be restored to perfect health.

Since I saw you, I have been in various parts of the world, and have had an opportunity of seeing several interesting countries, and must acknowledge I have had some providential escapes; but, thank God, I am returned to the best country in the world, in health and safety. I imagine the reduction of the 90th regiment will soon take place. I shall then have time to visit all my old acquaintances, and be assured, my dear Sir, I shall never pass through Chester without calling on you. I beg to be kindly remembered to all your family, and believe me,

My dear Sir,
Your sincere and obedient
R. Hill.

Rev. James Winfield, Chester.

The expectation expressed in this letter was not to be realised, and the reason is thus given in his own words:—

At the end of 1802 the affairs of Europe were unsettled; rumours of wars made it advisable to increase the army, and the 90th, instead of being reduced, had orders to use every exertion to get men, in consequence of which I sent out various recruiting parties in England and Scotland. I remained with the regiment the greater part of the winter of 1802, and beginning of 1803. In the spring of 1803 we received orders to proceed to Ireland; sailed from Portsmouth, and were quartered at Belfast till August following. During the period we were at Belfast, Ireland was in a very disturbed state. In August we were ordered to march to Ballinasloe. On arrival at Mullingar, I received an official letter informing me that I was appointed a Brigadier-General on the staff in Ireland, and was to be stationed at Loughrea.

This letter was dated August 20. 1803; and, of course, produced the trying separation between Colonel Hill and the distinguished corps he had so effectively and acceptably commanded. How much his removal was felt by his brother officers, is abundantly testified in the address presented to him with their unanimous concurrence, and which is here inserted from the original:—

> The officers of the 90th regiment, in expressing to Colonel Hill their unfeigned and heartfelt pleasure on learning of his appointment of Brigadier-General to the Forces, must, at the same time, assure him that his resigning the command of the regiment fills them with sentiments of the most lively and deep regret.
>
> On their taking their farewell of an officer who has ever stood so high in their estimation, they feel themselves called upon to declare that the discipline he maintained in the regiment, has ever gained it the distinguished praise and approbation of all the general officers they have ever served with,—a discipline so tempered with mildness that must have endeared him to every individual in the regiment, as well as his general attention to their private interests.
>
> But their gratitude and private feelings must now give way and be subordinate to the public service, and it is only left for them to indulge the hope that it may be their good fortune to serve under his command, and eventually in his brigade.
>
> They are proud to think and reflect on the distinguished honours they gained in Egypt, when he gloriously fell wounded at their head, and hope under his command they may acquire additional glory in future and no less important services.
>
> They finally beg leave to assure him that their best wishes for his welfare and happiness ever attend him; and that in every honour he may acquire they will, though absent, always participate.
>
> Signed, in the name and at the request of all the officers of the 90th regiment,
>
> Ruthven,
Major Commanding 90th Regt.
>
> Athlone, 1st September, 1803.

The duties performed in Ireland by General Hill were of various kinds, partly arising out of the internal disaffection which at that time prevailed, and partly out of the threatened danger of a French invasion. The latter was in some degree connected with the former, through the conduct of certain Irish exiles in France, during the bubble peace of Amiens, blown by the deceitful breath, of Napoleon, only to glitter and to burst rather sooner than suited either his own schemes, or those of the wily Talleyrand. At this time the services of General Hill in Ireland, thus sketched by himself:—

> On being appointed a Brigadier-General in Ireland, I was stationed at Loughrea, having under my immediate command some fine light infantry corps formed from the militia of Ireland; also having charge of the whole western part of the country. Ireland at this period was threatened with the invasion of the French, and was much disturbed by disaffection in the country. On the 20th of October, 1803, Lieutenant-Colonel Skinner, who commanded at Galway, informed me that he had received by express an account of an enemy's fleet being seen off the coast, in consequence of which the troops were kept in readiness to move on the shortest notice. Reports of this kind, many without foundation, kept us on the alert. General Dalrymple, on the 20th of October, sent a report of the enemy's actual landing at Killala Bay. This report originated from the circumstance of two English frigates coming in to water. Their empty casks were all floated to the shore, and each was considered a boat full of French troops.

This imaginary alarm of the Irishmen who were on the look-out, is probably without parallel in the category of blunders, and must have afforded infinite amusement at their expense, especially as the report stated "they were landing very fast!" Lord Hardwick was at this time Lord Lieutenant, and General Fox commander of the forces, and General Hill was soon brought into more useful service than attending to summonses to repel incursions of empty water-casks, he says:

> About the 10th of November, 1803, I was ordered to Galway, and arrived two days afterwards at that town, to take the command of the western district. On the 10th of December, made arrangements for the police of the town, which was badly managed. Orders were also given to the commanding officers of corps, to be in readiness to march at the shortest notice. Various orders and regulations for the yeomanry corps, which were in general in a bad (state). The Light Company of Galway volun-

teers laid down their arms; and other troops behaved in nearly the same unmilitary manner.

In these difficulties, General Hill manifested the most admirable tact, the result of which was that the Light Company, who had acted so disgracefully, confessed their error with shame and regret. He considered that his duty was to ascertain the causes of this conduct, and then to deal with them accordingly, in the spirit of that mild but firm dignity which adorned his character and office. His first step, therefore, was to order "a Court of Inquiry, comprised of respectable yeomanry captains, to investigate the conduct of the men, and to inquire into the cause of their complaints." General Hill, considering the affair one of great delicacy, submitted their report to the inspection of Sir Eyre Coote, asking either his private advice or official directions. He was anxious to heal the matter in a wise and proper manner. His remark to Sir Eyre Coote was:

> It appears to me that government have not been regular in their disbursements to the corps in this town; but the conduct of the company in question is not the less reprehensible on that account, which they are indeed fully sensible of, and promise to atone for their past irregularity, by future obedience and observance of discipline. But notwithstanding their present contrition, I have some hesitation in restoring their arms.

At the same time he ordered two ringleaders into confinement, till Sir Eyre's answer should arrive. This prudent line of conduct had an admirable effect. On the 1st of January, 1804, he had the pleasure of making a favourable report on the state of Ireland, yet, as usual, took no merit to himself, but said:

> This reformation probably may proceed in some degree from a failure of promise from the French, who it was generally believed would visit their friends here six or eight weeks ago, and from the present conviction in the minds of the people of the improbability of an enemy making any strong impression, from the vigilance and activity of government in the rebellious counties, and from the rigorous military measures adopted in the country.

In his own memoranda his proceedings are thus recorded:—

In the beginning of January, 1804 detailed instructions were given to the yeomanry corps for their conduct in the event of the enemy's landing on the coast, which was expected. I also examined all the places on the coast likely for the enemy to land, and visited more than once the wild country of Connemara, which chiefly belongs to Mr. Richard Martin, of Galway. In all these excursions I was accompanied and assisted by my friend and *aide-de-camp*, Captain Currie.

The precautionary measures which were the judicious result of this inspection, will be seen in the following letter, addressed by this officer to Mr. Martin:—

Galway, 5th Jan. 1804.

Sir,
In the absence of Brigadier-General Hill, who is gone to meet Sir Eyre Coote, I am directed to inform you that, in the event of an enemy's effecting a debarkation to the west of the Connemara country, he recommends to your immediate consideration to destroy Tindella Bridge, nine miles to the west of Oughterard; as also to occupy an important hill, three miles west of the last-mentioned place, over which the road runs, and which may be considered as a very strong hold in the hands of a small number, and capable of stopping the progress of an enemy advancing upon that quarter from Galway. There are also three small bridges to the westward of Ballynahinch, which it would be of importance to break up and destroy.

It is unnecessary to point out to you the impracticability of an enemy's advancing with artillery, &c., if these precautionary measures are adopted in time. The natural obstacles which the country presents, and the facility with which the road, the only road of approach, can be destroyed, must be obvious to every person possessing your local knowledge of it.

I have the honour to be. Sir,
Your most obedient humble Servant,
E. Currie.

Richd. Martin, Esq., &c. &c. &c.

General Hill, by various important steps, did effectual service, civil as well as military, in those trying times. His proceedings are little known, because eclipsed by the splendour of his Peninsular glory; but they will be duly appreciated by all who trace the satisfactory gradations of his rise to the highest pinnacle of military honour. At this time, the vigilance he exercised and the plans he adopted commanded great admiration; and one of them was, the raising effective bodies of native Irish, to act under their superiors, as guards of passes. A gentleman of the name of Ireland may be given as the example, and General Hill wrote respecting him in these terms to Sir E. B. Littlehales:—

> Mr. Ireland is a Protestant, and a very respectable loyal subject; and I conceive a corps of such people of his own persuasion as he would be enabled to associate together, might be rendered extremely useful in guarding the pass of Cong, and thereby cutting off the communication of the disaffected with the Connemara country.

In order to be prepared in case of necessity, General Hill opened a communication between Loughrea and Galway by signal, and how carefully he arranged the necessary preparations, appears from what he wrote on the 9th of January, 1804, to Sir Eyre Coote:—

> Captain Trench, Royal Navy, has been employed for some days in preparing a dictionary containing every word that can possibly be used. Each word is numbered; and as the ten signals agreed upon are capable of expressing any number whatever, you will perceive the facility with which the most detailed information may be communicated, and that *with the most profound secrecy*.

After this, the following account will be read with surprise:—

> In this month (January) I also established a telegraph between Loughrea and Galway, and had considerable trouble in recovering the expenses incurred on the occasion. I also had a survey of the country made."

This money was advanced out of his own private resources; but he bore this conduct on the part of the Government with his usual placidity, and obtained a reimbursement at last, after a long and tiresome correspondence. Towards the end of February, the disloyal portion of the Irish people were firmly persuaded that the French would come, and General Hill's view of their expectations is thus expressed in a private letter:

> I cannot avoid remarking that it is too evident that disaffection has not yet subsided; and although it is not possible for me to speak positively on a subject of so much delicacy, yet I am led

to believe that the disaffected, particularly of the middling class, rather begin to show themselves, and look forward with much confidence to the invasion of this country, which they pretend to say will take place in the course of this month.

The instructions from the Lord Lieutenant were to keep a vigilant watch, and to communicate all the information that could be acquired. He had scarcely received these injunctions, when an intimation was conveyed to him that "the country was laid out in departments, and commissioners of various ranks assigned to fill those departments," and also that the French would probably land in two or three places, and the conflict be very severe. The precautionary measures he took in consequence of this information, to which he attached some credit, were extensive and decided. He issued a circular of private instruction to the captains of yeomanry, so to dispose of the boats on Lough Carib that they could not be available to an enemy, and himself paid a visit of inspection to the isles of Arran, as being "particularly well situated for a look-out post on the western coast." He likewise issued orders how to deal with those who appeared disposed to welcome the invaders; and having still in remembrance the empty-cask bugbear, gave instructions for preventing false alarms.

In these laudable measures General Hill was cordially assisted by the well-disposed Irish of all grades and persuasions, while the Athlone militia tendered their services in any way, and in any place in the United Kingdom, that might be deemed expedient; nor was there the slightest reason to apprehend that attempts made to tamper with the yeomanry would be of any avail, so well were they organised and disposed. The result was, that on the 9th of May he was enabled to report to the Lord Lieutenant that "nothing had occurred in the district under his command to interrupt the public tranquillity;" and further, on the 1st of June, "the country is perfectly quiet, and I have no reason to think that there are any improper meetings held." The same also was stated in his official communications in July. But General Hill was not inactive; he was engaged on an important work. His own account states:

> In the summer I was employed by government to build towers for signals on the coast. This duty gave me considerable trouble and anxiety, which was greatly increased by the irregular manner in which government made their payments.
>
> This irregularity embraced every department, and was the subject

of harassing correspondence, especially on behalf of the arrears due to the yeomanry, in which General Hill was warmly supported by General Pigot, who had taken the command of the western district. Lord Cathcart was commander of the forces; and on the 9th of August General Hill received from him the subjoined secret communication relative to the long anticipated arrival of the French, who were again suspected of an attempt to land in Ireland:—

      Camp, Curragh of Kildare, 9th August, 1804.
Dear General Hill,
There is a tolerably well-grounded report that nine sail of the French fleet have got out of Brest, destination said to be the Mediterranean, but of course that is quite uncertain. We must keep a good look-out.
Any report to me will be forwarded either by the Secretary's office or Adjutant General's office, Royal Hospital, if I am not there.
    Yours, dear General, truly and faithfully,
              Cathcart.

This, however, was altogether a false alarm, for two days afterwards he received another letter on the subject from General Pigot in contradiction of the report.

         Ballinasloe, August 11. 1804.
My dear Sir,
I have received a letter from Colonel Anstruther, informing me that government have received advice that the report of a French squadron having escaped from Brest is unfounded. The whole of the French fleet in Brest harbour remained on the third, in the same state in which they have been for some time past.
   Believe me
      Most truly yours,
             H. Pigot.
P. S. Be so good as to inform Captain Trench of this, and make it known where you may think necessary.

Thus, between alarms and their contradictions. General Hill was at this time kept in a state by no means enviable, while his patience was tried to the utmost by obstacles of the most reprehensible kind, raised by proprietors to the erection of the signals on their properties, which became a source of great annoyance to him. He overcame all these difficulties with the most praiseworthy forbearance, and manifested infinite tact and kindness in settling certain disputes between Irish officers of yeomanry, commencing in bluster and ending in mutual apologies made under his directions, who never in his life seems to have had a dispute with any man. Besides these unpleasant circumstances, he had to submit to a continual change of *aides-de-camp*. His own narrative of events at this time makes mention of these circumstances:

> I was deprived of the services of Captain Currie, in consequence of the embarkation of the 90th Regiment to the West Indies. On November 17th Brigade-Major Foster repaired to Galway, for the purpose of being attached to me in the situation held by Captain Currie as Brigade-Major. In the early part of this year (1805), I was chiefly occupied at Galway in the erection of Naval Signal Posts. Mr. ———'s opposition to the erecting a post near his house in Connemara, was most reprehensible and troublesome to me. On the 26th January I received a letter from the adjutant-general, informing me that a large ship full of troops had been seen off the coast of Scotland, and desiring me to take every possible precaution.

As usual nothing came of this announcement, while General Hill was obliged to write thus to headquarters:—

> I have to request that his Lordship will be pleased to recommend the payment of the money advanced by me upwards of a year since.

This letter was crossed by one of an official character to the effect described by himself.

> On the 25th of April I received a letter from headquarters informing me that a large French fleet with troops on board had been seen near Gibraltar, and desiring me to keep a good lookout.

Then came another change of *aide-de-camp*.

> On the 14th of May, Brigade-Major Foster, who was afterwards killed in action, was ordered to join his regiment. He was, at my request, replaced by Captain Palmer of the 15th Foot.

At the same time General Hill wrote to Sir Eyre Coote, under whom Major Foster was about to serve, recommending him to his friendly attention as having been "unremitting in his duty as an officer, and circumspect in his behaviour as a gentleman." He manifested in all his recommendations the same impartial patronage of merit, and merit alone, which enabled him when at the head of the army to repel every insinuation of political opponents. An officer applied to him, while in Ireland, on the score of relationship, for a vacant company, alleging at the same time that several officers junior to himself had received this promotion. His answer was:

> Although it is my wish to serve every deserving officer, and particularly those I have the honour of being related to, yet, in your case, I am sorry I do not feel myself warranted to recommend you for promotion, as I could only do it on the plea of your merit, with which I am not acquainted.

He then added, that he had never seen him as a soldier, and that if his pretensions were just, his own commanding-officer would not overlook them.

In October, 1805, General Hill joined the camp on the Curragh of Kildare, with which he remained till it broke up, and then returned to Galway, after which he finally departed from that town, to the great regret of the inhabitants, who were unanimous in presenting him a most gratifying and justly-merited address.

This address, and General Hill's reply, were published in the *Dublin Post* and *Connaught Journal*.

The Amicable Society, of which he had been elected President in the month of November, 1804, enrolled him in the list of their honorary members, and addressed to him a most touching farewell. Under his influence, they said, they had "experienced all the advantages of the strictest military discipline, without any of its austerities." Thus General Hill quitted the district in which he had commanded, leaving the impression which a tender heart, a most courteous bearing, and a firm hand could not fail to make on the well-disposed of all ranks.

The Earl of Buchan, who first saw him in Scotland in 1792, remarked in a letter to Sir Richard Hill:

> By all the rules of Lavater, as well as my own, I should have augured well of that young gentleman from his appearance and manner.

The same impression was made upon every individual, of whatever grade, who had the good fortune to have intercourse with him, while experience more than confirmed the highest expectations.

CHAPTER 4

General Hill Brings Home Troops to Plymouth

The cause of General Hill's departure from Galway will be seen in a letter addressed to Lord Cathcart, by his Royal Highness the Commander-in-Chief.

Horse Guards, Oct. 19. 1805.

My Lord,
Having caused it to be intimated to your Lordship that a force of 5000 men would be immediately ordered to embark from Cork for this country, in consequence of the intention of government to send a considerable force from hence to the Continent, I have now to desire that your Lordship may be pleased to direct the under-mentioned regiments to be immediately embarked on board of such transports as have been provided for their reception, and to sail for England with the first fair wind. The regiments will take with them respectively their battalion guns, camp equipage, and as much spare ammunition as will complete them, if possible, to 300 rounds per gun, and 300 rounds per man.

As it is very probable that the *Middleton* transport, which was ordered to proceed with Sir Eyre Coote to Jamaica, with camp equipage and medical stores for 6000 men, may yet be at Cork, your Lordship will be pleased to cause her to be detained, and to return to England with the regiments hereafter mentioned.

"The battalions to be embarked are as follows: *viz*. 1st battalion 8th regiment, *ditto* 9th, *ditto* 28th, *ditto* 30th, *ditto* 36th, *ditto* 89th.

The general officer whom your Lordship will be pleased to embark with the above force, will be *Brigadier-General Rowland Hill*, and the whole to be placed for the present under the command of that *Brigadier-General*.

   I am, my Lord,
     Yours,
         Frederick,
         Commander-in-Chief.

In consequence of this letter, Lord Cathcart addressed the subjoined friendly notice to General Hill:—

      Royal Hospital, Oct. 21. 1805.

My dear General Hill,

I have directed the adjutant-general to forward to you by express, the copy of a letter which I have this day received from his Royal Highness the Commander-in-Chief. You will, therefore, be pleased to report by express to Lieutenant-General Lord Rosslyn, and to acquaint Brigadier-General Stuart, at Cork, and the officers commanding at Ballinasloe and at Loughrea, as well as at Athlone, of your motions, and proceed as expeditiously as you can to Cork, in order to superintend the embarkation of the troops.

There being no battalion guns on this establishment, there is considerable difficulty in supplying the demand on that subject. If, however, I can muster twelve guns, they will he prepared at Cork, and due attention shall also be paid to the stowage of the spare gun and musket ammunition on board the transport.

I have to request that you will give to Brigadier-General Stuart what information you can in regard to Galway, as he will probably, for the present, command there; but you must not delay your departure on any account relating to the service here, as you are entrusted with a command, by order of the Commander-in-Chief.

I will use my best endeavours to procure for you the price of your map.

I am myself under orders for departure, having received a notification that I am appointed ambassador to the Emperor[1] of Russia; but I have as yet no instructions relative to making over the command here, and I do not expect to leave this place be-

---

1. Lord Cathcart did not at this time go to Russia, but to the Weser.

fore the middle of the week.

Wherever you may go, my dear General, you will carry with you my sincere regard, and you will be followed by my best wishes for your health, honour, and happiness; and I beg to assure you of the grateful sense I shall always entertain of your active assistance and attentions since I have been in this command, and of the very great regard with which I remain,

My dear General,

Your faithful and obedient Servant,

Cathcart.

P.S. The ladies of my family send you their compliments and best wishes.

I have inserted these letters as evidences of the just impression made in the highest quarters, as well as on the inhabitants of his district, by the military talent and private demeanour of General Hill in Ireland. The map alluded to by Lord Cathcart, was a survey he had caused to be made according to instructions; and though he had advanced a considerable sum in payment for it, he could not obtain a reimbursement, and was obliged to memorialise the Commander of the Forces on the subject.

General Hill lost no time in proceeding to Cork according to order. His own memorandum contains the following notice of events at this exciting period:—

> On the 30th of October Lord Cathcart, as Commander of the Forces, took leave of the army, being ordered on service. The armies on the Continent at this period were in active operation. Bonaparte crossed the Danube. The capitulation of Ulm was signed by General Mack, and not a vestige of the Austrian force was left in Suabia. This armament from Ireland and England was hurried to the Weser, with the view of assisting the Continental powers to check the rapid success of the French.—21st of October: Lord Nelson's victory off Trafalgar.—In the early part of December the great armies of the Continent were engaged near Olmutz. The uncertain accounts of these operations which came to England, induced Mr. Pitt to risk everything to send troops to the Continent, and notwithstanding the season of the year, and the dangers of the North Seas, we were ordered to proceed. After a tremendous passage, and serious losses, some of us had the good fortune to arrive in the Weser on Christmas Day, 1805.

And a miserable Christmas it was, clouded with disasters and ill-tidings. General Hill, says:

> When I reached that river the headquarter ship of every regiment belonging to me was missing; some were wrecked on the Dutch coast, and many souls perished on the Goodwin sands.

No sooner had the general and his lively *aide-de-camp*, Captain Peebles, stepped on shore, than they were met by an old sugar-refiner who had resided in England, who told them, in the most grotesque attempt to speak their native language, of the triumphs of the armies of Napoleon. Such was the unhappy Christmas of 1805; but General Hill had one consolation, that of having made the acquaintance, on his way from Cork, of his future commander he says:

> On our voyage from Cork we put into Falmouth, where we remained about a week. General Houghton was under my orders in command of his regiment. We also anchored off Deal, where I first saw Sir Arthur Wellesley. He dined with me at my lodgings at Mrs. Chitty's, and was much amused with Captain Peebles. Sir Arthur took the command of the troops collecting for the Weser.[2]

General Hill modestly leaves unnoticed the impression he himself made on the sagacious mind of that illustrious man, an impression which became more and more confirmed in each succeeding year of intercourse in war and in peace.

The great successes of the French in 1805 caused the return of the forces with which General Hill had gone to the Weser, and at the end of January, 1806, he found himself, once more at Deal. On his voyage to that port he anchored off Yarmouth, and as was natural, the first question asked of the pilot was, "What news?"

---

2. This expedition was fitted out under the command of Lord Cathcart, and Major-General Sir Arthur Wellesley commanded a brigade in it, and on this occasion General Hill first served with him. On the arrival of the tidings of the Battle of Austerlitz, they were recalled, and the troops were placed on our own coast for defence in case of an invasion. Sir Arthur Wellesley commanded a brigade at Hastings after this, and General Hill was at Hythe, whence he went to the staff in Ireland. It was in allusion to Sir Arthur's being only in command of a brigade on the Weser expedition, that this true patriot soldier said, "I am *nammukwallah*, as we say in India; I have eaten the king's salt, and am therefore ready to serve my king in any capacity." These are memorable words, which have indeed been proved to be sincere by the whole course of the Duke of Wellington's life, spent in willing devotedness to his sovereign and country in and out of office.

His reply was truly in accordance with the quaint ignorance and roughness of his class in those days, "Billy Pitt is dead, and Charley Fox come into Parliament."

General Hill says:

> This news we soon found to be true. Pitt died on the 24th of January, aged 48, and Fox was placed at the head of the government. Bonaparte at this time was triumphant over all the armies of the confederates. These calamities deeply affected Mr. Pitt, and it was supposed that the successes of the French at Austerlitz had hastened his death.

From Yarmouth this small British force proceeded to Deal, and thence to Ramsgate, where General Hill received the melancholy tidings of the death of his mother.

He thus announces his next movement:—

> On the 17th of April I arrived at Brabourne Lees to take the command of the troops in that neighbourhood, establishing my quarters at a small house between Brabourne Lees and Hythe. Lord Moira was appointed to the command of the Southern district on the 15th of April, 1806. Sir John Moore was stationed at Canterbury, and I was directed to report to him until the 5th of June, when he and General Mackenzie Frazer were removed to the staff of the army serving in the Mediterranean, when Sir George Ludlow was appointed to the command at Canterbury. On the 23rd of June, my brigade, consisting of the 9th, 45th, and 62nd, marched and encamped on Shorn Cliff. I encamped with the troops on a beautiful spot immediately above the Rev. Mr. Brockman's house.

There he lived a true soldier's life, under canvas, and produced by his exertions and example such perfection in the brigade, that the highest commendations were passed on it by Lord Moira and the Duke of York in two successive inspections. He had previously been advanced to the rank of Major-General, and was now appointed on the staff; and his brother, Captain Thomas Noel Hill, became his *aide-de-camp*.

In October they went into cantonments, and remained at Hythe till the end of December, when they were ordered to Ireland. Before their departure General Hill had the satisfaction of receiving a flattering communication from the mayor, to which he replied with his usual courtesy.

He next went to Ireland, where he remained the whole of the year 1807. The Duke of Bedford was Lord-Lieutenant, and Lieutenant-Colonel Stewart was Chief Secretary and Military Secretary, to whom General Hill's principal communications of an official character were addressed. His routine of duty was very similar to that assigned him before the expedition to the Weser, except that he had not to deal with alarms of French invasion. He was stationed at Fermoy, and the chief objects of his attention appear to have been the suppression of local disturbances, and precautionary measures against *banditti* infesting the mountains, in both of which he was eminently successful. Everything reported to the Vice-Regal Court and the Commander of the Forces, was carefully sifted by him and represented in its proper light, which occasioned considerable trouble, for the slightest insubordination, even a disturbance on a market day, or a quarrel about leases and lands, was construed by the vivid imagination of his reporters into insurrection and hostility to government.

He managed to quiet all these false alarms, and allayed private animosities between the officers, as he did during his previous residence amongst the sensitive people he had to deal with. In this way he proceeded, to the admiration of all parties, till, in the year 1808, he was ordered to join the then Chief Secretary of Ireland, Sir Arthur Wellesley, on his first campaign in the Peninsula, where his military talents had full scope for their exercise, in a series of achievements equally honourable to himself and serviceable to his country. Happily for General Hill, with a change of government there arose a change of projects, or he might have been sent on the proposed Quixotic expedition to Spanish South America, instead of going to reap victory and honour on the fields of Europe.

The ministers who succeeded "the Talents" had the sense to relinquish this scheme; and guided principally by the advice of the deputies who had arrived in England from the Asturias and Galicia, they bade *adieu* to the projects of the adventurer Miranda, and changed the destination of the troops in Ireland from South America to Portugal, appointing Sir Arthur Wellesley to command them. These troops, amounting to about 9000 men, formed at that time the most disposable army of this country, whose soldiers and treasure had been alike scattered without judgment.

Sir Arthur Wellesley soon opened his correspondence with General Hill, respecting the brigading and embarkation of the forces. In his first letter[3] on these subjects, dated "Dublin Castle, 23rd June, 1808," he says:

> My dear Hill, I rejoice extremely at the prospect I have before me of serving again with you, and I hope we shall have more to do than we had on the last occasion on which we were together."

After giving him the necessary instructions. Sir Arthur added:

> You may readily believe that I have plenty to do in closing up a government in such a manner as that I may give it up, and taking the command of a corps for service; but I shall not fail to attend to whatever you may write to me.

Nor did General Hill fail to attend to every particular of the directions he received from Sir Arthur Wellesley, relating to the embarkation of the troops on board the transports in which they were to sail. The most anxious care was taken of their health and comforts, and the men were occasionally ordered on shore for air and exercise. Sir Arthur prepared for sailing with his usual promptitude, and on the receipt of his instructions, wrote to this effect:—

> Dublin Castle, July 3rd, 1808.
> My dear Hill,
> I have received my instructions, and I understand that the cavalry and some ships to receive the 36th and 45th regiments sailed from the Downs and Portsmouth on the 30th. I shall be at Cork on Wednesday, and I hope that we shall sail immediately afterwards. The horses of the commissariat will be at Cork on Tuesday and Wednesday, and I shall be obliged to you if you will arrange with General Floyd respecting the early embarkation.
> I would have taken horses of the artillery if I could have got them; but, alas! I could not, and have therefore those which will probably only do our work till we shall get others.
> I have written Malcolm a long letter respecting the arrangement of the transports into divisions; a code of signals for the army; and return of transports and flat-bottomed boats; so that

---

3. The principal part of the letters which passed between the Duke of Wellington and Lord Hill, during the Peninsular War, have been already published by Colonel Garwood. But the originals, written by the former, and Lord Hill's own copies of the latter, are in my possession, and from them I have made such extracts as I have thought it expedient to introduce into the present volume.

we may make all our arrangements for landing while we shall be on the passage. He will probably speak to you on these subjects, and I shall be obliged to you if you will give him all the assistance and information in your power.

Tell Arbuthnot that I have desired my groom to apply to him for orders when he should arrive at Cork; and that I shall be obliged to him if he will have the horses embarked in the transport allotted to the staff horses. He had better send up to Cork to one of the officers of General Floyd's staff, to desire that the horses may be forwarded to Cove when they will arrive.

Ever yours most sincerely,
Arthur Wellesley.
Major-General Hill.

Sir Arthur's instructions were dated the 30th of June; and on the 6th of July he arrived at Cork, where he was delayed longer than he expected, and became anxious to go in some small separate vessel to Coruña. He however sailed with the troops on the 12th; but on the 13th quitted the fleet, and went on board the *Crocodile*, commanded by the Honourable G. Cadogan, in which he arrived at Coruña on the 20th. The exact number of the rank and file who embarked at Cove was 9505, besides 215 horses, staff, field officers, 550 Sergeants, and 227 drummers, which appears to a civilian a goodly allowance; but they were going against the French, who out-drum every other nation upon earth. The voyage proceeded prosperously, and progress was thus announced by General Hill to Lord Castlereagh:—

Lat. 48° 40', Long. 9° W.
H. M. S. *Donegal*, 18th July, 1808.

My Lord,

In the absence of Lieutenant-General Sir Arthur Wellesley, it affords me particular satisfaction to inform your Lordship by the *La Gloria*, that none of the transports that sailed with the armament from Cove on the 12th of this month are missing, and that the troops are perfectly healthy. Sir Arthur Wellesley went on board the *Crocodile* on the 13th, and in the evening proceeded for his destination.

I have, &c.
R. Hill.

Viscount Castlereagh.

After various events irrelevant to this memoir, as having no connection with General Hill, Sir Arthur Wellesley came on board the *Donegal*, on the 30th of July, and began to land the troops in Mondego Bay on the 1st of August under admirable regulations. The operations occupied till the 5th, when a reinforcement under General Spencer arrived, by which however the number of troops was only augmented, to 12,300 men. Before he commenced disembarking the armament, Sir Arthur Wellesley had been apprised of the arrangements for the future command of the several corps that the Government had determined should form one army in Portugal, under the new commander of the forces. Sir Hew Dalrymple, with Sir Harry Burrard as the second in command. His own great name stood last in the list of seven lieutenant-generals in this programme of service, but under these mortifying circumstances his noble disposition was fully manifested. He wrote to Lord Castlereagh:

> All I can say on the subject is, that whether I am to command the army or not, or am to quit it, I shall do my best to ensure its success; and you may depend upon it that I shall not hurry the operations or commence them one moment sooner than they ought to be commenced, in order that I may acquire the credit of the success.

He went on issuing his orders from Lavaos with that comprehensiveness of judgment which has never been surpassed by any man in a like situation, until the approach of the hostile armies to each other indicated the necessity of instructions in case of a conflict. On the 9th he enclosed to General Hill a copy of orders given to General Fane through Colonel Bathurst, Lieutenant-Colonel and Deputy Quartermaster-General. On the original General Hill wrote the following memorandum:—

> Sir Arthur Wellesley's instructions for the *first* movement that was made by his troops on the Continent."
> It is as follows:—
>
> Headquarters, Lavaos, 8th August, 1808.
> Sir,
> I am directed by Lieut.-General Sir Arthur Wellesley to desire that you will be pleased to march tomorrow morning, at three o'clock, towards Leyria, and take post in front of Gião. Captain Douglas, Assistant Quartermaster-General, will point out the ground.
> Captain Gomm will attend the column from the camp,

to show the road. In the evening you will be pleased to push forwards some dragoons, with a detachment of 200 infantry, as far as you may judge expedient; and should you receive intelligence that the enemy are not at Leyria, or in the neighbourhood, you will cause the town of Leyria to be occupied by this detachment either tomorrow evening or on Wednesday morning.

Should you find that the enemy are in any force at or in the neighbourhood of Leyria, you will withdraw the detachment, and remain in front of Gião, until you receive orders from Sir Arthur Wellesley, to whom you will transmit the earliest intelligence you may obtain. You will be pleased to cause a detachment to remain in camp, to deliver over the camp equipage of the 60th and 95th Regiments to the storekeeper, who will be on the ground at three o'clock a.m. to receive it.

The tents are to be packed up in bales ready for embarkation, with the number in each bale marked on the outside, and they are to be packed on the waggons by the detachments of the regiments.

An assistant commissary will attend the brigade to supply provisions, and he will also make every inquiry respecting the resources the enemy may be likely to find at and near Leyria, and you will be pleased to give him any assistance he may require to execute this duty.

I have the honour to be, Sir,
    Your most obedient humble Servant,
                James Bathurst,
    Lieut.-Col. and Deputy Quartmast.-General.

The next day General Hill was informed in a letter from Sir Arthur Wellesley, that having heard that the enemy might possibly be in some strength at Leyria, he had desired General Fane to wait for his brigade and the brigade of General Ferguson, all of which were to halt at St. Gião till Sir Arthur himself should join them at five or six o'clock in the morning, if the enemy were in possession of Leyria. If not, he was to endeavour to feel his way into the town with two hundred riflemen and a few dragoons, and the next day to take up his position in front of the place. Leyria was entered, the enemy occupying Alcobaça, about sixteen miles distant, under Generals Laborde and Thomiere,

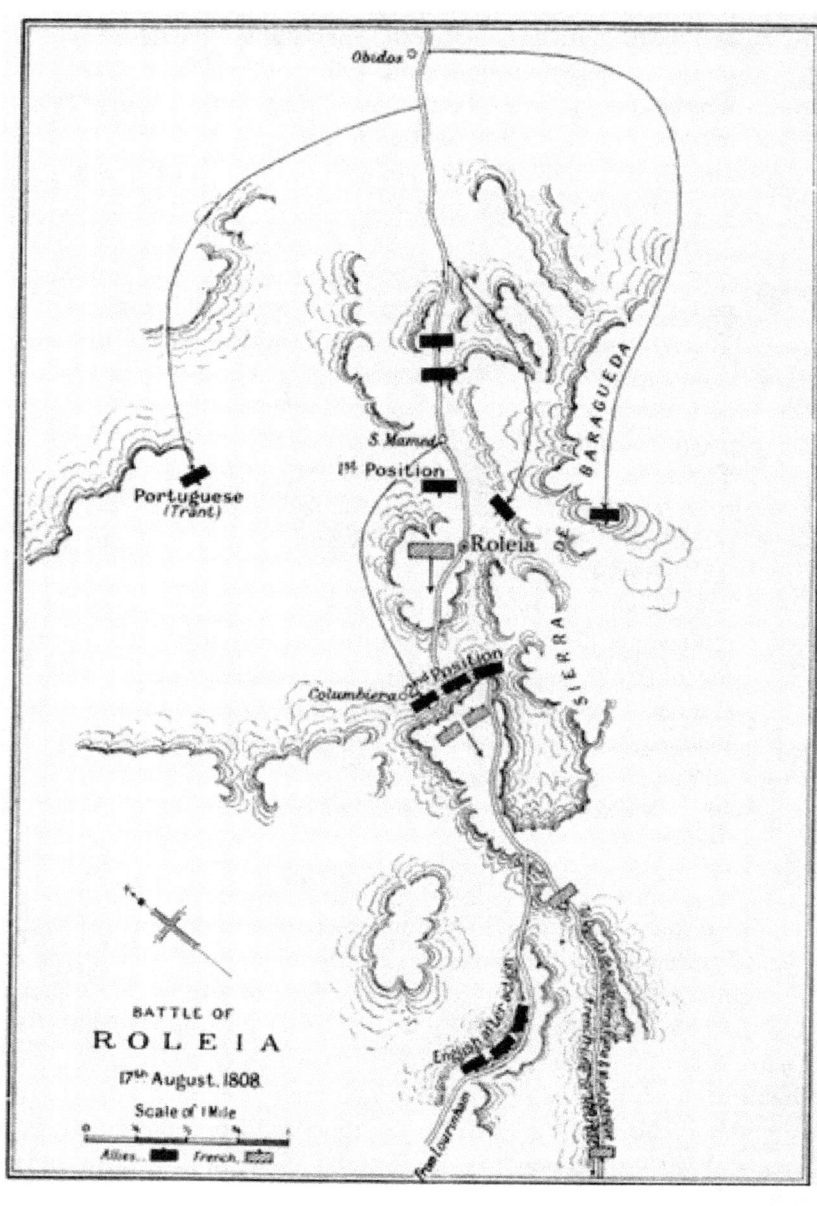

and Santarem on the high road to Lisbon, where Junot and Loison were established.

It is not my province to describe the plans, movements, and difficulties of Sir Arthur Wellesley at this moment, nor the conduct of the Portuguese general, Bernardim Freire, nor that of the ambitious meddling bishop of Oporto, who had assumed a character and displayed a spirit so contrary to that of his office as described by St. Paul—but to conduct the reader at once to the first action in which the subject of these pages gained his Peninsular laurels under his unrivalled leader. General Laborde, pressed by Sir Arthur Wellesley, had moved from his previous position to a small plain in front of the village of Roliça, with the advantage of an elevation enabling him to overlook the whole country as far as Obidos. Here it was determined to attack him on the 17th of August; and General Hill's brigade formed a portion of the central column commanded by Sir Arthur in person. After the repulse occasioned by the first attack, in which General Hill displayed the most eminent activity and skill, Laborde retired into a formidable position in the mountains, full of passes difficult of access, where he assumed, with consummate dexterity, an attitude of apparently impregnable defence.

Generals Hill and Nightingale advanced against this well-guarded front, approachable only by defiles where Nature had placed every conceivable obstacle of wood rock, and ravine, which seemed to render the steep ascent almost impossible to achieve by columns, whom the rugged paths could not fail to throw into disorder. But our generals pushed on undismayed by the difficulties of the passes, or the stern resolution of the enemy.

The mountain-hollows were soon heard to ring with the echoing roll of musketry, mingled with the war-shouts of the assailants and the still louder responses of the assailed. Laborde was driven from his stronghold with a considerable loss of men, and with that also of three pieces of cannon; but, owing to a want of cavalry on the side of the British, effected his retreat in good order. On this occasion General Hill received the highest commendations; and it may be added, that the conduct of all the troops engaged, in number by no means equal to that of the enemy, was worthy of the British name, and of the cause in which they fought.

At the celebrated Battle of Vimeiro, on the 21st of August, the brigade of General Hill was posted on a mountain at the back of the village, as a reserve to the whole army; and if Sir Harry Burrard,

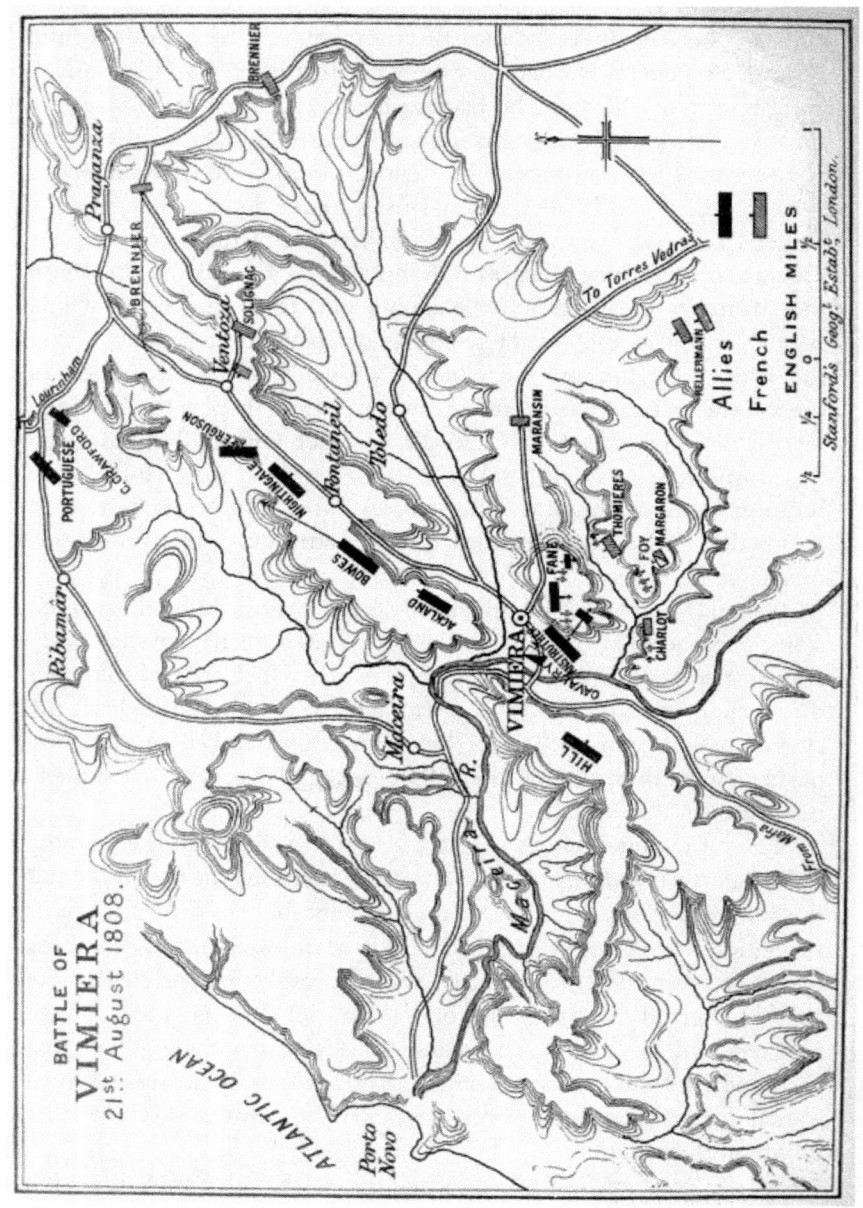

who landed during the action, had agreed to Sir Arthur Wellesley's proposal, he would have moved upon Torres Vedras to the right, while the victorious left pursued the advantages they had gained, and, in the opinion of Sir Arthur, would have ensured the entrance of the British into Lisbon before the French, if, indeed, the whole opposing army had not been annihilated. But the decision of Sir Harry, who, in the moment of Wellesley's triumph, assumed the command, was against all movement from Vimeiro, so that nothing remained for the victors but to dine with what appetite they could, under the conviction that they had been deprived of the glory of a consummation of their success, which, confiding in the genius of their superseded leader, few men doubt they would have achieved.

As it was. Sir Harry determined to wait at Vimeiro till reinforcements should arrive under Sir John Moore, and the French made good their retreat to Torres Vedras. The command of Sir Arthur Wellesley was now at an end, to the regret of every officer who served with him, evinced by a splendid testimonial. He arrived in London on the 6th of October, where the affair of Vimeiro, and the armistice and convention succeeding it, became the subjects of a court of inquiry, followed by the thanks to Sir Arthur of both Houses of Parliament, and his return to his duties as Secretary of Ireland. But the history of these circumstances belongs not to this memoir, as General Hill remained with the army.

In pursuance of the stipulations of the convention just alluded to, commonly but erroneously called the Convention of Cintra, Junot's army left Portugal in British vessels, and landed at La Rochelle in the month of October. Sir John Moore was appointed to the command of the British forces; Sir David Baird, with a large body of troops, arrived at Coruña; Bonaparte appeared in Spain; Madrid was once more occupied by the French; the usurper Joseph tenanted the palace of Saint Ildefonso; and Moore essayed his arduous and memorable movements in the north of Spain, during which Napoleon, alarmed at the demonstrations of Austria, departed, leaving Soult to encounter the English general, whose chief embarrassments arose from the inertness of the Spaniards and the undisciplined troops of Romana. General Hill, like the rest, was subject to the fluctuations of this trying campaign, the movements of which were of necessity uncertain, from the peculiarities of their situation. An example of this is afforded by the following instructions from Sir John Hope:—

>   Torricella, 14th December, 1808.

Dear Sir,
Circumstances have occurred which cause a change in our movements tomorrow. I enclose the proposed disposition of the right of the army on the 15th and 16th, in consequence of which you will be pleased to march with your brigade to Castro Nuño, on or near the Douro, and on the 16th to Toro.
    I remain, dear Sir,
            Yours sincerely,
                                    John Hope.
Major-General Hill.

These changes were due to an intercepted despatch from Berthier to Soult, which proved that the French were ignorant of the British movements, and inspired Sir John Moore with a hope that he might surprise and beat him before Bonaparte could come to his assistance. The French emperor himself was astonished at the boldness of the British movements, and pronounced Moore the only general fit to contend with him, for he could neither surprise him into an error, nor with all his energetic speed overtake him in his masterly retreat; so that he departed for his capital foiled in his designs, as Soult was when he pursued Sir John through Galicia, with the vain expectation that superiority of numbers would prevent the embarkation of the British Army at Coruña.

Under the guidance of this patient and sagacious leader our troops, after trials often described but never exaggerated, arrived within sight of the sea on the 10th of January, short of provisions, but supported by the expectation of finding transports in the harbour of Coruña, in which they might be securely embarked; but a few small craft were all that appeared in view. Contrary winds had detained the transports at Vigo, and the French Army, in larger numbers than our own, was rapidly advancing: but the mind of Sir John Moore expanded under the pressure of these adverse circumstances, and his measures were taken with prudence and decision. He first secured his sick on board the few small vessels at hand, put his wearied soldiers into quarters in the town, fortified its weak defences, and determined to effect his own embarkation by the repulse of his pursuers.

Fortunately, a magazine of English arms was in the town, which were exchanged for the battered muskets of the late campaign; but two storehouses of gunpowder, at some distance from each other, containing more than four thousand barrels, had been placed three miles off Coruña, and were in danger of being captured by the enemy. To prevent this it was unhesitatingly resolved to explode them. The train first reached the smaller store, and the town shook with the strong concussion; but scarcely had the larger taken fire when the result was like the eruption of a volcano, in the trembling of the earth, the bursting of the rocks, the upheaving of smoke, dust, stones, and sparks into the air, and the agitated foaming; of the disturbed waters of the sea, followed by a shower of white ashes that seemed to descend from the clouds.

Both armies, the secret being confided to one officer alone, were confounded: but the panic subsided, and the preparations for the fray proceeded; and the English troops, cheered by the arrival of the transports, were in high spirits, while their leader rejected with disdain a proposal to negotiate upon terms for leave to withdraw to them. He would have retired without bloodshed if possible, but would hear of no compromise, no convention. On the morning of the 16th he had removed all encumbrances to the ships, and was prepared to embark under cover of the shades of evening; but at noon the enemy attacked, and he won the victory of Coruña, at the price of his own life. The valour of those he commanded, the heroism of his lofty spirit, the awful nature of his wound, his death, his burial, his triumph, have been recounted by numerous historians, and will ever be remembered; though we trust the spirit of the Gospel will so pervade the earth, that a repetition of his departing words, "I always wished to die thus," may become impossible.

To the brigade of General Hill was assigned the office of protecting the British army as it proceeded to the ships, at the close of the engagement; and when the exhausted soldiers had ceased to file down from the field, feeble as the moon's wan beams on that chill and misty night, he himself went on board, and sailed for the shores of England. He reached Plymouth with a portion of the suffering troops towards the end of January.

The people of Plymouth and General Hill were most happily united in acts of philanthropy towards the soldiers on this trying occasion.[4]

---

[4]. In 1812, after the brilliant affair of Almaraz, the corporation of Plymouth voted him the freedom of that body; and the Mayor, George Bellamy, Esq., in communicating the tidings, made these remarks:—"When you were at Plymouth, I, in the midst of thousands, silently admired you, and had a greater opportunity than many of so doing, as I was employed in the Committee of Inhabitants to administer relief to the troops, their wives and children, when landed here from Coruña."

During the whole of the retreat of Sir John Moore General Hill's exertions were of the utmost service; and he stood high in the estimation of that distinguished man, who assured him, in a letter on private business, of the great interest he took in his welfare. On the inhabitants of Plymouth his humanity and kindness to the distressed soldiers made a lasting impression; while the men under his command looked to him as a father. During his absence on the expedition in Spain he lost his esteemed uncle. Sir Richard Hill; his father succeeded to the title and estates of Hawkstone; and he himself became possessed of the property at Hardwick Grange, bequeathed to him by Sir Richard, which he occupied as his favourite residence to the end of his life, breathing his last within its walls.

He had scarcely arrived in his native land before he found himself promoted to the Colonelcy of the Third Garrison Battalion; nor was he long before he was again ordered by the Commander-in-Chief to prepare for further service. By a letter from His Royal Highness the Duke of York, dated 17th February, 1809, it appears that he was appointed to take the command of the regiments then about to embark at Cork for the Peninsula.

He allowed himself only a few days of repose with his family in Shropshire, and proceeded at once to act on the instructions of Lord Castlereagh, conveyed to him in these terms:—

> Downing Street, 12th March, 1809.
>
> Sir,
>
> I am to convey to you the king's commands, that, so soon as the troops placed under your orders are embarked and ready for sea, you do proceed without loss of time to the Tagus, there to place yourself under the orders of Lieutenant-General Sir John Cradock, Commander-in-Chief of His Majesty's forces in Portugal.
>
> Three hundred artillery-horses are to accompany your corps. The necessary proportion of artillerymen and guns have already been forwarded from hence to Portugal.
>
> I am, Sir,
>
> Your most obedient and humble servant,
>
> Castlereagh.
>
> Major-General Hill, &c. &c., Cork.

General Hill's arrival in Portugal was anxiously looked for by Sir John Cradock, who had resolved to make no advance till he came, and was surrounded on all sides by difficulties created by the alarming spirit manifested by the troops and people, as well as by the chance of a decisive movement on the part of Victor and Lapisse, likely to be fraught with disastrous consequences. Marshal Beresford was also much relieved by the presence of these reinforcements, and urged Sir John Cradock to move forward.

Sir John's own intentions, and the duties he imposed on General Hill, will be seen in the subjoined communication from the former:

Leyria, April 22. 1809.

Dear Sir,

In sending forward the corps under your command, I beg to explain to you that it is more to procure accommodation for the troops than for any other purpose. Were I to entertain any apprehension of the approach of the enemy beyond Coimbra, I should not think it prudent to station your corps at Pombal, twenty miles distant, and so far from the main body. But lest any unforeseen occurrence should arise, I conceive it proper to give you these instructions.

I have reason to believe that there is a considerable collection of Portuguese armed persons, at and about Coimbra, even advanced as far as the Vouga River, under the command of Colonel Trant. Colonel Trant has written to me, that the enemy had pushed *patroles* and *videttes* as far as the opposite side of the river; and he states the enemy's force to be rather considerable. In one of his letters he estimates the cavalry at 2000, and the infantry at about 2500. But I understand that latterly their advanced posts had been retired. Colonel Trant, I am sure, will be very glad to receive any communication from you, and give you all the information he may possess.

Situated as you will be, your chief object is to gain as much intelligence as your distant situation from the enemy will permit, and prevent any predatory incursion, either to annoy you, or give us any alarm that would discredit the opinion of security from all insult which we imagine.

Should a small force of the enemy appear, I have no doubt but that you will make him repent his temerity; but if he approaches in superior numbers, or that you have reason to imagine his strength may be an increasing one, and such as would commit you in a general affair, I am to desire that you will fall back upon the main body, or towards them, giving me the most immediate notice.

    I have the honour to be. Sir,
      Your most obedient servant,
        J. Cradock, Lieut.-General.

Major-General Hill.

The cautious spirit attributed to Sir John Cradock breathes in every line of this letter: but two days after its date, in the midst of the enthusiasm enkindled by the arrival of Sir Arthur Wellesley in Lisbon, to assume the command, he departed to Gibraltar. The sickly aspect of uncertainty now changed into the flush of highest expectation, and all were roused by the conviction that the day of mighty achievements had dawned for the deliverance of the Peninsula.

CHAPTER 5

General Hill Takes the Command

Marshal Soult, having invaded the northern provinces of Portugal from Galicia, had taken possession of Oporto rather more than three weeks before Sir Arthur Wellesley reached Lisbon. He hesitated for a time as to whether he should combine with General Cuesta in an operation against Victor, who was on the Alemtejo frontier, or dispossess Soult of the town of Oporto, and the fertile province in his hands. The latter project was adopted; and the British leader assembled the chief portion of his troops at Coimbra, and, unknown to the French marshal—himself in a perilous position, from the disaffection pervading his own ranks—gained the advantage of securing two most important lines of movement: the one lay through Viseu and Lamego, by which he might turn the left of the enemy, and cut them off from Tras-os-Montes; the other was the direct road to Oporto, by which he could come suddenly on their right in superior numbers, and inflict on it a heavy blow, between the Rivers Vouga and Douro.

Sir Arthur availed himself of both these routes, but decided that his principal attack should be on the latter. Marshal Beresford, on the 6th of May, marched towards Lamego, by the Viseu road, with his separate corps, including six thousand Portuguese; and the bulk of the army was formed in three divisions of infantry, and one of cavalry. Major-General Hill commanded the third division of infantry; the first being under Lieutenant-General Paget, and the second under Lieutenant-General Sherbrooke. The cavalry was commanded by Lieutenant-General Payne. It having been discovered by Sir Arthur Wellesley that the lake of Ovar, extending twenty miles behind the French outposts, was unguarded, he decided on endeavouring to turn their right, by conveying troops by water to that town. This enterprise was entrusted to General Hill, to whom he wrote thus from Coimbra:—

Coimbra, 8th May, 1809, 2 p.m.

My dear Hill,

We halted yesterday, to give General Beresford time to get forward, and we proceed upon our operations tomorrow. You will receive from the quartermaster-general a paper fully explanatory to you of all that it is intended you should perform; to which I have only to add—first, that you will find the boats ready for you at Aveiro, and will have to get boatmen only, in which Douglas, whom I send to you, will assist you; secondly, that I mean you should bring to tomorrow night in such a place as that the enemy cannot discover you, in that part of the river or lake of which the banks are swampy.; thirdly, that you should land your light infantry below the town, where it is certain the enemy never is, in order to secure the unmolested disembarkation of the remainder of your corps at Ovar, where it is possible the enemy may have a small *patrole*.

I recommend you to cook a day's provisions at Aveiro, for your men for the 10th, and to refresh your men at Ovar, while you will wait there to learn the progress of General Cotton, with his cavalry.

Having communicated with that general, you will then move from Ovar by the road which leads from Ovar to Feira, till that road meets the great road from Coimbra to Oporto. You will halt there till you will be joined by the cavalry. My intention is to push the enemy as far as I can on the 10th, even into Oporto, if possible.

Ever yours most sincerely,

Arthur Wellesley.

Major-General Hill.

This letter I have copied from the original; and as the advance upon Oporto was one of the most remarkable movements of its illustrious writer, and an eminent instance of the talent and sagacity of the officer addressed, I subjoin the "paper" from the quartermaster-general. It is headed—"*Confidential* memorandum of arrangements for the advance of the army towards Oporto!":—

Headquarters, Coimbra, 8th May, 1809.

The brigade under M.-General Hill, which is already ordered to be at Aveiro on the 9th instant, will embark the same day on board boats to be procured there, so as the embarkation may be completed a little before low water, about 4 o'clock p.m.

M.-General Hill will then proceed from Aveiro towards Ovar, but he will give previous orders to the boats to bring to about two or three leagues short of Ovar (the object of this delay is to prevent the enemy being aware of General Hill's approach before M.-General Cotton has advanced upon his outposts), where the boats will remain until slack water on the morning of the 10th (about 4 a.m.), when the whole will again proceed.

M.-General Hill will cause three companies of light infantry to be disembarked at a landing-place about half a league from Ovar, upon the western side of the lake, which companies will advance by land to Ovar, so as to possess themselves of the town and harbour for the disembarkation of the remainder of the corps.

M.-General Hill will advance from Ovar on the morning of the 10th, but not until he has had communication with M.-General Cotton, or has ascertained that M.-General Cotton has reached Oliveira, upon the Oporto road.

M.-General Cotton is instructed to endeavour to communicate with M.-General Hill from that point, and M.-General Hill will be pleased also to use every endeavour to procure information of the movements of the enemy, and the advance of M.-General Cotton on the Oporto road. M.-General Hill will direct his march from Ovar by the road which leads towards the village of Feira, and which crosses the great road to Oporto, it is understood, in the neighbourhood of Santo Ridondo. M.-General Hill will, however, obtain more accurate information respecting his road at Ovar.

At the point where this road joins that to Oporto the junction of M.-General Hill's corps, and that under M.-General Cotton, will be formed, when both will proceed to Oporto.

M.-General Cotton will advance from the River Vouga at a very early hour on the morning of the 10th instant, supported by B.-General Stewart's brigade, and the King's German Legion. The object of this movement is to surprise and carry the posts of the enemy at Albergaria Nova, and along the Oporto road, and after the junction with M.-General Hill, to press back the enemy, and, should an opportunity offer, to pass the bridge of Oporto with the rear-guard of the enemy; at all events, to prevent his destroying the bridge, or removing the boats which may be upon the left bank of the river.

B.-General Cameron's brigade of infantry, with one brigade of light six-pounders, will arrive at Aveiro on the 10th instant, to follow M.-General Hill's corps. Boats are to be sent back, therefore, without delay, for the conveyance of that brigade to Ovar.

Precautions must be taken to prevent the escape of the boats, and ensure their proceeding direct to their destination.

M.-General Hill will inform himself at Ovar respecting the roads which lead from that place towards the River Vouga, lest events should render it necessary to use them. A *patrole* of Portuguese cavalry will be directed to proceed very early in the morning of the 10th, by the road which leads from Angeja to Ovar, there to join M.-General Hill's corps.

Geo. Murray, Q.-M.-G.

General Hill, having received his instructions, embarked at Aveiro on the evening of the 9th, and arrived at Ovar on the 10th, just at sunrise, having been assiduously helped in passing the lake by the fishermen. Various circumstances of a trifling character, however, arose to frustrate these arrangements, and the enemy was, for a short time, rescued from his peril by a masterly retreat on the part of Franceschi. He passed within a tantalizing distance of General Hill, who showed consummate judgment in refraining from attacking him, as it was contrary to the rules laid down for his guidance to act on the enemy's rear. His division, therefore, moved on quietly towards Oporto, which place the repulsed French reached with considerable loss, in time to destroy the bridge across the Douro, and to congratulate themselves on an imaginary security because that river rolled between them and their pursuers, while the veterans of Napoleon's army were ready to defend the passage of its wide and rapid stream.

Thus apparently foiled in his designs, Sir Arthur Wellesley ascended the height of Sarea, fully impressed with the importance, especially as regarded the operations of Marshal Beresford, of instantly crossing the Douro. The glance of his searching eye and the decision of his genius were almost simultaneous, and he determined to pass over, in spite of every difficulty, to a building called the Seminary, at the very point which, from the obstacles it presented, Soult supposed to be perfectly secure. He had previously ordered Major-General Murray to cross

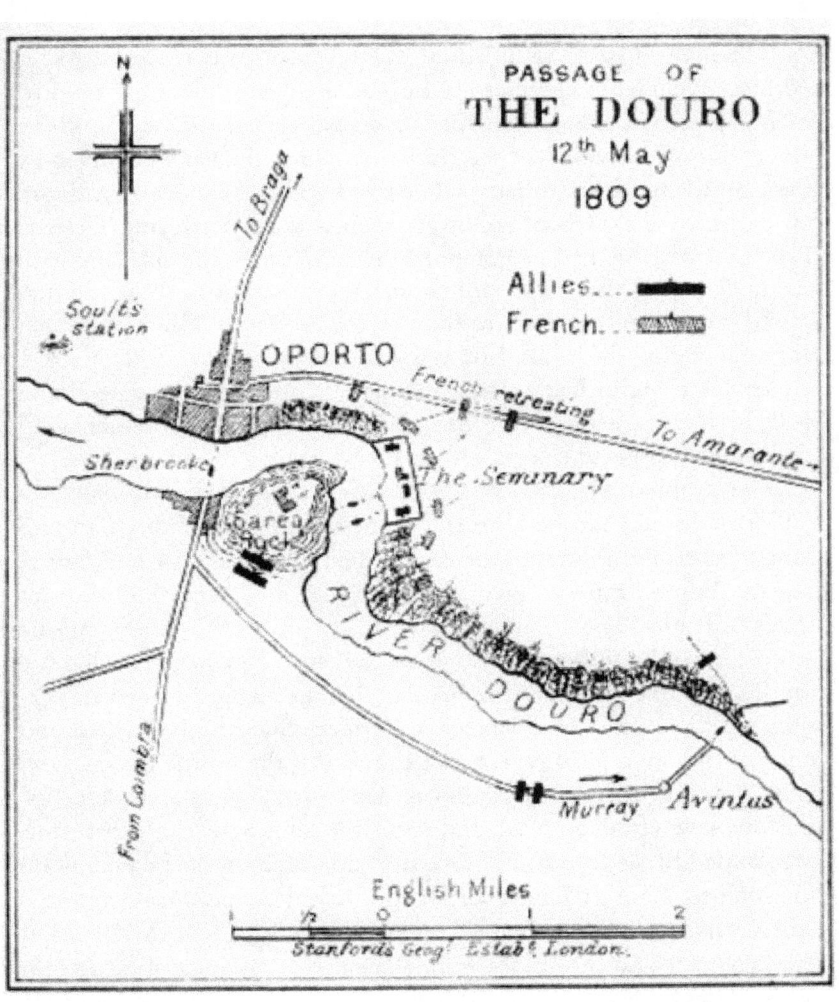

at Avintas, about four miles above Oporto, with a battalion of the Hanoverian Legion, a squadron of cavalry, and two six-pounders, if boats could be obtained for this purpose. For himself he was resolved, if only one boat could be found, to make his way over the river to the Seminary; and he succeeded in obtaining, unperceived, three or four barges.

When the first of these came up, its arrival was reported to Sir Arthur. "Well! let the men cross," he answered in an instant; and within a quarter of an hour after the words had passed his lips, an officer and twenty-five soldiers of the Buffs were upon the bank occupied by the enemy, and the Seminary was gained without the least symptom of alarm. A second boat followed, then a third conveying General Paget; and scarcely had they stepped on shore, when the city rang with the din of arms, the roll of drums, and the tumultuous shouts of surprised citizens and soldiers rushing to the Seminary. The brave Paget appeared upon the walls, but was instantly wounded and disabled. General Hill, who had crossed in splendid style with the 48th and 66th regiments, assumed the command. Soult was his opponent, and the assault furious in the extreme. Murray had not come up.

The moment was critical; but Sir Arthur had such confidence in Hill, that he was satisfied, on the earnest entreaties of those around him, to remain on the spot, surveying the scene of action, and directing the English guns to play upon the enemy. General Hill did not disappoint him. Three battalions were now in the Seminary; and he advanced coolly to the enclosure wall, whence he opened such a fire on the passing columns of the French, that the result was their dispersion and the capture of five pieces of artillery. Sherbrooke crossed, and entered the town in time to harass the rear of the hostile troops, who were quitting it. Then the forces under Murray were seen descending the steep from Avintas; and soon the shouts of the inhabitants proclaimed the evacuation of Oporto, and the flight of the enemy on the road to Vallonga. General Hill and his gallant *aides-de-camp* Captain Currie and Lieutenant Clement Hill received, with the other brave officers and troops, the cordial acknowledgments of Sir Arthur Wellesley, who had, by their aid, achieved the renowned passage of the Douro. His despatch said:

> They have marched in four days, over eighty miles of most difficult country, have gained many important positions, and have engaged and defeated three different bodies of the enemy's troops.

The results were briefly detailed by General Hill in a letter to his sister:—

Oporto, May 22. 1809.

My dear Sister,

On the 13th I wrote to you, and gave a hasty account of our proceedings to that day: the particulars you will have seen in the Gazette before this reaches you. I am this instant informed that a bag will be made up and despatched for England by seven o'clock: and as it is nearly that time now, I have not a moment to lose. Events have turned out exactly as I expected. Marshal Soult's army got so completely beat and frightened on the 12th, that their retreat became a perfect flight. I cannot, for want of time, enter into particulars at this moment, but beg to tell you that the morning after the enemy ran from this place our army pursued them, keeping close to their rear, and following them near 100 miles on the Braga road, to the frontier of Spain, about 50 miles on the other side of Braga. On this occasion the enemy suffered considerably, lost *all* their guns, greater part of their baggage and ammunition, and upon the whole are so much beaten, that it is thought impossible they can ever think of returning. The French loss, upon the whole, is upwards of 3000 men, including prisoners.

The French, having another force in the South of Portugal, under Victor, and knowing of our advance towards Soult, commenced moving to the North, in the direction of Castello Branco, which made our return to Oporto necessary; and, indeed, I fancy we shall lose no time in getting to Coimbra. When Victor hears of Soult's fate, I am pretty sure he will not advance further; and if he should, we have sufficient force to meet him. I assure you our prospects are good. Clement does not feel the least inconvenience from his *wound*, but his eyes are sore from the heat of the sun, and effects of the cold nights and long marches. I have not heard of John Holding.[1] Dido is safe. In the greatest haste,

    Yours ever most truly,

        R. Hill.

Miss Hill, Hawkstone, Shrewsbury.

Lieutenant Clement Hill's own allusion to his *wound* is character-

---
1. His servant.

istic of the coolness of that officer, whose name was so honourably mentioned in Sir Arthur Wellesley's despatch. In writing to his brother Robert, he said:

> Seeing my name among the wounded would, of course, alarm some of you, although it was mentioned as slight. You would not think much was the matter with me when you got my letter, as I never thought the knock I got worth mentioning, and had not the least idea I had been returned, and would not believe it till I saw it in print. The fact was, the officer who made out the returns happened to be standing near me at the time a ball struck me on the hip, just where my sash was tied. It was, of course, nearly spent, though it gave me a good rap, and I thought it was a worse job than it was, and was agreeably surprised to find the ball had not entered. The place was black for some time, and I was a little stiff, but I had nothing to call a wound. The more bloody the account of an action appears, the better it goes down with John Bull; and I suppose the officer who made out the list thought my name would add to the number; and I know he thought it would be of service to me, though I wish he had thought a little more of the feelings of my friends. The way in which the general and his staff are mentioned, in the other part of the despatch, is, of course, highly flattering to us all.

This letter was addressed to Major Robert Hill, of the Royal Horse Guards, Blue, afterwards Lieutenant-Colonel of the same regiment, and now Sir Robert Chambre Hill. The General, with his accustomed fondness for his pets, did not forget to mention his favourite "Dido," a most sagacious animal. His brother, and *aide-de-camp*, whose letter has been just quoted, also made allusion to her:

> I must tell you how careful she is of her family. Two of them have been brought in a basket; and the other morning, when the baggage was going off, she went up stairs by herself, and brought the basket in her mouth for the puppies to be put in.

In this simple and good-natured manner these brave brothers relieved the tedium of their campaigns, and diverted the attention of those who received their letters at home, from the weightier cares occasioned by solicitude for their safety.

The next communication from General Hill to his friends at

Hawkstone is dated "Abrantes, June 17th, 1809," where the British army was encamped, full of energy and spirit, but without money, shoes, or means of transport, while its energetic leader was assiduously endeavouring to overcome these and other impediments to his march into Spain:

> We have been at Abrantes about nine days, and I think probable we shall remain here some time longer to await events. The fate of this country and Spain, in my mind, depends entirely on what happens elsewhere. If Bonaparte subdues Austria, and can keep all quiet in the North, the Peninsula must fall. At present, our immediate neighbour and opponent. Marshal Victor, is rather retiring, but I dare say he will not go far, if he has reason to expect reinforcements. The last accounts were, that he had left Merida, and was falling back on Madrid.

After these remarks, he proceeded to make some observations on the interpretation put by Lord Castlereagh on the despatch of Sir Arthur Wellesley, respecting the passage of the Douro. His words will explain the point in question, and confirm the statement already made of the services he rendered at that critical juncture:—

> No officer is more deserving of praise than General Paget; but he was wounded so *very early* in the business, that he was not present when the *serious* attacks were made, and which, indeed, did not take place till after the greater part of the 66th and 48th had come up, although Lord Castlereagh, by his note to the (Lord) Mayor, would wish it to be understood that General Paget and the Buffs resisted the whole French Army.

History has corrected this mistaken version of Sir Arthur's official account; and the remarks of General Hill to his relatives are in unison with the view of Napier, in his narrative of the proceedings of that memorable day. In the same letter General Hill thus notices Mr. Mackworth, afterwards on his staff, and now Sir Digby Mackworth, of Glen Usk:—

> Mr. Mackworth is a fine young man: I wish I had it in my power to show him more civility. All I can do for him is occasionally to give him a bad dinner.

General Hill's opinion of this officer was confirmed in every step of his future life down to the year 1831, when he rendered such excellent service during the dreadful riots at Bristol, under circumstances of peculiar difficulty. His kind general, at the time of his receiving him in Portugal, was by no means well accommodated, for his brother thus described their position at Abrantes:—

> The troops are most of them encamped in huts near the town, and we are living in a small house near.

It was not till the 26th of June that the arrangements of Sir Arthur Wellesley permitted an advance towards Spain, when, having received the money he had applied for, but still without the expected reinforcements, he determined to move. On that day Mr. Clement Hill wrote home,—

> We shall be off in the morning. We have our route for eight days, which will bring us into Spain. The first town we enter is Zarza-la-Mayor, which is in the direction for Madrid; and I hope it will not be long before we are in that city."

The town here mentioned was reached on the 2nd of July, and by the 8th of that month Sir Arthur and the advanced guard had arrived at Placentia. Perplexities of every description surrounded the British general; but the ardour of his unquenchable spirit rose superior to them all, and was caught by the troops he commanded, though under the pressure of hunger and every species of privation. He sternly repressed all disposition to plunder, while he spared no exertion to relieve the wants of his soldiers. Their numbers had been much exaggerated. This arose out of the manner in which the returns were made, affording to Sir Arthur just grounds for the complaints he addressed to Lord Castlereagh on the subject from Castello Branco on the 30th of June, when the reinforcements announced had not arrived.

On the other hand, the French were in immense strength, under the most eminent marshals of Bonaparte. Victor, who was nearest the allies, mustered a large force in Estremadura; Sebastiani was in La Mancha; Dessolles defended Madrid; Kellerman and Bonnet occupied Old Castile, and a portion of Leon and the Asturias—the whole being nominally under the usurper Joseph, assisted by Marshal Jourdan. Soult, Mortier, and Ney were in the North, while Suchet and Augereau commanded large forces in Aragon and Catalonia. To these may be added the troops occupying ports or fortresses, besides such as were employed in keeping open the several lines of communication. Thus the allies were surrounded by an overwhelming superiority of disciplined forces, whom Bonaparte had directed to crush Wellesley in masses—a design this great general foresaw at the very time the French emperor, unknown to him, originated it.

To make Sir Arthur's situation even more difficult, his Spanish co-adjutor was General Cuesta, whom he found "more and more impracticable every day," and who, with the exception of certain ebbs and flows of rash courage, was the completest burlesque upon a commander of an army that can be conceived. For example, he came to meet the British general at a reconnaissance of Victor's position in a coach-and-six, out of which he was jolted by the roughness of the ground, and then he took a nap under a tree. But this drowsiness would have done no harm, had he not obstructed the plans of Sir Arthur by the most inconceivable obstinacy, which the latter mildly designated "whimsical perverseness of disposition." On the 24th of July, when the enemy had been dislodged without a battle, he actually, in a fit of mad jealousy, rushed forward singly in pursuit of the French, leaving Sir Arthur alone to exercise the caution he found it necessary to recommend to this heretofore sleepy, obstinate "old gentleman."

The Spaniards, as was foreseen, were soon driven back, and came towards the English Army near Talavera, in a state of confusion impossible to describe, till at length they passed to the rear, and ere long the movements of Victor plainly indicated that a great conflict was approaching. The genius of Wellesley rose with the perils thickening around him. Finally, the obstinacy of Cuesta gave way, and he consented to directions which placed him in front of Talavera on the right of the Tagus, where nature and art combined to defend him from serious attack. The left of the line was open in front, the extreme resting upon a steep hill, which was the key of the position, and there the trusty subject of these pages was placed with a division of infantry. Sir Arthur thus described this portion of his arrangements:—

> The position taken up by the troops at Talavera extended rather more than two miles: the ground was open upon the left, where the British Army was stationed, and it was commanded by a height, on which was placed *en echelon*, as the second line, a division of infantry under the orders of Major-General Hill.

It was on the 26th of July that Cuesta gave orders to retreat, after his sudden push to Torrijos; and on the 27th, as Napier observes. Sir Arthur, by virtue of his genius, assumed the command of both armies. The previous condition of affairs is described by General Hill in a letter to his sister, dated "Talavera, July 25."

> If you received my last from Placentia, you will have been informed of our movement towards Talavera, which commenced on the 17th, the day after I wrote to you, and was finished in six days. On the third day of our march we were joined by Cuesta's army, which advanced with the British to this place, where, as we expected, we found Victor *strongly posted*, having the Tagus upon his left, and a small river, the Alberche, in his front and on his right. Sir Arthur Wellesley, I understand, urged the necessity of an *immediate* attack. General Cuesta, *it is said*, wished to postpone it. Certain, however, it is that nothing was done on the day of our arrival or the next, during which time the French remained with every appearance of making a stand, which determined our two chiefs to attack them with our united force the next morning at daybreak, the British on their left, and the Spaniards on the right. Dispositions were made accordingly, and we began to move about one o'clock in the night.
>
> At daybreak we were at the points fixed on, fully persuaded that in a few minutes we should have been engaged, when, to the surprise of everyone, we found that the French *were off*, and not a man to be seen. They had departed during the night, and taken the road to Madrid. What the result of this will be, I cannot tell. If we can get the French out of Spain, (which I do not think unlikely) without an action, *I* shall be satisfied. If, however, that should not be the case, it may be an unfortunate circumstance that they went off; for although our loss must consequently have been great, yet I am confident, with God's assistance, that we should have beat them. It seems most annoying that we are not able to follow them, owing to a total want of supplies.
>
> The Spanish Government has not in any one respect fulfilled its promise in regard to supplying the British Army with provisions, in consequence of which, and our own bad commissaries, the troops and horses have been very badly fed of late. Instead of our having supplies to *take on*, the soldiers have not yet had meat or bread for *yesterday*, and it will not be possible for us to move on for some days, which probably will prevent our seeing the French again; for I am inclined to think we shall not follow them a great way unless *they wait*, which does not appear very

likely after giving up this country and their strong position. The people are in high spirits at seeing the French run—a sight they never saw before. The Spanish armies are strong, and will increase. It is true they are badly disciplined, but their inveteracy towards the French is so great that they are formidable. No Frenchman falls into their hands without suffering death. The general who was taken a short time ago was kept alive, not from respect to French generals, but as being a valuable prize.

At the juncture described in this letter, Cuesta advanced. Sir Arthur remarked:

I am only afraid he will get himself into a scrape: any movement by me to his assistance is quite out of the question.

His inglorious return has been already noticed, as well as his tardy submission to the master-mind of Wellesley. Hence arose the demonstration on the part of the French, which led to the disposition of the allied forces alluded to before the introduction of this account by General Hill. When he wrote it, he little imagined that the day of his danger, escape, and glory was so near.

King Joseph slept on the 26th at St. Ollalla, but was up before break of day, and his troops were put in motion ere the sun cast its early beams for the last time, upon numbers who had watched for its rise with eager hopes of a decisive day: but not till it had been three hours past its meridian did the fight begin. At that time Sir Arthur Wellesley was in the Casa de Salinas. To reach this place, the French had to ford the Alberche, and to march some distance through woods, out of which they emerged so suddenly, that they had nearly made him prisoner at the instant of surprise. Providentially, this disaster was not permitted to fall upon our army, and upon Europe. The impetuous onset of the enemy caused our troops to withdraw with some loss, but with such steadiness and discipline, that they returned upon and checked the forces which had attacked them. Victor soon exhibited a magnificent display, which issued from the forest, and advanced against the combined armies. It was dusk when he opened his cannonade on the left of the British position, and directed his cavalry against the infantry of Spain. Sir Arthur's despatch says:

This attempt entirely failed.
Early in the night he pushed a division along the valley on the left of the height occupied by General Hill, of which he gained

a momentary possession; but Major-General Hill attacked it instantly with the bayonet, and regained it.

It was a night of awful struggle; opposing flashes of musketry, seemingly close to each other, sparkled in the gloom. At length, cessation of firing permitted the conquering shouts of the British soldiers audibly to proclaim that their stern opponents were repulsed into the ravine below. Shortly afterwards the flames of the bivouac fires of both armies shot upwards to the darkened skies, and the fighting was over; but eight hundred English and a thousand French were lost in that tremendous fray. In the morning the French came forth again; and, to use the words of Sir Arthur Wellesley:

> The general attack began by the march of several columns of infantry into the valley, with a view to attack the height occupied by Major-General Hill.

Various as have been the descriptions of his brave conduct on that day, all agree in their estimate of the great military qualities he displayed. His own narration will be found in a letter to his sister, written on the spot:—

Talavera, July 30. 1809.

My dear Sister,
God has protected Clement and myself in two of the severest battles I ever witnessed, which took place on the 27th and 28th. For the particulars I must refer you to the public despatches, but cannot help mentioning a few circumstances which will show you the providential escapes we have had. About a week ago I told you that the French had retired from Talavera, on our approach towards them. It now appears they did this, not with the intention of going off altogether, but for the purpose of meeting their reinforcements, which being done by the junction of Sebastiani's force of about 12,000, and King Joseph, from Madrid, with 6000, they turned back with near 50,000, with a determination to bring the whole of it against the British Army, not half that number
In the field. Early on the 27th we heard of the returning of the French, and as the day advanced they approached nearer. By four in the evening their whole force was in sight, and continued moving forward, driving In our outposts, till they came within reach of shot from our lines, when they halted; and as

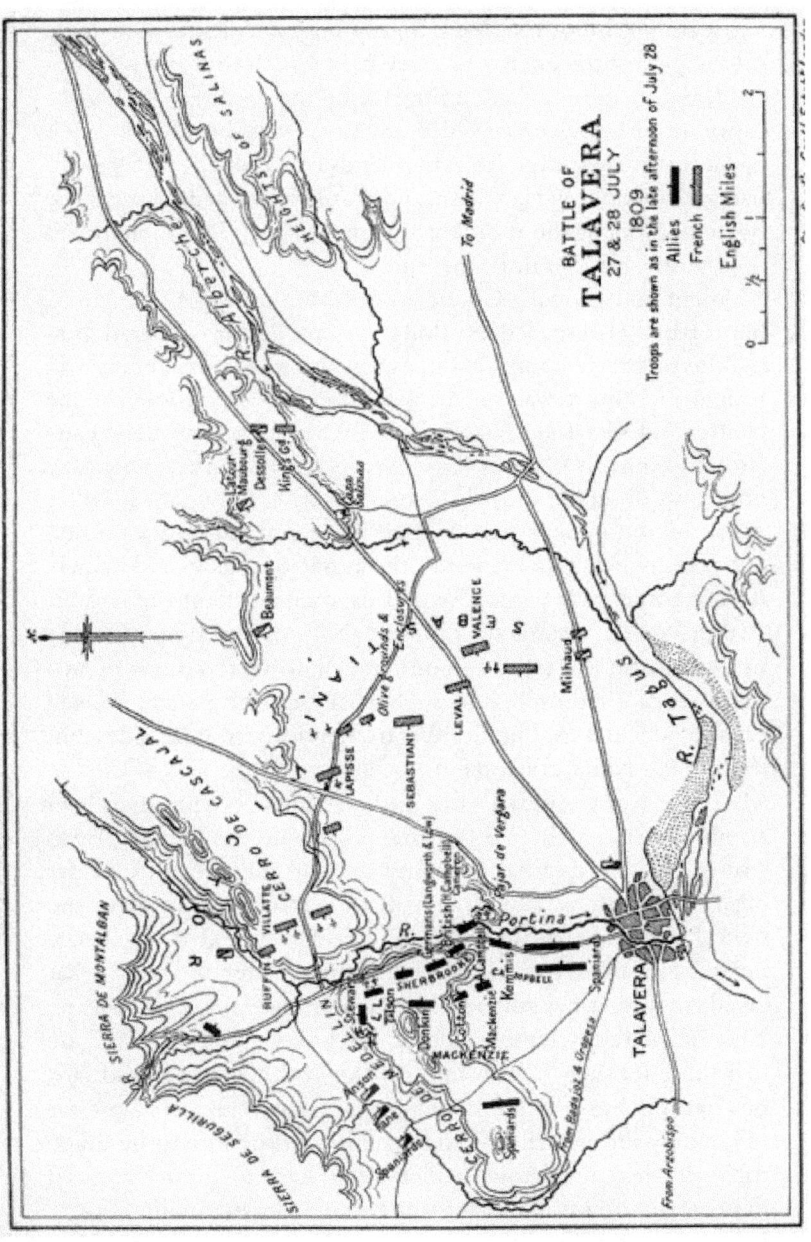

night was coming on we did not expect any serious attack till the next morning. It was, however, scarcely dusk, when there was a heavy fire of musketry on my post, and a severe struggle on the part of the enemy to carry it, in which they did not succeed, and in about half an hour gave up the contest. On this occasion poor Fordyce was killed, my horse was shot, and I myself had a fortunate escape from the hands of a French soldier, who had got hold of my right arm, and would have secured me if my horse had not at the moment sprung forward. The Frenchman fired at me, but did not touch me.

Clement and Captain Currie were in the midst of the whole, but fortunately escaped. Nothing very particular occurred during the night: we continued in our position, and the enemy was near us. My post was on the left. General Sherbrooke in the centre, and General Campbell to his right, and all the Spaniards to General Campbell's right. In the morning, when day broke, we observed the whole French Army drawn up in order of battle; the greater part of their force immediately opposite my post, which was evidently the point of attack, and which, if they could have gained, would have given them the day. Sir Arthur Wellesley came to it, and in about half an hour after the sun was up an immense column, since known to consist of two divisions of 7000 each, under Marshal Victor in person, moved on and attacked us. The fire was tremendous on both sides, but the French could not force us.

My horse was wounded early in the action. I got another from an officer. Shortly before the enemy gave up the conflict, I was struck by a musket-ball near my left ear and the back of my head. The blow was so violent that I was obliged to leave the field. I continued unwell the whole of the next day, and the next; I am, however, thank God, much better today. My hat saved my life; it has suffered as much as my helmet did on the 13th of March. Clement is safe; his horse was killed, and he had three musket-balls in him on the 28th. Currie is also safe, but had his horse killed under him. During the attack on me the enemy did not allow the remainder of the line to be quiet, for, with their numerous artillery, they kept up a constant and destructive fire on it, not regarding the Spaniards at all.

In about four or five hours the enemy's fire slackened for a short time; they, however, afterwards began as serious an attack upon

General Campbell as they did upon me, and, meeting with the same reception from him and the whole as they did in the morning, were fairly beat, and in the evening after dark went off. The loss on both sides is very great. Indeed, ours probably 4000, the enemy's 7000. King Joseph was in the field, though not in the fire. When it is considered that the French force was double ours, and solely employed against the British, we may count the battle of Talavera amongst the most glorious that ever took place. You must excuse this hasty account—indeed I must again refer you to the official details. The French are said to be still retreating. Kind remembrance to all our dear friends at Hawkstone, who, I am sure, will be sensible of and thankful for the providential escapes we have had."

On the 1st of August he wrote again:—

Talavera, August 1st, 1809.

My dear Sister,

Two days ago I wrote to you a long and hasty letter, giving you some account of the glorious actions which had been fought between the British and the French on the 27th and 28th. The letter, I dare say, will go to England by the same ship which will convey this, provided it reaches Lisbon; but as the communication between us and Lisbon is rather uncertain, I send this by a different route. There never was a more severe action fought than that of the 28th, or more honour gained by an army than was obtained on both days. I must, however, observe, that it was a dear-bought victory, for, out of 18,000 British, I fear you will find, by the returns, our loss to be near 200 officers killed and wounded, and about 5000 men.

Another such victory would be a serious one for us. The French have suffered *certainly* more than we did, and are still retiring towards Madrid, but I doubt whether they will go far. The Spaniards are very numerous, but have as yet done nothing either in fighting or supplying us with provisions. Unless a change takes place, I think we shall not agree long. The conveyance of letters has now become so uncertain, I must be careful what I say. My head, thank God, is much better; I have no pain, and merely a little stiffness about the neck.

My horses, I think, will recover. The one I rode on the 27th, when I was in the midst of the French in the dark, was wounded through the belly; the other had *two* shots through the withers, and one *in the saddle*. Your little mare is well, and so is Dido, and John Holding looks a great deal better than when he left England. Joseph may remain where he is, for I think our stay is rather uncertain. We shall not go to Coruña again, but, in case of accidents, we have fortunately Gibraltar and Cadiz under our lee. If the Austrians are successful, and the Spaniards will give us assistance, all will go on well. Clement joins in kind remembrance to all.

   I remain,
    Yours most affectionately,

                R. H.

In the year 1827 a military officer of high rank requested from General Hill the favour of a memorandum explanatory of his own escape, with which he complied as follows, in his truly unaffected style:—

I recollect on the 27th of July I got some dinner in my quarters in the town of Talavera about four o'clock. Immediately after I rode out, accompanied by Major Fordyce, towards the Alberche, in which direction we heard some firing. I returned to the bivouac of my division, I suppose about sunset, when I found it had moved to take up a position. I instantly followed it, and found it deploying in line, and was shown by somebody where the right was to rest. I pointed out the hill on the line of direction we were to take up. I found, however, I had not sufficient troops to occupy the ground without leaving considerable intervals between the regiments. During this operation I recollect perfectly well that I was with the 48th Regiment, in conversation with Colonel Donellan, when, it being nearly dark, I observed some men on the hill-top fire a few shots amongst us.

Not having an idea that the enemy were so near, I said at the moment, *I was sure it was the Old Buffs, as usual, making some blunder.* I desired Donellan to get into line, and I would ride up the hill and stop their firing. On reaching the hill-top, I found the mistake I had made. I immediately turned round to ride off, when they fired and killed poor Fordyce, and shot my mare through the body. She did not fall, but carried me to the 29th Regiment, which corps, by my orders, instantly charged the French, and drove them from the hill. I do not know what numbers the enemy had, but I think they were not strong—perhaps some of their light troops.

The poor old coach-and-six general had no further part in this affair than sending two pieces of cannon to Sir Arthur Wellesley, when he desired reinforcements against the powerful artillery of the French. He went, however, into a furious rage with his troops for being terrified into confusion, though not attacked, which ended in their *decimation*, and the execution of the decimated. Some, however, of the Spaniards showed true bravery, and the couple of guns just adverted to were most efficiently served; but the general condition of Cuesta's army, and the exhausted state of the British, who were upon the scantiest food, rendered all pursuit at the close of the second day's victory impossible, and the triumph was dearly won. The army of Sir Arthur passed that night on the cold damp field, amidst the dead, the wounded, and the dying, while as many of the disabled as they could remove, found their hospitals in the convents of Talavera. The morning after the last action General Cuesta wrote, for publication in the Spanish *Gazette*,—

> I cannot express myself sufficiently to celebrate the admirable courage of the English Army, and its excellent general, *and of our own troops also!*

Sir Arthur Wellesley was elevated to the peerage on the 26th of August, by the titles of Baron Douro of Wellesley, and Viscount Wellington of Talavera; but he did not receive the official notification till the 16th of September, and up to that period retained his old signature. His Majesty was also pleased to appoint General Hill to the colonelcy of the 94th Regiment; and Mr. Perceval, in the House of Commons, on the vote of thanks from the Houses of Parliament, paid him a distinguished compliment. The conduct of the Spaniards was disgraceful beyond all conception. They would neither supply provisions, relieve the wounded, nor help to bury the dead, refusing, as Sir Arthur observed, "assistance and necessaries which any other country in the world would have given even to its enemies."

At length this bad faith, and the consequent difficulties he encountered, together with the wants and privations of his troops, and the various movements of the French, induced him to contemplate withdrawing towards Portugal. There were many varying opinions at the time respecting Sir Arthur's speedy change from the victorious offensive to defensive operations; but it will be found that General Hill entirely approved of these celebrated movements, and denounced the Spaniards equally with his chief. He wrote thus from Merida:—

Merida, August 30th, 1809.

My dear Sister,

I must own I never entertained any sanguine expectations from the assistance we were likely to receive from the Spaniards. Their conduct last year was sufficient to satisfy all who witnessed it, that we were engaged in a hopeless cause. What has now happened I trust will convince our rulers at home that a small English force alone cannot drive the French out of Spain, and that Spaniards are neither willing nor able to do much for themselves. In the battle at Talavera, the Spaniards might have rendered us most essential service. There really appeared on that occasion, something like a mutual agreement between the French and Spaniards not to molest each other. During the whole of the actions the French employed all their force against the British, and at no time did the Spaniards attempt to give us any assistance.

The conduct of Spain with respect to supplying us with provisions is, if possible, worse than their behaviour in the field. Previous to our entering the country they promised every kind of supply, and carriages for the sick; *and I know they have done nothing*, in consequence of which many sick and wounded have been left behind, and the army has suffered great privations for want of food, and is now, I am sorry to say, much *reduced* and very ineffective. Under all these circumstances, I think Sir Arthur Wellesley has acted wisely in *retiring*, and we are now by easy marches proceeding towards Elvas in Portugal, where I imagine we shall wait until orders arrive from England. The French are not following us, and give as a reason that they have orders to that effect.

They say they shall remain on the banks of the Tagus about Talavera, until their expected reinforcements arrive from France, and on their coming they recommend the English should quit the Peninsula. . . . . . The French have likewise another report amongst them, which is, that Napoleon means to restore Ferdinand to Spain, and remove King Joseph to a throne in Germany—a measure I do not think very improbable, for Ferdinand would be quite subservient to the will of Bonaparte, and by being sent to Spain would quiet the people, who, although not formidable, are troublesome. The French are particularly kind and attentive to our wounded and sick.

7 o'clock.—I am just informed that the bag will be closed in a few minutes; I shall therefore only add that Clement and myself are perfectly well. I do not feel the least inconvenience from the blow I got on the head. We shall, I think, be in Portugal in the course of five or six days. If the accounts from Austria continue unfavourable, we mist quit this country, and it is the general opinion the sooner the better. Kind love to all.

Yours ever.

It was impossible that Sir Arthur Wellesley could go on with such a man as Cuesta, or with the cowardly Spaniards he commanded, of whom he wrote to Lord Castlereagh:

Nearly 2000 ran off, on the evening of the 27th, from the Battle of Talavera, not a hundred yards from the place where I was standing, who were neither attacked nor threatened with an attack, and who were frightened only by the noise of their own fire. They left their arms and accoutrements on the ground. Their officers went with them; and they and the fugitive cavalry plundered the baggage of the British army, which had been sent to the rear.

Afterwards the one corps said to have behaved well at Talavera ran away from the bridge of Arzobispo, leaving its guns; and the conduct of all parties had so deprived Sir Arthur of the fruits of his victory, that he determined to remain with them no longer. In this decision, as we have seen, General Hill entirely agreed, and, in fact, had made a formal complaint that one of his foraging parties had been fired at by Spanish soldiers.

But though Sir Arthur decided to fight no more *with* Spaniards, he was willing to fight *for* Spain, and consented, having consulted with his brother, the Marquis Wellesley, then in that country on a special mission, to remain for a time on the Spanish frontier, at least so far as to place General Hill's division at Montejo and La Calzada, and the heavy brigade of cavalry at Merida, where they could get forage. From the former of these places the General addressed the following interesting letter to Hawkstone:—

Montejo, 10th Nov. 1809

I wrote to you from here about a fortnight or three weeks ago, since which time we have been, as we were for some time before, in daily expectation of some change taking place. Nothing particular, however, has occurred. The French remain on the Tagus, occupying the towns from Toledo to Orapesa. The Spanish Army is in La Mancha; the British cantoned in the villages about 30 miles round Badajos. None of the three armies seem to be inclined to move forward; the French show their weakness by remaining where they are, and we prove ours by allowing them to stay so quietly. I do not consider our prospects at all mended of late, consequently I entertain the same opinion I have always expressed respecting the country.

The cause in my mind is hopeless, unless war with some chance of success should be renewed between Austria and France—an event which does not seem very probable. Too much jealousy, I fear, exists between us and the Spaniards to give hopes of doing any good by acting together, and little can be expected from our separate efforts, for the Spaniards do not understand the *business*, and we have not *numbers*. Our army is much reduced; it is generally supposed that we have upwards of 30,000, but I assure you we could not bring more than 13,000 into the field. The sickness which prevails is dreadful, and the mortality melancholy. There are not less than 10,000 in the hospitals, besides some hundreds in a convalescent state. The deaths during the last three weeks have, upon an average, been little short of fifty men a day.

The rains have now commenced, and we are told that we shall be more healthy. I thank God that Clement and myself enjoy good health. I do not know whether our future plans are fixed upon, but I really think we shall be *off* soon. It is generally thought that we shall move towards Lisbon, to wait events, and at the same time to be in readiness to quit the country if necessary. We have heard of Lord Wellesley's appointment to the head of the new administration. He intended to leave Seville this day, and will probably reach England about the time you receive this. I am glad he is come into office; he is certainly a very able man, and must know the Spaniards, and also our *real* situation in this country.

It is now forty days, a very unusual time, since we heard from

England. We anxiously look for the next arrival, which will bring us the new arrangements respecting the administration, and in all probability a confirmation of the peace between France and Austria—an event which the French at Madrid have announced. I dare say you will see in the English papers that the Spaniards have adopted a new mode of government, and established a regency, a change which I fear will benefit them very little.

You will likewise see an account of an action fought between the Spaniards and French at Tamanes, not far from Salamanca, in which the *valorosi Spaniards* claim a great victory. The fact is, the French with a small division attacked the Spaniards, who were *five times* their number, posted on strong ground near Tamanes. The French were at first successful, took six guns, and made their cavalry go off. The Spanish infantry, however, not only maintained their ground, but in the end retook their guns, and the French retired with some loss. A Spanish officer writes to his friends in this village, and after giving an account of the action, he says he followed the French to Salamanca, and finding that they had quitted it, they entered the town, but that it was with "*shaking chins,*" a Spanish proverb, which you may easily conceive implies great fear. Being in daily expectation of a move towards England, I will not desire Joseph to come out. We heard from Thomas lately; he was well. Kind remembrances to all.

I remain, yours very affectionately.[2]

At Montejo General Hill and his brother were comfortably lodged in the house of a large farmer, whom they found a good kind of man; and they had the satisfaction of seeing a degree of plenty and happiness around them, to which they had been hitherto strangers in Spain. They were about twenty miles from Badajos, where headquarters were. One part of this house was occupied by General Hill and the remainder by the farmer's family, who were "all very civil without being troublesome." Lieutenant Clement Hill described him as having "a wife and two daughters not quite of the first class, but dressing smart when they went to mass on a Sunday." In Badajos, he said, there was:

A great display of beauty and fashion. Almost all the wool is

---

2. General Hill frequently arose from prudential motives, in omitted to sign his name to his case of their being intercepted, letters at this time. Probably this.

sent from this part to England. I cannot say much for the beauty of the sheep that produce it. Rowland has bought four from our landlord, which are to accompany our milk goats, till we have an opportunity of sending or bringing them to England, to improve the Shropshire breed. We lead quite a quiet country life, going out a-coursing three times a week, though I should not wonder if Bonaparte gave us a chase of another sort some of these mornings.

This sort of life suited the tastes of these heroic brothers, who "liked it much better than the gay town "of Badajos, where the inhabitants were far from being as civil to those who fought for their independence, as at the pleasant rural Montejo. Here the division of General Hill was reviewed by the commander-in-chief, who had then assumed the title of Viscount Wellington; and the services of its leader were acknowledged in his promotion to the rank of Lieutenant-General, which had indeed been some time previously urged by Lord Wellington as his just due.

The general himself wrote word home:

We have excellent coursing here, and now and then a fox-hunt, and sometimes attack a wild boar and the deer.

With regard to more important matters he expressed himself, towards the end of November, to the following effect:

Affairs in this country seem to be drawing to a crisis. The Spanish Army imprudently advanced towards Madrid; the French allowed them to get within eight leagues of the place, and then attacked them, and the result is that the Spaniards were entirely defeated and dispersed, lost fifty pieces of cannon, 15,000 prisoners, and about 8000 killed. Reinforcements are said to be on the march from France, the Spanish Government are quarrelling amongst themselves, and the British Army is greatly reduced by sickness, which, I am sorry to say, is by no means abated since I wrote last.

In December he thus described his own position and views:—

Montejo, Wednesday, 6th Dec. 1809.

My dear Sister,

A mail is despatched to England every Wednesday. I wrote to you by the last, since which time nothing very particular has occurred, and I have little to tell you now. The Spaniards, in consequence of the late dastardly conduct of their troops, seem to be a good deal alarmed. The government at Seville find their flowery addresses and patriotic proclamations to he of little avail, and will not make the people fight. I understand there is the greatest consternation amongst the rulers of this unhappy country; it is also said that their main army is entirely dispersed: indeed, we have daily opportunities of witnessing their *runaways* passing through this neighbourhood.

We likewise see the inhabitants of this part of the country burying and hiding their property, in expectation that it would otherwise fall into the hands of the enemy. The French are upwards of 150 miles from hence, and I do not hear of their having made any movement towards us since the victory over the Spaniards. Here we are in the same situation and same state of uncertainty as when I wrote last. Our long stay here, I imagine, must be from political motives; I, therefore, in some degree look forward for a change when Lord Wellesley's sentiments respecting this country are made known by himself in London, and which we may expect to hear of in the course of a week. Our army continues to suffer much by sickness; my division has lost, in the last seven days, 60 men, besides the deaths which must have happened at the distant hospitals, and which I am sure cannot be less than 20 or 30.

John Holding, the only invalid in my family, I am glad to say, is nearly recovered, and enjoyed our two last days' hunting with great spirit. By-the-by, I will enclose you a portrait of our Spanish huntsman, which Clement has hit off to a nicety; the instrument in the mouth is not a *vulgar tin horn*, such as our huntsmen use, but a sort of pipe-lute, or whistle, with which the bearer occasionally plays a tune, to collect the dogs and animate the sportsmen. General Cotton is off for England, and I suppose will arrive there about the time you get this. He has represented that urgent business requires his presence at home, and his request has, of course, been granted. He says he shall soon be back.

I think I told you that Colonel Leighton was well. You shall hear from Clement or myself by the next packet. In the meantime believe me to be

                Yours very affectionately,

                                    R. H.

In the midst of all these uncertainties Lord Wellington, now Marshal-General of Portugal, was contemplating the defence of that country; and I copy from the letter written with his own hand his announcement and offer to General Hill:—

"Badajos, Dec. 18. 1809.

My dear Hill,

In the arrangements for the defence of Portugal I shall form two principal corps, both consisting of British and Portuguese troops, the largest of which will be to the northward, and I shall command it myself, and the latter will be for the present upon the Tagus, and hereafter it may be moved forward into Alemtejo; and I will not make any arrangement either as to the troops that are to comprise it, or as to the officer who is to command it, without offering the command of it to you.

At the same time, I will not separate you from the army, and from my own immediate command, without consulting your wishes; and I shall be glad to hear from you on this subject as soon as possible, as the arrangements for quartering and disposing of the troops depend upon your decision upon this point.

You will therefore send back either a messenger, if you can get one, or an officer, with your answer as soon as possible.

I send your letters arrived by the English mail.

Ever yours most sincerely,

Wellington.

How the general felt such a mark of confidence, is expressed in his own words in a letter dated "Abrantes, January 4. 1810."

You will not, I am sure, be sorry to learn that we have quitted Spain, and are once more clear of the unhealthy plains of Estremadura. The whole of the British Army is now in Portugal: how long our government mean we shall remain here, or the French allow us, I cannot say. It, however, seems to be the intention of the present rulers to try to defend Portugal, for which purpose Lord Wellington has formed, as he calls it, two *principal* corps, composed of British and Portuguese, the largest of which is gone to the northward, and he commands it himself; the other remains on the Tagus, which he has in the handsomest manner offered to me. I am aware of the importance of the situation I am placed in, and trust I shall be attended with the same good fortune I have hitherto experienced.

General Hill deserved this trust, and the entire course of his subsequent services showed the wisdom of the selection.

Chapter 6

Abrantes

The beginning of the year 1810 was spent by General Hill at Abrantes, where Captain Patton of the Engineers was carrying on works of great importance, as part of Lord Wellington's plan for the defence of Portugal. The general supplied artificers from his corps for this purpose, and awaited his instructions, which were promised him as soon as possible in the following kind note:—

Coimbra, Jan. 6. 1810.
(Dated in the original 1809 by mistake.)

My dear Hill,

I just write you a few lines to tell you that I have not forgotten you, but my hands have been so full of business since I saw you that I have not had time to attend to your affairs yet. But you shall be fully instructed in the course of a day or two.

Ever yours sincerely,

Wellington.

Lieut.-General Hill

The instructions were given on the 9th, under which date they appear in the volumes of Colonel Gurwood.

The troops were at this time much recruited by the change of air and the fineness of the weather, while General Hill and his *aide-de-camp* had the gratification of being near their brother, Colonel Thomas Noel Hill, who was serving with the Portuguese Army. He was then at Oporto, and proposed to pay them a short visit. His regiment was reported as in the highest order.

During the whole of January Lord Wellington and General Hill were in constant correspondence. Their letters related to movements of troops; accommodation for cavalry; payments; commissariat; ammunition; magazines; bridges; and other kindred matters. At length, on the 12th of February, Lord Wellington directed him to move forward to Portalegre, in consequence of the French having approached Badajos. He was likewise desired to take measures for the safety of the convalescents and sick, and to provide for the conveyance of the latter to Elvas. Much was left to his discretion, which was most satisfactorily performed. He soon effected the removal of his corps, and was himself quartered at Portalegre, in the house of one Señora Donna Francisca Rosa Barba, a most attentive hostess. The farmer of Montejo, their former landlord, whose name was Don Alonso Botello, would have been too glad to have changed situations with the Señora Rosa, for his house was now occupied by the French. In all his foreign quarters, the habits of the general in private were as domestic and unpretending as if he had been residing at his own country seat.

One object of this advance was to protect Elvas and the sick in that town, but they were as quickly as possible removed to Lisbon. When the enemy heard of General Hill's arrival at Portalegre, they retired from Badajos. The general had with him his own British division, two brigades of Portuguese infantry, about 4000 strong, under Major-General Hamilton, one brigade of British cavalry, amounting to 1000 in number, under Major-General Slade, the 4th regiment of Portuguese cavalry, and one brigade of German, and two of Portuguese artillery. He was instructed to co-operate with certain Spanish troops, then supposed to have crossed the Tagus, and to prevent the French, if possible, from attempting any serious operation against Badajos, from which, as we have seen, they retreated on his approach. The strength of the enemy, as to numbers, and the celebrity of Napoleon's marshals[1] who commanded them, were enough to have made the British generals pause, for much of the force they had to oppose to them was of at least doubtful efficiency, while every possible impediment was cast in their way. But in the consciousness of a good cause they persevered and triumphed.

It was in the month of March that the French corps in Estremadura broke up, and Mortier departed to the South; but Regnier, with Soult's corps, remained in the neighbourhood of Merida. General Hill was much complimented by Lord Wellington on the way in which he had strengthened his position at Portalegre, as well as on his arrangements for communication, and the punctuality of his advices. At the end of this month the French threatened them on all sides,

---

1. *Napoleon's Marshals* by R. P. Dunn-Pattison is also published by Leonaur.

but menaced too many points at a time to create much uneasiness as to any particular one; and Lord Wellington pronounced himself "in a situation in which no mischief could be done to the army or any part of it." He also characteristically observed:

> I am prepared for all events; and if I am in a scrape, as appears to be the general belief in England, though certainly not my own, I'll get out of it.

The Marquis de la Romana, who was in constant communication with General Hill, was afraid that the French would annoy Badajos from Caceres; and if this should be the general's opinion, he was permitted to show himself beyond the Sierra, but he was directed to incur no risk or unnecessary loss. The British commander was determined to follow out his own great plan, and not to harass his troops by marches and counter-marches in conformity with the motions of the enemy; and the issue proved that he was right. Towards the 11th of April the French appeared to be preparing to attack Ciudad Rodrigo or Almeida, which it was thought expedient to prevent, and certain movements were made with a view to these objects. A correspondence also took place between General Hill and Marshal Beresford respecting the disposition and food of the Portuguese cavalry. The marshal wrote:

> I regret, though I am not surprised, to find how much the Portuguese corps with you have wanted provisions. It is impossible to deal with the rascally *junta de vivres*, that provide, or rather do not provide, for this army."
> I was some time since thinking of paying you a visit, and to see Elvas, and the other places on that frontier; but the gathering at Salamanca indicating some intention on the part of the enemy against Ciudad Rodrigo or Almeida, I cannot stir your way till something more decisive of their intentions appears.

At length, on the 3rd of May, Lord Wellington wrote to General Hill that the plot seemed to thicken; but that, after a careful perusal of previous instructions, he did not think it requisite to add to them. He also approved of a movement made to assist O'Donnell, which gratified the worthy Romana, who wrote to the general in English:

> I am very anxious to give many thanks to your Excellency at this purpose.

The nature of his next intercourse with both these personages will be best explained by General Hill himself:—

Portalegre, 18th May, 1810.

My dear Sister,

A few days ago Clement wrote to you to inform you that we were on the move—an advance I thought it right to make under the following circumstances:—On the 14th I received a letter from the Marquis of Romana, stating that 'the enemy presented themselves before Badajos to mask an attack they intended to make, and perhaps are actually executing, on our position of Zafra. The fewness I have of troops to succour said post induces me to request your Excellency will please to order some regiments to march to support my troops. This is a movement highly interesting for the safety of the province of Alemtejo, therefore I dare pray the orders for its execution may be given immediately without any delay—if possible, even today, for tomorrow the attack will be made, if not already this day. I have the honour to renew to your Excellency my ardent desire that this movement of the troops under your Excellency's command may take place, and at the same time the distinguished sentiments,' &c. &c.

Another Spanish General, O'Donnell, informed me at the same time that 'the enemy, having collected the greater part of his forces on the left banks of the Guadiana, has made a movement towards Olivença, intending, it is supposed, to *cut off* and attack Ballasteros'—the Spanish general at Zafra.

In consequence of the above I moved forward, and in the night of the 14th, when I was at Arronches, I received three expresses, stating that the enemy had retired, and an official message from the Marquis Romana in the following words: 'The marquis is most particularly obliged to you for the move you were pleased to make with the British and Portuguese troops, and is extremely anxious to have an interview with you tomorrow at Campo Mayor. His Lordship appears desirous that the British troops should not advance further, fearful it might attract attention, and cause Regnier to be reinforced.'

I accordingly met the *marquis*, who confirmed the above, though at the same time expressed a wish that we should move on to near Merida—a proposition so imprudent and contrary to my instructions, that it was out of the question my complying with it. I returned to Portalegre, a point I do not like to be far distant from, in the event of our being wanted in another quarter. I had a very civil letter from Romana this day: he tells me the enemy are still retiring, but I must confess I do not think they will go far.

I have had a letter from Colonel Campbell this day: he desires his compliments to all at Hawkstone. He was well on the 29th *ultimo*. I am,

> Yours most affectionately,
>
> R. H.

Fully aware of the consequences of quotations from private letters of officers in English newspapers, he added, with his usual caution:

Do not allow the contents of this letter to appear in public.

And well, indeed, had it been for the British leader's satisfaction, if all the officers of his army and their friends had possessed similar prudence. That prudence in every respect was fully estimated: and with regard to his movements at this time, Lord Wellington wrote to him:—

I am convinced that whatever you decide upon will be right. I recommend to you, however, to proceed with great caution in respect to intelligence transmitted to you by the Marquis de la Romana and all the Spanish officers. It is obvious that there is nothing they wish for so much as to involve our troops in their operations, which could lead to no advantage, and might end in the loss of every thing.

To this General Hill was quite alive; and the account he sent to his Lordship, proved his interview with Romana to have been conducted with equal sagacity and good feeling. What he said corresponded entirely with the views of his chief; yet his bearing was so courteous, that Romana, though his request was declined, manifested no resentment. The marquis was much respected by those who co operated with him, and showed every possible civility to British officers. Nevertheless, it had been reported to Lord Wellington that Captain Cotton had been insulted at Badajos. The captain's report, however, to General Hill completely exculpates Romana:—

In reply to your inquiries relative to whether the people of

Badajos insulted me when I was sent there by your orders, I have the honour to acquaint you, that on the evening of the day on which I arrived I went to the public Alameda, and some people, who were at the entrance and on the walls, certainly did hiss, and otherwise expressed disapprobation: but it was momentary; and nothing could exceed the civility and marked attention of the Marquis Romana and all his staff during the time I was there the first time, and also the last time you sent me there. The circumstance never occurred a second time.

But O'Donnell and his staff were not satisfied, although, as Lord Wellington observed in a letter to General Hill, both he and Ballesteros had recently had the advantage of his assistance, and were "thereby saved from being destroyed by the enemy."

May passed off without any incident of importance. At the end of the month General Hill wrote as follows:—

Portalegre, May 29, 1810.

My dear Sister,

I have nothing new to communicate to you. The armies remain nearly in the same situation as when I wrote last. The French, however, are strong, and Massena is arrived to take the command of that corps destined to attack Portugal, and which is said to be upwards of 80,000..... Our troops are very healthy, and every thing in the best order.

I had a letter from Cadiz this day of the 13th. The enemy in that neighbourhood is supposed to be about 15,000 or 16,000—too weak to do more than invest the place, and keep the garrison shut up. The Spaniards there, as well as in other quarters, do very little, and do (not) seem to consider themselves as the principals in the cause. The stories you see in the papers respecting Romana's march to Seville are all nonsense. It is true that the French occasionally quit that part of the country, upon which small parties of Spaniards enter it, but very prudently retire from it on the return of the French.

Ever yours most affectionately,
R. H.

Lieutenant Clement Hill, on the 5th of June, gave an account of their situation:—

We are perfectly quiet here, and have no more immediate prospect of being disturbed than we have had ever since we came. It appears something was expected to be done in the North a few days ago, but we since hear that all is again quiet. We have been so long in a state of uncertainty, that every one appears tired of conjecturing what the instructions of the French are; and, from all accounts, they are still more tired of the kind of war they are carrying on. They are kept almost constantly marching, and harassed by small parties of the Spaniards. The German troops in their service, and some few French, take every opportunity they can of deserting. There is scarcely a day that some do not come into Badajos; and I understand it is the same in the North.

You will have seen that General Massena calls himself King of Portugal, and intends having the honour of conquering this country. Whether he is really serious in making the attempt before Spain is subdued, I suppose a short time will show, as also what we are to do in the event. The army are all in high health, and fit for any thing, and the French, I am sure, will not be very anxious to meet them. We heard from Tom yesterday; he is very well; and the marshal says his regiment is in high order. . . . . We thought our rainy season was at an end, but it began again a few days ago. Yesterday, the king's birthday, it rained almost all day, and was as cold as ever it is at that time in England—so much so, that we found a fire comfortable. We hear nothing of going into camp. The country is now in the highest beauty: I wish I could transplant some of the orange-groves to Hawkstone. We have had many days fixed for a wolf-hunt, but have always been prevented by rain.

On the 24th of June, the report of certain manoeuvres of the enemy induced Lord Wellington to write to General Hill:—

> I conclude that you will have moved across the Tagus, and I shall immediately send you information and instruction respecting your position, &c.

It, however, became unnecessary that the river should be crossed; and the Marquis de la Romana arrived at General Hill's quarters on the 27th, on his way to pay a visit to Lord Wellington. The 2nd of July, being post-night for Lisbon, Lieutenant Hill was deputed to write to his sister instead of the general, who was too much engaged.

I believe we have been two weeks without sending you any news from these parts, for the best reason, having none to send. You must, of course be expecting interesting accounts of this army. It is certainly very extraordinary that we have so long remained quiet: however, we continue to have no immediate prospect of being otherwise. Both this and the French Army are much as they have so long been, the latter certainly not daring to come near us, nor is there any probability of our going to them. We heard yesterday of the bombardment of Ciudad Rodrigo having commenced. It is not thought likely that it will hold out long; but the Spaniards often fight longer than they are expected, when they get behind a wall. Till the French get possession of that fortress, it is not probable they will make any attempt on this country: and we must wait with patience to know what their intentions are. . . . . . . I can answer for Rowland and myself never being in better health. The weather is warm, but we are seasoned to the climate."

The day previous to the date of this letter Lord Wellington had received intercepted French letters, which acquainted him with the orders of Bonaparte to Regnier; which were "to cross the Tagus at Alcantara, and to manoeuvre, in conjunction with Massena, on the right bank of that river." His Lordship had some doubt if this order would be executed: if it was, General Hill's directions were to cross the Tagus at Villa Velha, leaving a portion of Fane's cavalry on the left bank. Lord Wellington said four days afterwards:

> If, however, the second corps should remain in Estremadura, it is desirable that you should, without loss of time, co-operate with the Marquis de la Romana, in an effort to dislodge Regnier from Estremadura, during such time as it may be necessary to collect such parts of the harvest as may be required for the formation of magazines.

His principal restriction was from crossing the Guadiana; which Romana, whom he expected to see shortly on his return from visiting Lord Wellington at Alverca, did not like. In reference to this, his Lordship wrote to General Hill:

> You will observe that I have put this point, '*it is desirable*' that you should not cross the Guadiana. This only expresses my opinion; but you on the spot must be the best judge whether you can

effect your object without crossing that river.

On the 9th, Lord Wellington again instructed the general relative to crossing the Tagus, and the proposed expedition into Estremadura; his letter also conveyed intelligence that Ciudad Rodrigo still held out: but on the 11th another was written, to say that it had surrendered by capitulation at six o'clock the night before.

The breach was open, and the French army were about to enter, when they offered terms of capitulation, which were accepted.

On the 13th, Regnier showed symptoms of an intention to cross the Tagus; and General Hill immediately apprised Lord Wellington of this intelligence. He stated that he should, "in consequence, incline to his left, and hold everything prepared to cross at Villa Velha, if he found him serious in crossing the river." He also wrote to Romana the same day; and the next received a letter from the marquis in English, and written with his own hand. How the worthy Spaniard picked up enough of our language to write as he did, is quite a marvel.

Badajoz, 14 July, 1810.

Dear Sir,
It is no doubt that the enemy is crossing the *tagus* at the same points you have the goodness to inform me, and consequently i have not other to say to you that if you deem convenient to make a movement, for my part i am ready to support them, i have ordered to Gl. Odonell to move towards Alcantera.
I have the honour to subjoin a copy of a letter send me by Genl. Odonell, wich i preay to you to forward His Excellency Lord Wellington.
On the side of Seville no was a movement of the ennemy. Rumour was spread yesterday that he began his retreat towards Sierra Morena, but that deserve confirmation.
I have the honour to remain, with the highest esteem,
   Your most humble servant,
           Mis. De la Romana.
i fear that Ciudad Rodrigo is surrendered, but I pray to you to conceal that, whatever i have no the least intelligence of this succes.

The plans of General Hill, consequent on his information respecting Regnier's movements, were entirely approved at hea quarters; and on the 15th he set off to Apalhaõ, to be ready to act on either side of the Tagus. On the 19th the civil marquis wrote him another English letter:—

Badajoz, *19 de Julio*, 1810.

Dear Sir,
i have the honour to inform to you that after the latests reports of banks of Tagus, it appears that the whole Regnier's corps had crossed this river, and are in movement towards Placentia and Ceria. i expected today the reports from Truxillo, and wil be not a lose for time in sending to you the notice. two thousand infantry and 300 cavalry were laying the 15 at Cancaveral.
  i am, with the highest degree of estim and regard,
    Your most faithful servant,
      Mis De la Romana.

Lieut.-Gen. R. Hill.

At the beginning of August, after some days of much anxiety, and great display of military skill, General Hill dated from Sarzedas:—

Sarzedas, near Castello Branco,
August 4. 1810.

My dear Sister,
Clement has, I know, been writing to you by this day's post; and if he has told you every thing that has been done of late, he has given you a tolerably long letter. Hitherto I have been fortunate enough to be aware of the enemy's movements, and to anticipate Lord Wellington's wishes. I trust and think matters will end well. I can only say that everyone seems most anxious to do his duty; and we have every confidence in our chief, who has a difficult game to play: at the same time, I am sure he will not risk too much. My situation at this moment is a good one; the position is strong: and if I find I cannot maintain it, I can get out of it, the country in my rear being mountainous, and the passes few and easily defended.

One of my Portuguese cavalry regiments was engaged with the enemy's cavalry yesterday. I have not received a report of what was done, but it is certain the French fled, leaving sixteen prisoners, and twelve dead. I believe the Portuguese were superior in numbers to the French; it is, however, the first affair they have had, and will have the best effect. Deserters come in daily, and represent the French Army to be tired of the war: that, however, is of little consequence so long as Bonaparte is not. Kind remembrance to Sir John and all friends.

> I remain most affectionately yours.

Truly did he say that he had anticipated the wishes of his chief, for the day after the date of this letter Lord Wellington wrote to him:

> It appears to me that the disposition which you have made of your corps will answer perfectly.

Regnier's whole body of cavalry had crossed the Tagus, and had become troublesome to General Hill's outposts in the flat country in his front. On the 8th he received a letter from the Frenchman relative to the exchange of an officer, in which he coolly says:

> *Je n'ai jamais été assez près de vous pour vous proposer son échange.*

He had approached one who was quite ready to encounter him at the proper moment, and from whom he must have wished himself farther off before the next month had elapsed, as will be seen in the sequel. Regnier dated his letter "Zarza la Mayor;" but Lord Wellington, with his usual caution, remarked to General Hill:

> When you send your answer, do not date where your headquarters are.

Though there was little fear of his giving his opponent any gratuitous intelligence. On the 17th he was again in the receipt of information from his Lordship, by the hands of Lord Clinton, to the effect that the enemy had broken ground before Almeida, and that he himself should soon "strike a blow" if he had the opportunity. Lord Clinton found General Hill occupying a small chapel by the road side; and as his strictness of discipline and character for integrity had attracted the peasantry, he was enabled to spread before his noble visitor bread, milk, honey, eggs, poultry, and excellent country wine. Men who had lived on coarse beef and hard biscuit for a long time, felt the full luxury of such supplies. The general had the pleasure of transmitting to head quarters, by Lord Clinton, an account of a successful attack upon a detachment of the enemy's cavalry, which had been reported to him by General Fane as having been made by a squadron of cavalry, consisting of a troop of the 4th Portuguese cavalry, and one troop of the 13th British dragoons. Amongst the prisoners of this party was the man with the horrible countenance, mentioned by Major Moyle Sherer in his *Recollections of the Peninsula*.[2] Still nothing of any moment occurred; and the general himself thus describes the posture of affairs:—

> Sarzedas, August 21. 1810,
>
> My dear Sister,
>
> I am sending letters to Lisbon, and will therefore write you a few lines to let you know that we are going on well, and that your three brothers in this part of the world are in perfect health. There is nothing very particular in this quarter. Regnier continues in my front, with his headquarters at Zarza Mayor. I have had frequent communications with him: and we are very civil to each other as far as words go. I sent an officer to him the day before yesterday. He dined with the general, who was exceedingly polite.
>
> The French did not seem at all sanguine upon the subject of the war, but, on the contrary, talked of being heartily tired of their present circumstances; complained of our never being quiet; and said they never heard from France. Deserters come in almost every day; three arrived this morning. They are in general Germans, and all agree in saying the French are heartily tired of the unjust war in the Peninsula. The peasants murder them wherever they are found in small parties; and no communication can be kept up through the country without strong guards, which is very harassing to the troops. Massena has commenced the siege of Almeida, and Lord Wellington moved a few miles nearer to him yesterday.
>
> We are in hourly expectation of the packet from England. Kind remembrance to Sir John and all dear friends.
>
> Yours ever most affectionately,
>
> R. H.

On the 28th he informed his friends at Hawkstone:

> Nothing very particular has occurred during the last week. The enemy are making formidable preparations for the siege of Almeida, which place, I fear, cannot hold out very long; and when the enemy have taken possession of that place, probably they will commence their operations upon Portugal.

The same day Lord Wellington wrote to him:

> There is no doubt but that the place has fallen.

---

2. *Recollections of the Peninsula* by Moyle Sherer is also published by Leonaur.

Observe Regnier well; his movements will be the clue to everything else: I expect that he will move tomorrow.

On the 1st of September General Hill was informed by his Lordship that the magazine at Almeida was blown up, which destroyed the town. Regnier's movements still remained doubtful; and on the 5th Lord Wellington's communication was thus expressed:

> Nothing has occurred this day worthy of attention. I rely upon your prudence and discretion not to engage yourself in any affair of which the result can be at all doubtful. Retire gradually if you find the enemy threatening you in too great force; and let me hear from you constantly. If we can avoid any accident before we all join, I have confidence of our final success.

On the 12th General Hill quitted Sarzedas, which he announced in the following terms to his chief:—

Sarzedas, September 12. 1810.

My Lord,
From the intelligence I have already sent your Lordship, and that which I now enclose, it is pretty certain that the whole of Regnier's corps have marched to the northward, and that some part of them have already reached Guarda. Therefore, adverting to your Lordship's instructions of the 31st of August, I have prepared to cross the Zezere, as therein directed. The British infantry and my artillery will be at Sabrera Formosa this evening; and until I find it necessary to proceed from that place, I shall continue Le Cor at Fondão, and General Fane at Castello Branco. Should the enemy return to this part of the frontier, I am in as good a situation to defend the passes from Sabrera Formosa as from Sarzedas, as your Lordship observes.

I have, &c.
R. Hill.

Viscount Wellington, K.B.
&c. &c. &c.

Sarzedas was left with regret by the household of the general; but they had given up all hope of coming in contact with Regnier for some time. Lieutenant Hill observed, in writing to his sister:

> I do not wonder at your anxiety about us; but I wish you would think no more of our danger than we do. To be sure, as Mr.

Moore says in his *Almanac*, '*when armies are in the field, a battle may be expected,*' and such an event may take place; but I assure you we have no more prospect of it than we have had for some time, nor so much, for the enemy certainly show no disposition to come near us.

When General Hill arrived at Sarzedas, the village was completely deserted, except by the priest, their landlord; but the inhabitants soon found out that they might return in confidence of protection, and even profit by the sale of provisions; so that a forsaken and desolate place became speedily converted into a luxurious market, supplied not only from the neighbourhood but from Lisbon itself.

The enemy's whole army had, by the 17th, entered the valley of the Mondego, and on that day General Hill was directed "to collect his corps at Espinhal, &c., and remain there till further orders." He arrived at Espinhal on the 20th, and was at Foz d'Aronce on the 21st. Lord Wellington occupied the Convent of Busaco—a formidable position. From the lofty summit of that mountain he bade defiance to the gathering hosts of the veterans of France,—firm in his purpose, clear in his calculations, and full of assurance that a day of reward for his unexampled patience was at hand. Nearly 70,000 of Napoleon's conquering troops were a fearful array, commanded as they were by three Marshals of France,—their chief Massena himself, whose life had been one perpetual success. But Wellington had counted the cost of being attacked by such assailants in his stronghold, and had decided that the loss should not be his, but theirs. The eventful moment was daily approaching. He wished to have an interview with General Hill, but neither could quit their post. On the 24th the former wrote from Busaco,—"I was not able to go to you as I intended;" and the communication of the latter was as follows:—

Villa Chem, September 25, 11 p.m.

My Lord,

It was my wish to have waited on your Lordship, but the circumstances of our present situation will, I trust, plead my apology for not having done so. My brother is the bearer of this, and will take charge of any commands your Lordship may send me.

I was in front this day, with General Fane, posting his cavalry, and returned by the bridge of Val del Espino. I cannot learn that any thing but a few parties of cavalry had crossed the Mondego,

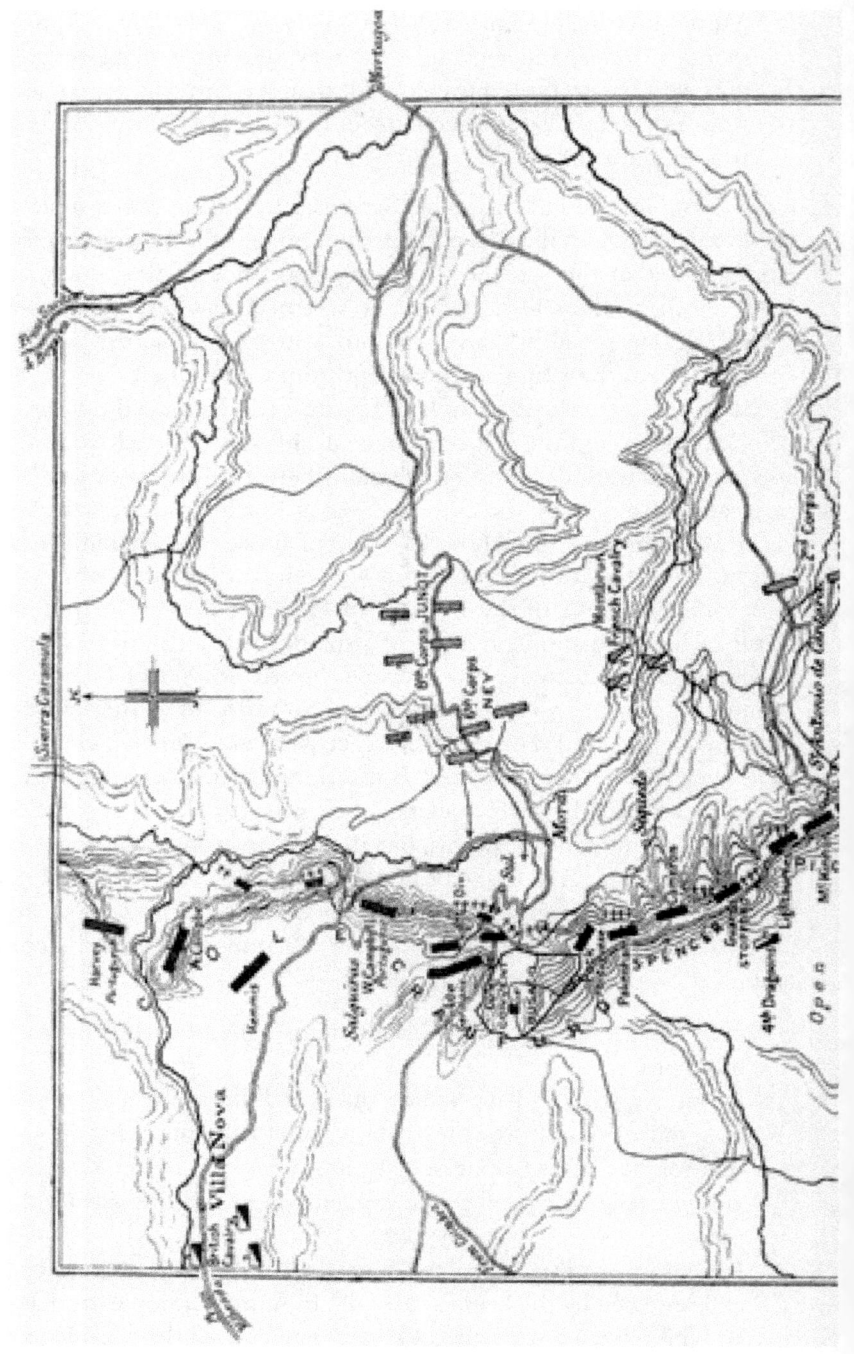

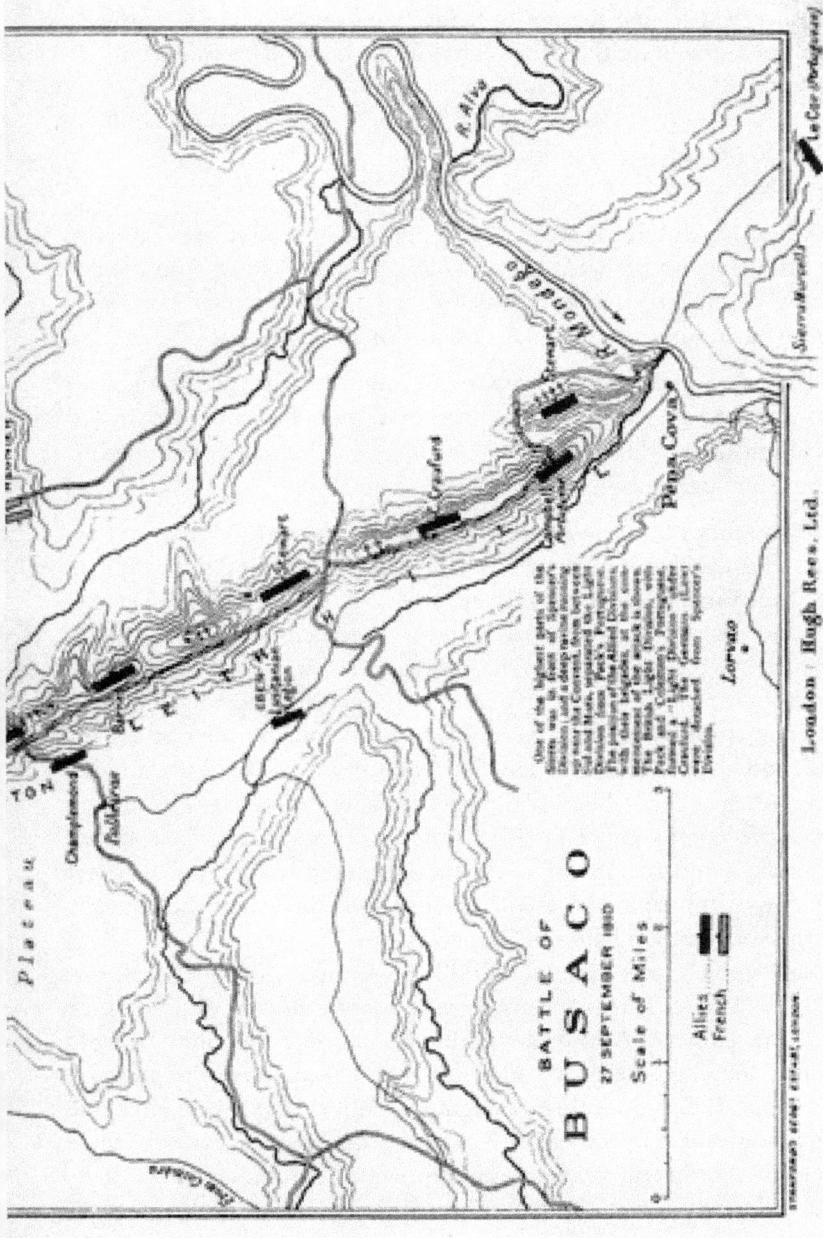

and they appear to have gone back. This is confirmed by Captain Cox, who has joined General Fane.

I have had several reports of firing being heard this day at the left of General Leith, and am anxious to know the result of it.

I have, &c.

R. Hill.

Lord Viscount Wellington, K.B.
&c. &c. &c.

A few hours after this letter was penned its writer moved across the Mondego, and led his gallant soldiers up the steep mountain of Busaco, where he quickly disposed them on the right of Lord Wellington's army, in order of battle. Major Sherer says:

> Our position extended nearly eight miles along this mountainous and rocky ridge, and the ground on which we formed, inclining with a slope to our own rear, most admirably concealed both the disposition and numbers of our force.

At the foot of this position reposed that evening the forces of Portugal, who were wont at sunset to gather in circles round their officers, and chant forth their vespers. Their eyes now first beheld the seventy thousand invaders of their fatherland—an appalling spectacle, as the rays of the setting sun were reflected from their arms. Only twenty-five thousand Portuguese were about to engage with them in their first great combat; but they were aided by an equal number of British, commanded by Wellington and Hill. The dawn of the 27th ushered in the decisive day. While yet the grey mists rested on their mountain couch, the enemy came on. The watchful picquets had heard their preparation, and the British were standing silently to arms. Regnier with two columns, and Ney with three, rushed up against the convent, and the well-known battle of Busaco ensued.

The whole corps of General Hill was thrown into open column, and moved to its left in the most perfect order and in double quick time. The effort of Massena was directed against the right of Lord Wellington, which he expected to turn; and, ignorant of the presence of Generals Hill and Leith, he imagined that his troops were engaging with its extremity. To the surprise of the French, the forces under these officers suddenly emerged from their previous concealment, and halted at the spot whence the brave 74th had just driven back a column of the enemy, and were retiring in line, regular, compact, invincible. The only signs of recent encounter were their colours ragged with the shot of their opponents. Soon after the British commander and his staff galloped to the spot, he said, in a decisive tone:

> Hill, if they attempt this point again, give them a volley and charge bayonets, but do not let your people follow them too far down the hill.

But they had had quite enough. Regnier now found what it was to be *near* the British; and the French, instead of returning to the onslaught, occupied the remainder of the day in removing their wounded; and some of them actually shook hands with the English soldiers as they slaked their common thirst from a narrow rivulet that ran at the bottom of the hill. The Portuguese behaved valiantly; while on Marshal Beresford and the English officers, amongst whom was Colonel Thomas Noel Hill, rested the high honour of their discipline and military bearing. General Hill's division was, as has been seen, ready in the exact place where it was needed, but was not engaged; still his presence rendered essential service. Every other general's conduct also, including the names of Picton, Pack, Cole, Crawfurd, and Leith, was worthy of their leader, their country, and the cause in which they fought.

The night which succeeded this memorable day, afforded to the victorious occupants of the mountain scenes of indescribable grandeur. The whole country beneath them glowed with countless fires, showing thousands of shadowy forms of men and horses, mingled with piles of arms glittering amidst the flames. These gradually subsided into glowing patches of red embers gemming the black bosom of the earth, and all seemed to threaten another mighty conflict at the dawn of day. The men under Hill were kept in their full accoutrements, and each with his musket by his side, front and rear ranks, head to head, lay upon the mountain, awaiting the morn, and expecting that an assailable gorge near at hand would be the point of attack. This expectation was not realised. Towards evening the French moved with the design of cutting off the allies from Oporto, or bringing on an action where the ground was more in their favour. Lord Wellington, foreseeing this intention, withdrew from the Serra de Busaco, and General Hill, crossing the Mondego, marched on San Miguel, where he endeavoured to ascertain the movements of the French.

> If you find that the enemy cross the Mondego, send Le Cor immediately to Arganil, and depend upon my being with you, with the whole army, in a few hours. If they try our left instead

of our right, I shall give you instructions for movements corresponding with ours.

To this letter, dated "Tormes, 29th September," he thus replied:—

> St. Miguel, 30th Sept., 1810, 10 a.m.
>
> My Lord,
>
> I have received your Lordship's letter of the 29th from Tormes, and have issued orders accordingly. By the enclosed reports you will see that the enemy had not shown near the river yesterday, and that the bridge of Tabra may be destroyed if thought necessary.
>
> I have, &c.
>
> R. Hill.
>
> P. S. The movements of yesterday were well executed, and the guns got off without any material injury.

In consequence of his anticipations respecting the enemy's proceedings, Lord Wellington wrote to General Hill:

> Your movements therefore become a subject of some anxiety to me. I understand half, possibly the whole of your infantry will be at Santarem this day. Everything that arrives at Santarem this day should march in the morning to Azanibuja. Any part of your corps which makes a short march into Santarem tomorrow morning must move on to Cartaxo, and the whole must move early the next morning upon Villa Franca.

To this and another letter of the same import he replied the next day from Santarem:—

> I hope your Lordship will have received the letter I wrote last night, in answer to yours of yesterday morning, informing your Lordship that the whole of the infantry and artillery under my command had arrived here yesterday, with my intention to pass Azambuja this day at least. I will, however, halt on the Villa Franca side of that place. I shall be ready to proceed further if your Lordship should deem it necessary.

The next communication from Lord Wellington informed him,—

> Your whole corps, even including that part of Fane's cavalry which will not leave Santarem until tomorrow morning, will

be in good time.

On the afternoon of the 8th they entered Alhandra, about four leagues from Lisbon. From this place, on the 12th, Lieutenant Clement Hill sent home tidings of himself and his others.

> You will probably, before you get this have heard of the army having fallen back to near Lisbon, which, no doubt, people in England will be disappointed to find, after the victory at Busaco. It certainly was always Lord W.'s intention to do so in the event of the enemy advancing in force, as of course the farther they are drawn on the more difficulty they will meet with when defeated, which most certainly they will be if they are mad enough to attack us in our strong position, which extends from this place, on the Tagus, to Mafra, on the sea, the whole country between which is fortified; and I believe Lord W. has now as many troops as they have. He seems quite confident of success.
> They made a show of following the army during our retreat; but I believe it is not yet ascertained whether their whole force is come on. Our giving up so much of the country has certainly distressed the inhabitants dreadfully. They are all ordered, on pain of death, to leave their houses and to destroy all the property they cannot carry away with them; and very few having means of transport, you may imagine what misery it causes. But they all submit with the greatest patience, knowing it has the desired effect of completely annoying the French. Our post is at this place, about eighteen miles from Lisbon. We are in every respect well off, get all the good things from Lisbon, and live in a palace.
> We are both quite well. Tom is not far from us; but I have not seen him lately. We hear almost every day of his being well. I hope you received my letter, (written) as soon as I had an opportunity after the Battle of Busaco. Rowland and I were not much in the fight, but had the pleasure of seeing the French get a drubbing, in which Tom's regiment helped. Marshal Beresford and Lord W. have not forgot his name amongst others that are mentioned.

The strong position here alluded to was on the lines of Torres Vedras. Lord Wellington had carried on these celebrated works silently but perseveringly, for the defence of the seat of government and capital of Portugal, that he might there achieve the deliverance of a nation, and crown his own and the British name with imperishable honour. At this time the rains had commenced, and the men suffered much from the want of tents, which had been ordered, but had not arrived; on which Lord Wellington observed, drily, "They swear they have been sent from Lisbon." General Hill found time for a short letter, descriptive of his position;—

Alhandra, Oct. 13. 1810.

My dear Sister,

The enemy, finding he could make no impression at Busaco by force, endeavoured to get round our left, which obliged Lord W. to fall back. We now occupy a position about 20 miles in front of Lisbon; it is strong, but rather too extensive for our numbers. The enemy followed us pretty close upon our march, and is now immediately in our front, and I have no doubt will soon bring matters to a crisis. We are confident of success, and I trust you will soon receive favourable accounts. My post extends from the Tagus about four miles to the left, and I am, as you may suppose, a good deal occupied; but hearing there is an opportunity of sending letters, I will not miss it. I thank Sir John for his very kind letter, which I will answer in a few days. . . . . Tom and his regiment distinguished themselves much in the late action at Busaco.

Most affectionately and truly yours,
R. H.

On the 14th the general's old friend Regnier was near him again, of which he apprised Lord Wellington. He wrote on the 15th:

I have to inform your Lordship that the enemy reconnoitred us on the high ground in front of our position yesterday about noon, having obliged our picquets to fall back. His force appeared to consist of about three battalions of infantry and some squadrons of cavalry. An officer and a large suite were observed in front.

After mentioning the successful result of some skirmishing, he continued:

A prisoner, brought in late yesterday evening, states that the officer who reconnoitred us was Regnier, and that the whole of his corps is in our front, the main body being near Villa Franca, where our armed boats observe considerable smoke and the appearance of encampments.

During the remainder of this month, several changes of position took place in consequence of the marches of the enemy, who retired without venturing on any attack, completely foiled by the strength of the lines and the skill of their opponents. On the 27th, by desire of his gallant brother. Lieutenant Hill sent word home from Alhandra:—

> We have now not the least idea of their attacking us here, and they must give up all thoughts of getting Lisbon. I really believe they never have been more deceived or were in a greater scrape than they are at present, and they will have some difficulty in getting out of it. They cannot remain near us much longer without being starved, as they have very few supplies here, and the Spaniards and Portuguese are intercepting all from their rear: in fact, part of their army has already begun to retreat. We are all three quite well. Tom is about ten miles from here: he made us a *morning call* yesterday, and today we expect him to dine and sleep. The people in Lisbon have now quite got rid of their alarm, and the ladies begin to come up by water to look at the French. Our house is near the river, and Rowland is just gone down to do the civil thing to the admiral's family, who are come up on a party of pleasure, or he intended writing himself.

The worthy Romana had once more joined the allied forces in front of Lisbon with a considerable detachment of Spaniards, and Lord Wellington found him friendly and attentive. The subjoined letter of General Hill to his father affords very interesting information:—

Lobral Pequeña, near Alhandra,
Nov. 3. 1810

My dear Father,

Clement, I know, wrote by the last packet, and I sent a few lines the week before. when I wrote, I expected the enemy would not have remained many hours without attacking us; but not having done so at that time, I think it is pretty certain they will not meddle with us now, at least in our present position, and with their present force. It is difficult to foresee the result of this contest: it is, however, evident the enemy did not expect the resistance he has met with from the Portuguese troops; indeed, an intercepted letter from Bonaparte to Massena shows that he holds the Portuguese very cheap. I have not seen the letter, but know that it gives Massena a tolerably correct statement of the

British force, and directs him to attack it, making no mention of the Portuguese; and adding, that with his 65,000 men he cannot fail to drive the British 30,000 into the sea.

At the same time, he directs Massena to *press on*. Massena has accordingly endeavoured to obey his emperor's commands, and foolishly attacked the strong position of Busaco; and although the battle at that place was by no means so desperate as the Battle of Talavera, yet the enemy's loss was considerable: and finding he could not force the position, he turned it, and obliged Lord Wellington to fall back to this line, where he has his left on the sea, and his right here on the Tagus. On our march, Massena did press on as fast as he could, and I verily believe he and his army thought we were off to our ships, and consequently were a good deal disappointed when we halted here to meet him, in which situation I thought he would have attacked us. He has, however, given us so much time, that we are now twice as strong, from the works constructed, as we were when we first arrived; therefore, as I said before, I do not think he will have anything to say to us *here* at present.

The enemy give out that they expect considerable reinforcements; and, although I believe there can be none near, yet I dare say Bonaparte will, when he finds he has not sufficient troops, send more. Many are of opinion that Massena will not be able to keep his ground, and must either quit the country or surrender. I must own I am not quite so sanguine as they are; but, at the same time, I think he is rather in a scrape if he does not get more troops soon. Clement and Thomas are quite well. The former writes by this day's packet, as I told him I thought I should not have time. I return you a thousand thanks for your kind attention to my affairs. Believe me, my dear Father, to be your ever obliged and dutiful

R. Hill.

Sir John Hill, Bart.

Another letter also explains the proceedings of the two armies.

Lobral Pequeña, near Alhandra,
November 10. 1810.

My dear Sister,

On this day week I wrote to Sir John, since which time nothing of consequence has occurred. The two armies remain as they were, the British in the position I mentioned in my last, with the right on the Tagus, and the left on the sea near Torres Vedras, a distance, probably, of about 25 miles.

The French advanced regiments are close to us; that is, some of them not more than a mile and a half from the place where I am now writing, with the sentries within musket shot of each other. In this situation we have been for the last month, and I dare say it will appear rather extraordinary when I tell you that we are perfectly good neighbours, and never think of molesting each other.

On the contrary, I have been obliged to put a stop to the intimacy which was going on. It was by no means uncommon to see the soldiers of each army getting grapes out of the same vineyard, water from the same well, and asking each other to drink wine.

Indeed, I know of some instances, though not quite correct, of our officers sending to Lisbon for boots and shirts for some of their *friends* at outposts. By this intercourse, however, we have procured some information. The French certainly seem tired and dissatisfied with the war, and say that Massena's intelligence must have been very bad. They, however, hold out; at least, are told that reinforcements are coming to them, and that they shall be able to keep their ground until they arrive, and will then drive us into the sea.

The only reinforcements I have heard of are about 10,000, said to be on the march. It was supposed by some that the French could not remain where they are for want of provisions: it is, however, a difficult matter to starve a Frenchman; and although the destruction and misery have been very complete in the great towns, and on the line of the great roads, yet I fear the Portuguese, with all their boasting, have been very deficient in the essential point of clearing the country we have left of its provisions and cattle...... I trust the day will come for us all to see our dear friends at Hawkstone. God bless you all!

        I am,
            Yours ever most affectionately,
                              R. H.

Miss Hill.

A third letter soon succeeded the other two.

LINES OF TORRES VEDRAS

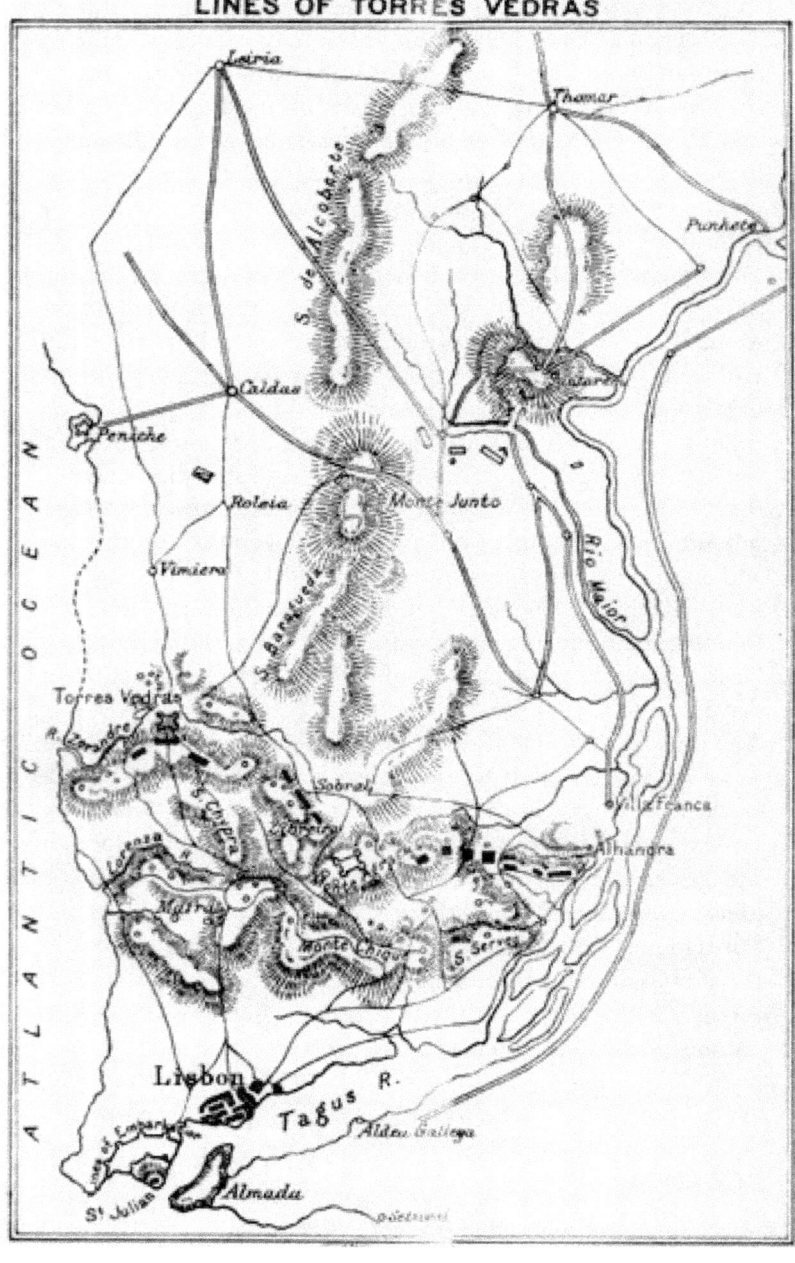

Villa Nova, 18th Nov. 1810.

My dear Sister,

On the morning of the 15th, at daylight, we descried that the enemy had retreated during the night. They have continued their march to their rear, ever since followed by our army. What the real situation of the enemy is I cannot pretend to say; it is, however, the general opinion that they are going to quit Portugal. It is certain the French Army has suffered a good deal in this country,—what with losses sustained at Busaco, the desertions, sickness, and want of comforts. I cannot, however, help thinking they are not in that state to justify their going off altogether. Some of their troops were in Santarem last night, and I dare say are gone from thence this morning. Our light troops are close after them, and have taken some prisoners, about a hundred a day, in general, weakly sick men, which shows that the enemy is rather in a hurry, when they do not wait to protect their sick.

I am going to cross the Tagus this day with my corps, and shall move up the south of the river towards Abrantes. I saw Tom yesterday. Kind remembrances to all.

      I remain,
         Most affectionately yours,
                R. Hill.

Miss Hill.

General Hill had been instructed to cross the Tagus, but Lord Wellington wrote to him on the 19th, to say that a letter from General Fane had almost induced him to believe that he had made a mistake in sending him over that river at all. He added:

> I am certain that you should proceed no further up that river than Chamusca at present, with the head of your corps.

Accordingly his next letter is dated "Chamusca, Nov. 23rd, 5 p. m." It states:

> I wrote on Saturday last, and told you that the enemy had retired from the front of our former position. They continued retreating till they arrived at Santarem, where they now are in considerable force, and from whence I think it will be difficult to drive them if they are inclined to remain. My corps passed the Tagus on the 17th with the view of recrossing at Abrantes, should the enemy retire into Spain by Castello Branco. They

either intend to retire by that road, or by Espinhal and the Ponte Marcella, or to remain in the country till they get reinforcements. I am inclined to think the latter, though the former is the general opinion. Clement has of course told you our present position, which at this moment is very safe, having the Tagus between us and the enemy.

Towards the middle of December, General Hill was obliged to retire to Lisbon by a severe attack of fever, which at first gave hopes of speedy abatement. His illness had been communicated to his family by his brother, and he wrote himself on feeling somewhat better.

Lisbon, December 15. 1810.

My dear Sister,

Clement will have informed you of my having been indisposed. The feverish attack which I had is by no means unusual in the interior of the country, and particularly on the south bank of the Tagus, where we have been lately. The fever is seldom attended with fatal consequences, and a change of air to the neighbourhood of the sea, has almost always an instantaneous effect for the better. I was therefore removed to Lisbon, and since my arrival here have been daily recovering. I have just been out riding for nearly two hours, and do not feel the least fatigued; on the contrary, I feel myself better. I have received your last kind letter. Nothing, I assure you, would give me greater pleasure than to obtain permission to visit Shropshire, which, if I were to ask, I am sure I could procure; but under present circumstances, in my mind, it would not be right to think of it, provided my health will admit of my returning to my post.

Surely affairs in this country cannot long remain in a state of uncertainty. I do not, however, think the French have sufficient force in Portugal to drive us out of our strong position, nor do I think Lord W. has sufficient strength to drive them out of the country. It appears as if Massena was waiting either for instructions or reinforcements. It is certain that his adjutant-general was despatched to Paris about three weeks ago; it is also certain that some small reinforcements, about 4,000, which were on the march to Massena, have returned into Spain.

I am now living in Lord W.'s house here. He was here about a week ago; he is in high spirits, and seems very confident. He goes out hunting about twice a week. . . . . . We are anxiously expecting the arrival of the next packet from England; its contents must be very interesting to us, as we have heard nothing since the 27th of last month. Kind remembrances to all friends, and believe me, my dear Sister,

Most affectionately yours,

R. H.

By the 22nd he was so much better, his brother expressed a hope that in about a fortnight he would return to his corps at Chamusca. These expectations were not realised, and he could not regain his strength, which he reluctantly acknowledged in writing to his sister.

Lisbon, 30th December, 1810.

My dear Sister

Clement wrote to you by the last packet, and I must send you a few lines by this day's. I find it is much easier to lose one's strength in this country than to regain it. I have not for some time had the least fever, but I feel the effects of it, and cannot get appetite or strength. I do, however, hope soon to be better; but if I find I do not recover in this country, I shall leave it. General Fane, who has been all along with me, sails to England in the packet which takes this; he was ill about the time I was, and with nearly the same complaint, but his attack was severer than mine.

Things are again becoming interesting in this country. When Massena went from before Alhandra, it was generally supposed that he was off altogether. I think I then told you that I thought he would not go far, which turned out to be the case. It now appears to he certain that the whole of the 9th French corps, about 15,000, has entered Portugal to reinforce Massena, and that the junction once effected, which I think will be in the course of a week, it is probable he will carry into immediate execution one of the following operations—a general attack upon the position before Lisbon, or the passage of the Tagus, and the occupation of the province of Alemtejo. . . . . . . I fear I shall not be able, at all events, to join the army for a fortnight at least. Excuse this hasty letter, and believe me,

Most truly yours,

R Hill.

Major-General Stewart filled for a time the post of General Hill, but was extremely desirous that he should himself return to the command. As he was unable to do so, Sir William Beresford crossed the Tagus and took charge of affairs; and the kind letter of Lord Wellington, announcing this to General Hill, expressed much anxiety that he might soon resume his situation, but urged him not to attempt it till quite able. He also wrote to him in the most friendly manner, advising frequent change of air; but all was of no avail; and the physicians recommended his going home for a time, to which, on the strong solicitation of Lord Wellington, he became willing to yield, the more especially as he had been visited with a severe attack of jaundice.

Accordingly, after a passage of three weeks, he reached Falmouth on the 6th of February, 1811, and was at Exeter on the 9th. On the 11th he arrived at Wells on a visit to his uncle, Mr. Tudway. Before he left Exeter he heard of the "sudden death of his friend Romana," by an officer just come from Portugal. A very few days in his native country proved the excellence of the advice given him, for he began rapidly to mend, and was very anxious to proceed to Hawkstone, accompanied by Lieutenant Clement Hill and Captain Currie. He wrote from Wells:

> I mean to go by Bath, and as I really have no coat except a uniform one, I believe I must *halt* there one day for the purpose of getting one made, and to purchase a few necessary articles.

Although much better, he was still unable to encounter the evening air, and therefore proposed to take three days in going from Bath to Hawkstone. His arrival was a source of much comfort to his friends, who saw him daily advancing towards a renovated state of health. But he was most anxious to return to the army, which, by the blessing of God on repose and the comforts of home, he was enabled to rejoin in May, almost immediately after Marshal Beresford's desperate Battle of Albuera.

CHAPTER 7

General Hill's Return to the Army

General Hill, on reaching the Peninsula, was welcomed by the following letter from Lord Wellington:—

Elvas, May 27. 1811.

My dear Hill,
I am very glad you are returned in good health, and I hope that we shall see you soon.
You will have heard of events here, which I hope will enable us to obtain possession of Badajos, upon which we are busily employed.

Believe me, &c.

Wellington.

He proceeded at once to headquarters, and wrote to his sister, to apprise her of his arrival.

Elvas, May 31. 1811.

My dear Sister,
I have the pleasure to acquaint you that after a prosperous journey, we arrived here yesterday, and as I have been but one fortnight coming from Spithead to this place, little time has been lost. Indeed, I believe few ever made the voyage and journey in less time. Beresford's battle, which you will have heard of long before this reaches you, has been a bloody one, and as the French retired, we claim the victory, but alas! it has been a dear bought one. When I was in England, and heard that the French had possession of Badajos, I said I thought I should be in time to see it retaken.
The opportunity exists, and the enemy seems determined to

keep it as long as he can, in consequence of which preparations are making to besiege it, and it is the general opinion that it will fall in about ten days. In the mean time my corps, which I shall resume the command of tomorrow, will prevent the enemy from relieving the place. I saw Lord Wellington yesterday, and shall dine with him today. He is, as usual, very civil, and expressed pleasure at my return. I assure you, I never felt in better health than at present, and trust I shall continue well. Clement[1] joins in kind remembrance to Sir John, and all at Hawkstone.

  I remain,
    Yours very affectionately,
        R. H.

The return of General Hill not only gave pleasure to Lord Wellington, but excited, as is truly stated by Napier, "the eager rejoicings of the army." After various movements, which it is not essential to trace, he arrived at "Torre Moro, one league from Campo Mayor." On the 20th of June he sent home news to this effect:—

My last letter to you was from Elvas, on my way to Almendralejo, to assume the command of my corps, which I did about seventeen days ago. I had scarcely been there a week, when accounts from every quarter confirmed what had been for some time expected, the advance of the French from the North as well as the South towards Badajos, for the purpose of relieving that place, and in doing which they have completely succeeded. Lord Wellington, not wishing to risk a battle to save it, sent orders for me and all the troops in front, to fall back upon the approach of the enemy. We accordingly came here, and as the enemy was bringing all his force towards this point, Lord W. ordered the whole of his army from the North to march in this direction, and to this neighbourhood, where the whole will be assembled in the course of two or three days. The enemy, on their part, have concentrated nearly all their force about Merida, and having gained their first object, the raising of the siege of Badajos, it is thought they will not at present make any further attempt on Portugal.

He had, on the same day, been taking a long ride with Lord Wellington, and when he came home, could not help congratulating him-

---

1. Mr. Clement Hill was promoted to the rank of captain in April, 1811.

self on having had nothing to do with the unsuccessful siege of Badajos. But he perfectly coincided with his chief as to the wisdom of not risking a battle in the open plains near that place, "where the enemy was bringing the whole of his force, and which force in cavalry was far superior to ours." On the 11th of July he observed, in another letter:

> The enemy, having now completely succeeded in their object of relieving Badajos, and throwing abundant supplies of provisions and ammunition into the place, do not appear desirous, nor, indeed, I ought to say equal to undertake any further operations against us at present.

Besides, the French had said, in their official papers, that none but madmen would continue in the unhealthy spot they then occupied, during the hot months, which being a just remark, he concluded they would retire, and expected Soult was going to Seville, and Marmont about to recross the Tagus. The same reasons also operated on the mind of Lord Wellington, who marched to Beira, leaving the troops under General Hill cantoned in Alemtejo. The Prince of Orange had just joined the army, and General Hill had met him at dinner at headquarters, when his Serene Highness and himself commenced an acquaintance, which afterwards ripened into mutual esteem and confidence. Soon after, Lieutenant Mackworth, whom the general had taken as his extra *aide-de-camp*, was made prisoner by the French *patroles*, but was very well treated by them, and eventually, after a long correspondence, exchanged. This affair, and the nature of his position, are noticed in a letter to Miss Hill, which will preclude the necessity of tracing his movements at any length, during a period comparatively dull.

Villa Viçosa, August 28. 1811.

My dear Sister,

Your letters have duly arrived, and I beg to thank you for all you have been kind enough to write to us. If you received a letter I wrote from Torre de Moro, you will find that my prognostics have in some degree been verified. The French retired to a short distance for the purpose of giving their army a little rest. The army of Portugal, as it is called, was in consequence cantoned with its right off Placentia, and left at Truxillo, where they were enjoying the comforts of the towns on that line, when Lord Wellington marched the main part of his force towards Ciudad Rodrigo, where it now is, and which I imagine will oblige the French to make a move on some point; but whether it will be directly upon his lordship, or more in this direction, I cannot tell. I do, however, find that they are preparing for a march: at the same time I do not apprehend they can do any thing serious against us at present. My principal object is to watch the 5th French corps, which is at and about Zafra. It consists of about 10,000 infantry and 2000 cavalry. My corps is stronger than that. The 5th, however, may be joined by some others from Truxillo and Seville.

Nothing could exceed Lord W.'s attention to my request respecting Mr. Mackworth; and it has been the means of procuring his release from the hands of the French, where, in justice to our enemy, I must say he was extremely well treated.

I am fully persuaded that if I had not gone home at the time I did, my health would not have been established; at least, if I may judge from others who were *ailing* at the time I was ill, and were kept lingering in the country without doing duty, and in the end have been obliged to quit.

Yours very truly and affectionately,
R. H.

The division of General Hill remained at Villa Viçosa till the 3rd of September. It is a handsome town, distant about five leagues from Elvas, and there was much in the place and its environs to render it very agreeable, particularly the hunting palace and preserves, together with the picturesque rides and walks in the park, which had in former days caused it to be a favourite country residence of the royal family. The confidence reposed in our troops brought abundant supplies as usual to the market, and within two miles lay the famous vineyards of Borba, affording the best wine of Portugal. The Chapel Royal was also an attraction to some of the officers, from the excellence of the music, which was, however, frequently of a description ill suited to the sanctuary. Early in September they removed to Portalegre; but nothing of an exciting nature occurred for some time. Three letters of the General give every requisite explanation of his own circumstances, and events affecting the army. The two first are to Miss Hill; the third to his elder brother.

Portalegre, Sept. 17. 1811.

My dear Sister,

I have nothing particular to communicate to you by this day's post; I will however send you a few lines to tell you we are all well. The enemy are, I think, concentrating their force in the direction of Ciudad Rodrigo, with the intention of preventing Lord W. from *meddling* with that place, and I should not be surprised if they succeed. The French Army is certainly weak and sickly. Marmont is, I am told, assured that he shall have reinforcements of 40,000 from France, and he is now enabled to draw some of the troops to this side, in consequence of the fall of Tarragona and Figueras, and Soult's late success over Blake in Granada. General Castanos *tells* me the Spaniards in Galicia have had some advantage over the French.

Castanos is in my front, and when you hear so great a name, you will imagine I am well protected by a large army. The following statement of Castanos' force, contained in an intercepted letter from the French general at Merida, to Marmont, now before me, is a pretty correct one:—'Morillo, commander of the Spanish infantry, and the Count de Penne, commanding the cavalry, in all about 3000 *mauvaises troupes mal armées sont à Caceres. Hill, commandant d'une division Anglaise, est entre Villa Viçosa et St. Olia. Castanos, avec sept ou huit cent officiers, et fort peu de soldats, a son quartier général en Valencia d'Alcantara*.' The troops at Caceres belong to Castanos; but, as the French say, he has very few soldiers at Valencia, not more than two or three hundred.

Portalegre, Sept. 24. 1811.

My dear Sister,

Clement is gone to Lisbon, and I dare say will write to the colonel from thence to thank him for his kindness regarding some hounds which have arrived safe and well. Things are becoming interesting again in this country. Lord Wellington has a large army in his front, and by an intercepted letter, and the movements of the enemy, we are not likely to be idle this side. The 5th corps has advanced to Merida, and by the above-mentioned intercepted letter it appears that it is to manoeuvre upon me, to prevent our going to Lord Wellington. I do, however, think it probable Lord W. will give up the idea of attacking Ciudad Rodrigo, with which the enemy will for the present be satisfied. Kind remembrances to all, and believe me

Yours very affectionately,
R. Hill.

Miss Hill.

Portalegre, Oct. 1. 1811.

My dear Brother,

Circumstances have a good deal changed since I wrote to Maria on this day week. Lord W. was then in a position covering Ciudad Rodrigo, and Marmont was on his march to relieve it; and the question was, whether Lord Wellington would risk an action to prevent supplies being thrown into it. The question has now been decided by his Lordship's declining it; a measure deemed most advisable, considering the force of the enemy. Lord W. has, in consequence, fallen back towards Sabugal, and yesterday it was supposed the enemy were also on their return to the quarters from whence they came, having succeeded in their object of supplying Ciudad Rodrigo.

You will perceive from what has happened, that the enemy is not so weak as we were inclined to suppose him to be last year, when he was running out of Portugal. I am, however, of opinion, that although he probably would have no great objection to meet us in an open country, yet I do not think he is sufficiently strong to undertake offensive operations against this country. Therefore, under all circumstances, it strikes me that Marmont will be perfectly satisfied with having gained his object at Ciudad Rodrigo, and that we shall remain for the winter quiet. Next spring will probably decide the campaign in favour of England or France, according to the reinforcements which may arrive to either army. With respect to my situation, I have been rather on the alert the last ten days. Marmont sent a request to the commander of the 5th French corps, Girard, to manoeuvre on this side, while he marched upon Ciudad Rodrigo; at the same time telling him that the English had very few troops in the Alemtejo.

Girard, who does not belong to Marmont's force, called the army of Portugal, so far complied with the request, and came as far as Merida, and I made a disposition of my troops in hopes of falling upon him should he have come much nearer. He, however, knew better than Marmont respecting the force on this side, and is again returned to Zafra. Soult, who commands all the troops on the south of the Guadiana, has been employed, as you will see by the papers, in destroying Blake and Freere's people, and he is now near Malaga, collecting troops to attack Ballesteros, who has landed at Algeziras.

Thomas has been moving a good deal lately with Lord W.'s army: I dare say you will hear from him. Clement returned last night, and tells me that he did not write to you from Lisbon; but he promised to do so by this day's packet. If I had thought he had not, I should not have so lightly mentioned in my last my best thanks to you for your kind attention respecting the hounds, which have arrived safe and well, are now within four days' march of this place, and I am sure will afford great amusement to the officers of this part of the army, who, I am persuaded, are entitled to every recreation circumstances will admit of.

Kind remembrances to all at Hawkstone, not forgetting Rowland and John.[2] Pray tell the former I will endeavour to procure him a beautiful Spanish horse: they are in general much handsomer than the Portuguese.

Yours ever most affectionately,

R. Hill.

On the 25th and 27th of September the combats of El Bodon and Aldea Ponte took place, when Lord Wellington had much reason to be satisfied with the Portuguese soldiery trained by British officers. In the despatch announcing those affairs his Lordship observed:

> General Girard had collected at Merida a small body of troops, I believe with the intention of making an incursion into Portugal, under the notion that I had withdrawn Lieutenant-General Hill's corps from the Alemtejo for the purpose of maintaining the blockade of Ciudad Rodrigo. But I imagine that he will break up this collection again, as soon as he shall hear that General Hill is at Portalegre.

In reference to this. General Hill remarked in a letter to Hawkstone, dated September 8:

> Lord Wellington's despatches will, I dare say, make you acquainted with the events which have taken place in the north. Marmont has, I believe, fallen back to the cantonments he occupied previous to his relieving Ciudad Rodrigo, and Girard is gone to his former quarters at Zafra. We are, however, a little on the alert again on this side, in consequence of the return of Soult to Seville; and it is supposed he is coming to Estremadura; in consequence of which, I am getting back some of my troops

---

2. Later Viscount Hill, and his brother the Rev. John Hill.

which I *lent* to Lord W. when he was threatened by Marmont.

Towards the middle of October Girard's division crossed the Guadiana at Merida, and inflicted the greatest annoyances on the northern district of Estremadura, in consequence of which, General Hill proposed to operate against him in conjunction with the Spaniards under Castanos. His principal objects were, first, to drive the enemy from Caceres; secondly, to force him to re-cross the Guadiana; and thirdly, to endeavour to cut off the retreat of the whole or part of the hostile forces posted at Caceres, before they could be augmented or supported. As no ulterior advantage could be derived from the first object without the accomplishment of the second, this became the chief consideration in the general's disposition of his troops. Lord Wellington fully approved his design, if it could be undertaken "without risking the safety of Campo Mayor and Orguela," which he was assured might be done, as both these places were considered secure from assault; but the general was instructed not to pass Caceres with his headquarters and main body; and when he had driven off Girard, he was to replace the Conde de Penne Villemur at Caceres, and bring back his troops, who had endured the greatest sufferings from the weather, towards the frontier.

The French retired from Caceres on the 26th; but their pursuers had no certain tidings as to the direction they had taken, and therefore the suffering British and Portuguese soldiers were halted by their considerate leader for that night at Malpartida, while he himself used efforts to discover the route of the retreating enemy. His information rendered it certain that they were gone to Torremocha, and he endeavoured, by taking a shorter road than theirs, to intercept and bring them to action. While on his march, General Hill discovered that Girard was at Arroyo de Molinos, and not aware of his movements, which at once induced him to decide on overtaking and surprising the whole force of the French, or at all events compelling them to an action. The weather was wretched in the extreme; but the soldiers did not fail in a long forced march instantly undertaken in the most perfect quietude, that no symptom of their approach might alarm the enemy.

By the evening of the 27th they were at Alcuescar, within four miles of their unconscious foes. Every conceivable precaution was resorted to. The light companies were thrown into the villages to prevent the natives from alarming the enemy; and the cavalry, artillery, and infantry were disposed of in the neighbouring fields, with the strictest orders not to cheer the cold and gloomy night with a single fire, the flickering of which might give indication that they were near. The wind blew furiously; the rain fell in torrents; and the patient soldiery had no protection from the storm, except the drenched coverings of their tents, which the gale had thrown down; but their patience and confidence in the leader they loved deserted them not. They were warmed by the flush of expectation that the morning would recompense them for all their toils; and the first streaks of dawn had not appeared in the horizon, when the various columns fell in, without a single note of a bugle or the beat even of one solitary drum.

The ground was admirably chosen with a view to concealment: they filed quietly through the village, and having crossed an intervening mountain, found themselves, just as the day began to break, within half a mile of Arroyo, where Girard was yet in security, ignorant of their presence and his own danger. At this instant a violent hailstorm, pouring on the rear of the allies, caused the faces of the French picquets to be turned from them; but just as they were ready to make the decisive movement the clouds cleared away, the sky became serene, and the hostile corps was preparing for their march, in expectation of a propitious day. The decisive moment had arrived. General Hill was himself inspired, as was every brave man he commanded, with the enthusiasm of the scene. The usual calmness of his demeanour, rendered even more than commonly striking by the precautions he had taken for silence, became suddenly converted into an animation that cheered and almost amused every witness of his ardour. It seemed kindled in an instant.

He drew his sword,—gave a loud hurrah,—spurred his horse,—and led the charge on the astonished ranks of the French, then forming without a thought that he was so near at hand. The first brigade, headed thus vigorously by himself, moved at once on the village of Arroyo, and the Highlanders catching up the humour of the hour, were heard playing on their bagpipes *"Heigh, Johnny Cope, are you waiting yet?"* The second brigade, under General Howard, moved quietly round to the other side of the place, to intercept the troops which the first should drive out. In the centre came the cavalry, ready to act in whatever way might be deemed expedient. Presently the 71st and 92nd Regiments dashed into Arroyo, and came upon the French just as they were filing out, with the exception of one brigade, which had marched for Medellin before daylight. This charge first announced to them the snare into which they had fallen; and with only a feeble effort on the part of their cavalry, they were driven before the bayonets of the British.

The French infantry, nevertheless, having emerged from the town, tried to form into two squares with cavalry on their left; but the 71st lining the garden-walls of the town, poured into them an awful fire, which was soon succeeded by that of artillery. They fled in utter confusion, and the capture of prisoners, cannon and baggage, rapidly followed. Then came the memorable pursuit of that extraordinary day. Just behind the routed forces of Girard rose the rocky and steep Sierra de Montanches, up which they clambered in a state of utter confusion, throwing away their arms, ammunition, and knapsacks, and yielding their persons as prisoners to their pursuers at every step, in the excitement of such a chase the British, the Portuguese, and the Spaniards, seemed all to forget that they had been without rest, and soaked with rain and mist all the night before. They laughed, shouted, jumped in their heavy accoutrements, or caught the scrambling horses of the fugitives, who could not ride them over the mountain, and came down mounted in triumph, till fatigue caused some to desist, and the rest being too much scattered, were judiciously stopped on the summit of the Sierra by General Howard.

Nearly fifteen hundred prisoners were taken, and some of them of high rank. Lieutenant Blakeney, of the 28th, leaped over a wall, and seized the Prince D'Aremberg in the midst of a group of officers. General Brun was also taken, with a colonel of cavalry, an *aide-de-camp* of Girard, two lieutenant-colonels, a *commissaire de guerre*, and no less than thirty captains and inferior officers. Girard himself, with a handful of men, escaped by the bridge of Medellin, declaring he would rather die than surrender. It was altogether a most brilliant achievement, and is thus eloquently adverted to by Major Sherer in his *Recollections* of the day.

> One thing in our success at Arroyo de Molinos gratified our division highly; it was a triumph for our general—a triumph *all his own*. He gained great credit for this well-conducted enterprise; and he gained what, to one of his mild, kind, and humane character, was still more valuable, a solid and bloodless victory; for it is certainly the truest maxim in war, '*that conquest is twice achieved, where the achiever brings home full numbers.*'

Indeed, the loss in his division was most trifling, while a deep blow was inflicted on the enemy. Girard was wounded before he escaped, and Soult afterwards arrested him, and reported him to Bonaparte, who, knowing that he was, notwithstanding this misadventure, a thoroughly brave soldier, pardoned him in the expectation of future services. In his official reports to Lord Wellington, General Hill did the utmost justice to the officers under his command, and rejoiced in the opportunity of bringing into notice his *aide-de-camp*, Captain Currie, who was rewarded by subsequent promotion. Lord Wellington received the announcement of this distinguished service with unequivocal tokens of satisfaction; and in a letter to Lord Liverpool thus expressed his sense of the merit of him to whom the success was due:—

> It would be particularly agreeable to me if some mark of the favour of his Royal Highness the Prince Regent were conferred upon General Hill; his services have been always meritorious, and very distinguished in this country, and he is beloved by the whole army.

He adverted to his various gallant acts, from the passage of the Douro to the last operation at Arroyo, and continued:

> In recommending him, as I do most anxiously, I really feel that there is no officer to whom an act of grace and favour would be received by the army with more satisfaction than on General Hill.

Lord Wellington justly described the sentiments of the army towards the subject of these deserved commendations, whose name was never mentioned by those who served under him without some affectionate expression. General Hill gave a brief account of the action in a letter to his sister.

Portalegre, Nov. 5. 1811.

My dear Sister,
I am sure my dear friends at Hawkstone will rejoice to hear of my good fortune, and share with me the satisfaction I feel, in having, under the will of Divine Providence, given a severe blow to the common enemy, and, thank God, almost without loss on our side. My official report on the business, which I dare say Clement will carry to England in the same ship which will take this, will give you a detailed account of what has happened; but in case it should not, I have time merely to inform you that on the morning of the 28th, at daybreak, I succeeded in surprising, attacking, and annihilating the French corps un-

der General Girard at Arroyo de Molinos. The enemy's force when attacked consisted of about 3000 infantry, 1600 cavalry and artillery. The result is the capture of one general, Brun, one colonel, the Prince D'Aremberg, thirty-five lieutenant-colonels and inferior officers, 1400 prisoners, and probably 500 killed. The others dispersed, having thrown away their arms: we have also got all the enemy's artillery, baggage, and magazines—in short, everything that belonged to the corps.

Clement, I am pretty certain, will go in the ship that carries this, otherwise I would send you a more detailed account, although I should lose my dinner, which is now going on the table. The prince and most of the French officers dine with me. The British here have been very kind to the French since they have been in our possession, and they seem very grateful for it. Clement behaved very gallantly, as indeed did all.

Yours most affectionately,
R. H.

Clement is now gone to Lord W. with my report.

The congratulations received by General Hill from his brother officers were numerous and flattering. General Murray wrote:

> I feel a peculiar pleasure in this fortunate affair, as it concerns yourself personally, and assure you that I only repeat the sentiments which are in the mouth of everyone whom I have heard speak upon the subject.

Marshal Beresford remarked:

> I confess I did not think Girard would have allowed himself to be overtaken; but you completely outmanoeuvred him, and the thing is complete.

Lord Wellington, after the arrival of Captain Clement Hill at headquarters, addressed a brief but gratifying letter to the general.

Freneda, Nov. 9. 1811..

My dear Hill,

I have not written to you since the 22nd; as I have had nothing new to interest you, and I would not interrupt your operations. Nothing could be more satisfactory to me than all you did; and I am happy that I had determined to send home your brother with the report of your transactions, before I had heard that it was your wish that I should do so.

He and Churchill will tell you how we are going on here.

Ever yours most sincerely,

Wellington.

Lieut.-General Hill.

His old friend, General Graham's note was kind and characteristic.

Lagiosa, Nov. 12. 1811.

My dear Hill,

I rejoiced most truly on hearing of your success, but I delayed writing to congratulate you on it, till I should see your despatch with the particulars. Lord Wellington sent me your letters two days ago, at the same time expressing his high approbation of your conduct, a testimony more valuable than any other, but one which in every body's opinion is most justly deserved by the judgment, activity, and admirable arrangements which produced so brilliant a result with so trifling a loss.

Currie has been good enough to send me sketch of the ground and disposition of the troops, which I prize much, and which perfectly explains the movements described in your report. I beg you will make him my best thanks, and pray remember me too to Squire, who, I am happy to see, is such a favourite with you. I hope your health has not suffered by the fatigue and bad weather. *Adieu.*—I hear you have got hounds, and have you a tolerable country and good sport? At headquarters I am told they have already done up all their horses. Here we have only a little coursing and shooting, neither in much perfection. Once more *adieu*, and believe me ever most faithfully yours,

Thos. Graham.

Pray remember me to Sir W. Erskine.

Captain Clement Hill, who carried the news of his brother's success to England, had a very bad passage of eighteen days' duration, so that on arriving he found the tidings had preceded him; but happily the accounts, instead of having been exaggerated, fell short of the reality. Captain Hill described his own reception in a letter dated, "Mr. Codd's Office, Horse Guards, 2nd December." He says:

I got here yesterday with the despatch. Lord Liverpool was at his country house at Coomb, where I went to him. He read the contents of it, and then sent me on with it to Oatlands for the prince to see. His Royal Highness is still confined to his bed, and I did not see him. I saw the Duke of York and a great many other of the great people there, and every one spoke in the highest terms of the business. I returned to Lord Liverpool's at night, and dined there: he was uncommonly kind, and, like everybody else, pleased. In short, I am sure nothing that has been done during the war has given so much satisfaction.

General Hill's proceedings were worthy of all the admiration they excited. He gave the artillery he had taken to the Spaniards, for which he received a glowing letter of thanks from Castanos; and he treated his prisoners not only with the courtesy of a gentleman, but with the kindness of genuine heroism. Lord Wellington attached much importance to the capture of the Prince d'Aremberg, from his connection with the Imperial Family, and enjoined strict vigilance over him; yet General Hill executed this delicate duty so as to elicit from his illustrious charge the warmest expressions of gratitude. We have seen how his friends wrote to him: the letter of his prisoner just before he was sent to England equally deserves attention:—

Lisbonne, ce 3 Xbre, 1811.

Mon Général,
Au moment do m'embarquer pour l'Angleterre, je regarde comme un devoir do vous renouveller mes remerimens pour toutes les bontés dont vous m'avez comblé pendant le tems que j'ai été avec vous. Croyez, mon Général, que je serais heureux, si l'occasion se présentait, d'être utile à quelques officiers de votre division; ils pourront partout me reclamer avec confiance.
J'ose de vous prier de faire passer les lettres ci-jointes à Badajos; c'est une affaire d'intérêt que je désire terminer avec mon chef d'escadron.
Veuillez agréer l'assurance du profond respect avec lequel j'ai l'honneur d'être, mon Général, votre très humble et très obéissant serviteur.
Le Duc d'Aremberg."

Much reason, indeed, had the writer and his fellow-prisoners to thank General Hill, who not only showed them every civility while with him, but provided for their kind reception in England, as appears from a sentence in a letter of Lord Mulgrave. His Lordship said:

If your prisoners should come to London, I will show them every attention in my power, and will take care that they shall know they owe it to your favourable report and recommendation of them.

You have nothing to wish beyond the impression you have made on the public mind.

A second letter was also addressed to him from the same quarter:—

Harley Street, Dec. 5. 1811.

Dear Hill,

I had written and sealed my last letter immediately on the receipt of yours, and before it was in my power to congratulate you, as I do most cordially, on the professional distinction which awaits you, as soon as it can be bestowed on you. It will be satisfactory to you to know that in the letters which I have received from the part of the army which is immediately under the command of Lord Wellington, your brother officers all do justice to the mode in which the service was conducted and success prepared, and appear to rejoice at your victory almost as much on personal as on public feelings.

Believe me with the greatest regard,
Ever yours most faithfully,

Mulgrave.

The honour referred to in this letter was thus announced to General Hill by Lord Liverpool:—

(Private.)

Downing Street, December 4. 1811.

Sir,

I have had particular satisfaction in transmitting to Lord Wellington, by the mail of this day, the Prince Regent's most cordial and decided approbation of your conduct in the late operations against the French force under General Girard. His Royal Highness does the fullest justice to the distinguished ability with which you have conducted this important service, and I can assure you, that His Majesty's confidential servants, and the public in general, most entirely participate in the Prince Regent's feelings upon this occasion.

I have great pleasure in being enabled further to add, that the Prince Regent has authorised me to assure you that as soon as the restrictions upon the regency have expired, it is his intention to confer upon you the Order of the Bath, as a proof of the sense which has Royal Highness entertained of your services.

As it may be a satisfaction to you to be in possession of the original document, containing his Royal Highland assurances upon this point, I have the honour to send it to you, together with an extract of my note, to which it was an answer.

I am, with great truth, Sir,

Your very faithful and obedient humble servant.

Liverpool.

The approbation of his Royal Highness the Commander-in-Chief, was conveyed to him by Colonel Torrens, the Military Secretary:—

Private.

H. Guards, Dec. 8. 1811

My dear General

I beg your acceptance of my most sincere congratulations upon the brilliant success which has attended your expedition against the French force under General Girard. After the flattering testimony which has been borne of the public approbation, I shall not render myself liable to the imputation of flattery, by the expression of my individual opinion that the previous arrangements of the surprise of the enemy, and the promptitude of execution, reflect upon you a degree of credit as a general which few indeed have had the good fortune to attain.

The whole country are united in the voice of approval; and I heartily rejoice that such a distinguished reward has attending your unremitting and laborious services. The public approbation, though inconstant and whimsical, has charms in it, which, as a soldier, I should appreciate much beyond any favour unsupported by general and well-earned applause: and therefore I take double pleasure in the justice which is universally done to your distinguished conduct.

Captains Currie and Squire will be promoted, on your earnest recommendation, to the rank of major, and your brother also, upon the expiration of his period of service, will be advanced to the same rank. I assure you his Royal Highness had great pleasure in giving effect to your wishes respecting Captain Currie; and he will also be ready to show every possible attention to the other officers whom you have recommended to notice, when he has the means of facilitating their advancement.

I imagine that this *coup* on your part will close the scene of any active operations, until the opening of the spring.

I beg you will command my services here in any manner in which you think I can contribute to the accomplishment of your wishes; and when you have time to write a line upon what is going on, I shall be most grateful to you to think of me.

His Royal Highness's official letter to Lord Wellington, will sufficiently show the extent of his approbation to render any further assurance on my part quite unnecessary, to convince you of the high sense his Royal Highness entertains of your distinguished conduct.

Believe me, my dear General, to be,
Ever yours most faithfully and sincerely,
H. Torrens.

In reflecting upon this exploit, so many excellences present themselves to the mind, that it seems disposed to rest on each till another is exhibited to its view. First we see a quick conception of an advantage, followed by an effort in the face of fatigue and the elements, that placed his enemy in his hands without a sound of his approach; then the silence of the approach itself was succeeded by a burst of heroic animation that cheered on his wearied followers to new energy; the achievement completed, his generous spirit applied every possible alleviation to the condition of his captives; and at last, when his honours were accorded to him by a grateful country, the meekness of his bearing raised the estimation of his merits, and augmented the interest with which he was regarded by all men, citizen and soldier, friend and foe.

Not many weeks elapsed alter this blow to the hostile army, ere tidings of new movements on the part of the French reached General Hill in his cantonments, and he was directed by Lord Wellington to move also. The object will be found described in a letter written to his brother, then in England:—

Portalegre, Dec, 26. 1811.

My dear Clement,

We are again in motion, not on account of the enemy being near us, but because he is pressing Ballesteros and the town of Tarifa; and it is hoped that my movement upon Merida and Almandralejo may make a diversion in favour of our friends in the South. I shall be at Albuquerque tomorrow, and move directly upon Merida.

A courier arrived here yesterday, bringing me a letter from Lord Liverpool, and a correspondence between him and the prince, full of flattering expressions. The purport of the correspondence is 'the prince's most cordial and decided approbation of my conduct;' and he assures me, that as soon an the restrictions upon the regency have expired, it is his intention to confer upon me the Order of the Bath.[3]

You cannot possibly be in time for this march, therefore you need not hurry.

Yours very faithfully,
R. Hill.

On the 27th of December General Hill passed into Estremadura, and discovering some lack of vigilance on the part of the French, he meditated giving them another surprise, and had almost hoped to have gained a march on Dombrowski as he did on Girard. A *patrole*, however, from a detachment discovered his advanced guard on the 29th; and though he used every effort to prevent this small body from retiring to Merida, the retreat was effected by the skill and gallantry of Captain Neveux, who knew the nature of the country, and how to take the fullest advantage of it. Our cavalry could only inflict upon him the loss of about forty men. But General Dombrowski, not relishing the idea of the approach of General Hill, retired from Merida in the night, leaving a magazine of bread, and 160,000 lbs. of wheat, besides several unfinished works. On the 1st of January, 1812, General Hill marched on to Almandralejo, in hopes of coming up with Count D'Erlon. The count, however, moved off as soon as he was apprized of his danger. But a portion of the allies under Colonel Abercromby—a worthy son of the hero of Egypt—had a small affair of great brilliancy with a strong party of the French cavalry at Fuente del Maestre. The subjoined letter gives an account of all these proceedings:—

Merida, Jan. 6. 1812.

My dear Sister,

The mail arrived here last night, bringing your letter of the

---

3. A similar intimation had been received by Lord Wellington, who, in communicating it to General Hill, observed, "It may fall to my lot to be the instrument of conveying to you the honour intended for you, as I have acted in a similar capacity in respect to others; but I assure you that I shall perform this duty, if it should devolve upon me, with at least as much satisfaction as I have on any former occasion."

12th, for which I beg you will accept my best thanks. I wrote to Clement on Christmas-Day to tell you that I was on the point of making a movement to draw the enemy's attention from Ballesteros, who was hard pressed near Gibraltar. On the 30th I entered this town, from whence the enemy retired on our approach, leaving some stores of corn, I having obtained a little advantage over him the preceding day.

On the 1st I marched to Almandralejo, in hopes that Count D'Erlon would have given me an opportunity of coming in contact with him. He, however, retreated, and was yesterday in full march towards and near Llerena. The dreadful state of the weather and the condition of the roads, render any further operations on my part impossible without incurring great risks, and exceeding my instructions. I returned here two days ago, and my stay will depend chiefly on my supplies.

I must conclude, as it is post-time. Kind remembrance to all.

Yours very affectionately,

R. H.

My movement has occasioned great alarm to the enemy, and I trust I have effected the object in view. Clement will be glad to hear that Abercromby has had an opportunity of doing something. The affair of Fuente del Maestro does him and all engaged great credit.

On the 19th of January Lord Wellington terminated the celebrated siege of Ciudad Rodrigo, in which Colonel Thomas Noel Hill behaved most gallantly. The general was too happy to apprise his family of his brother's distinction.

Niza, Jan. 23. 1812.

My dear Sister,

Before you receive this you will have heard of the taking of Ciudad Rodrigo. Things seem to have been very well managed there by all concerned in the capture; and I am happy to find that Tom and his regiment had an opportunity of distinguishing themselves.

Lord W. having conceived that my late movement to the southward of the Guadiana had created every diversion in favour of Ballesteros and Tarifa which could have been expected from it, he directed me to return to Portugal, and take up a position with my right at Portalegre, centre here, and left at Castello

Branco. The object of taking up this position was the probability of the enemy making an attempt on this side to draw Lord W.'s attention from Ciudad Rodrigo.

Clement has not yet arrived: by his last letter we may, I think, expect him daily. Lord W. sent me his despatch to Lord Liverpool to read, and by it I am glad to find that honourable mention is made in it of Colonel Campbell and the 94th, for their conduct at the storming of Ciudad Rodrigo. Kind remembrances to all, and believe me to be,

Yours very affectionately,

R. H.

On the 28th of January Lord Wellington addressed a letter to General Hill from Gallegos, the original of which is marked *secret and confidential;* but as it appears in Gurwood's eighth volume, a quotation from it is all that is requisite. After informing him that the enemy had not advanced from the Tormes, that the re-establishment of Ciudad Rodrigo was proceeding, and that it was proposed to replace the army in their old cantonments, his Lordship acquainted him that he was "turning his mind seriously to Badajos." He then proceeded,—

> When we shall attack Badajos we must expect that the army of Portugal, consisting of eight divisions of infantry, the whole of which are now in Castille, and the army of the South, will co-operate to oblige us to raise the siege. The army of Portugal would naturally cross the Tagus by their bridge at Almaraz; and they would be obliged, at the season of the year in which I propose to undertake this operation, to go round even by Toledo, if we could destroy their bridge and other establishments at that place. This is what I wish you to attempt.

The general's reply to this communication shows how thoroughly he entered into all the plans of Lord Wellington, and what grounds there were for the confidence reposed in him:—

Niza, Jan. 30 1812,

My dear Lord,

I have the honour to acknowledge the receipt of your Lordship's letter of the 28th, marked *secret and confidential,* and will use my best endeavours to fulfil the instructions which it contains. Your Lordship will perceive, by Mr. Hillier's report on Almaraz, dated the 16th instant, that I have not been inattentive to your wishes on the subject of the destruction of the enemy's works at that place. You will likewise observe, that on the 16th the enemy had only two boats on the river, and the others, nine in number, were on the north bank of the river, mounted on carriages, and two spare carriages. I have, &c.

R. Hill,

Viscount Wellington, K. B.,
&c. &c. &c.

The report of Lieutenant Hillier was called in Lord Wellington's answer a "very clear" one; and he proposed to supply General Hill with the means of sending a detachment to the right of the Tagus, to cut off the retreat of these boats, which was the principal object of his expedition.

At this time General Hill had the satisfaction of seeing in the English papers the complimentary allusion to his exploit at Arroyo de Molinos, in the speech of his Royal Highness the Prince Regent at the opening of Parliament. It was thus deservedly commended:—

> The successful and brilliant enterprise, which terminated in the surprise, in Spanish Estremadura, of a French corps by a detachment of the allied army under Lieutenant-General Hill, is highly creditable to that distinguished officer, and the troops under his command, and has contributed materially to obstruct the designs of the enemy in that part of the Peninsula.

In writing home on the 30th of January, he alluded to this honourable mention of his name with evident gratification, and also to a letter he had received from Mr. Henry Wellesley, then at Cadiz, relative to his diversion in favour of Ballesteros and Tarifa. Mr. Wellesley, in allusion to the loss of the French at Tarifa, assured him that it "was certainly not less than 2000 men, leaving behind them all their artillery, ammunition, &c." Then he proceeded,—

> It is probable that your movement in Estremadura contributed greatly to this event.

In quoting this passage. General Hill himself observed:

> I confess I think it is most likely that it did, for on the 1st, 2nd, and 3rd we advanced rapidly, the alarm of which must have reached Tarifa on the 5th, the day the enemy retired suddenly from before the place.

By the 10th of February General Hill had formed an opinion that the expedition against the enemy's boats on the Tagus near Almaraz, was not practicable; and Lord Wellington entirely concurred in the reasons he assigned. He was, however, fully prepared to make any attempt deemed advisable, "at the shortest notice." Eight days after this he wrote from Portalegre,—

> The greater part of Lord Wellington's army is marching to this side of the Tagus; I therefore think we shall soon try what can be done with Badajos.

By the 3rd of March he was enabled to say:

> Things are becoming a little interesting again in this quarter. Lord W. is on the point of undertaking the siege of Badajos, for which purpose the whole of the army is on its march to this side of the Tagus, and the enemy have not at present shown any disposition to oppose him.

Shortly after this announcement of the state of things around him, he received from Lord Wellington the insignia of the Order of the Bath, accompanied by an invitation to Elvas for investment.

> Portalegre, March 10. 1812.
>
> My dear Hill,
>
> I send herewith the letter from the Secretary of State, and the insignia of the Order of the Bath, and the copy of a letter to me, directing me to invest you therewith.
>
> I am going to Elvas tomorrow; and as I believe the earliest occasion will be on every account the most suitable, I would invest you there on the next day, the 12th, if you can make it convenient to come over.
>
> Pray invite the general and staff of the 2nd Division to come over to Elvas to be present on the occasion, and to dine with me; and likewise General Hamilton and General Long, if they should be near you.
>
> I'll take care that you shall all be quartered in Elvas.
>
> Ever yours most sincerely,
>
> Wellington.
>
> I understand that you wish to know by what road I shall pass tomorrow.—By the direct road by Assumar.
>
> Bring the insignia of the Order with you on the 12th.

The day after the ceremonial he let his family know that it had taken place:—

Elvas, March 13. 1812.

My dear Sister,
Lord Wellington arrived here the day before yesterday, and desired General Graham and myself to come over for the purpose of being invested with the Order of the Bath, which ceremony took place yesterday.

Nearly the whole of the army Is on this side the Tagus. Our operations against Badajos will commence immediately. It is not intended that my troops should have any thing to do with the duties of the siege, but will form a covering army on the north of the Guadiana, in the direction of Merida, whilst General Graham, with a similar corps, will be on the south of that river.

Adieu, my dear sister.
Yours ever affectionately,
R. Hill.

Those who knew Sir Rowland Hill, by which title he must now be called, will not wonder at the brief dismissal of the subject of his new honour in this letter. Never did the insignia he so nobly won rest upon a breast that wore them more meekly. An esteemed officer on his personal staff says:

> When he was knighted there was not one of us dared for nearly six months to call him *Sir Rowland*: he was quite distressed at being called any thing but *General*; and it was only very gradually that he could be driven to bear his honour.

A letter to his brother on the subject of supporters to his arms, at once manifests his simplicity of mind, and the way in which he could, under circumstances of the most exciting nature, coolly divest himself of their influence to attend to the minutest affairs claiming his notice.

Guerena, four leagues in front of Merida,
March 31. 1812.

My dear Brother,
I have received your letter, enclosing one from General Wynyard, recommending Mr. Nayler. That gentleman has been recommended to me by several of my friends. I have in consequence appointed him to transact the *requisite* business for me

in the College of Arms. Mr. Nayler, in his letter to me, says, on being favoured with my wishes on the subject of supporters, proper sketches shall be sent to me.

Now, my dear brother, I do not wish you to go to town on purpose, but when you do go I shall be obliged if you will see Mr. Nayler; and knowing you to be a man of taste, I wish you would give him some hints on the occasion. Perhaps by consulting our friends at Hawkstone my acquirements might be arranged to the best advantage: for my part I do not care much what the supporters are, but, I must confess, I do not much like fancy figures, such as I have seen to some arms, supported by a *jolly tar, a grenadier, a light infantry man, or a heavy or light dragoon*; such, I think, are bad. It strikes me that animals are the handsomest. Some have lions: you and I, probably, would have no objection to a *greyhound*, while there are others who would prefer the *foxhound*: but upon the whole I should be glad to leave the choice to the ladies; they have more taste than we have.[4]

You will get later accounts from Badajos than this can contain, as it will pass by that place, which every day now are extremely interesting; and before this quits the Tagus the fate of that garrison will probably be decided. Everything is going on well there. Soult is certainly in full march, in hopes of relieving it; but as Marmont is still at a great distance, I do not think Soult will, by himself, venture to attack us. His advance is pretty near me now. Two of his cavalry regiments arrived at San Benito, four leagues from hence; but we are ready for a *start* in the first instance, and a fight, should he persist.

Yours ever most affectionately,

R. H.

In consequence of the movements of the French forces, Sir Thomas Graham was ordered to fall back upon Villa Franca, and Sir Rowland Hill upon Merida, the bridge of which place he was desired to destroy on leaving it. In writing to Lord Wellington, Sir Rowland remarked, "The preparations for breaking up the bridge appear to have created some sensation in the town:" to which his Lordship replied, with that consideration which he always manifested:

---

4. The part here omitted refers merely to details of business relating to the governorship of Blackeness Castle, which had also been given to Sir Rowland for his services.

Tell the *alcalde* or *corregidor*, that if we destroy the bridge I will render it passable again for them; that it is to answer a military purpose, and must be done if necessary.
This promise was most faithfully fulfilled a few weeks afterwards.

Sir Thomas Graham, who fell back towards Albuera, was in almost daily communication with Sir Rowland Hill at this time, but their letters referred chiefly to the various reports of the enemy's approach; and though, perhaps, of great interest to persons qualified and inclined to trace the fine manoeuvres of these generals, they are by no means suited to this memoir. The siege of Badajos went on; Drouet and Darican only advanced to hear that the place had fallen. Such was the slaughter, that Wellington himself shed tears over his own conquest, when he thought on the valiant dead that fell in that scene of carnage. The town was bravely defended, but a British army under Wellington bore with it irresistible power. Sir Rowland Hill shall again give his own impression, and describe his situation.

Almandralejo, April 15. 1812.

My dear Sister,
Clement and Thomas, I know, wrote to you by the last packet, giving you an account of the fall of Badajos, which is certainly a glorious and important event, though at the same time a dear-bought victory, as will appear by the long list of killed and wounded which will accompany the official accounts.
Marmont's movements in the North have made it necessary for Lord Wellington to recross the Tagus; and my corps is again advanced to this part of the country fur the purpose of covering Badajos while the works of that place are repairing.
Soult, at present, is moving towards Seville; and I do not think he will be inclined to have any thing to do with us here.
Yours very affectionately,
R. Hill.

We will now pass on to the next achievement of Sir Rowland Hill—the surprise of Almaraz. He was directed by Lord Wellington to undertake this enterprise, in order to destroy the only means possessed by the French of effecting a passage of the Tagus. This was a boat-bridge laid down by Marmont, and secured by strong defences. His Lordship thus instructed him on the 24th of April:—

Marmont has retired, and I shall immediately get provisions

into Ciudad Rodrigo. I propose, while this operation is going on, to send some troops back across the Tagus, and to distribute the whole in such a manner as that they can be easily subsisted. I think that you might avail yourself of this opportunity to strike your blow at Almaraz. I think that one of your British brigades and two Portuguese brigades, or one-and-a-half British and one strong Portuguese brigade, would do your business as to the French in that neighbourhood. . . . . . Make all your preparations in secret for this expedition. I shall watch from hence the course of the enemy's retreat, and will let you know if it should appear to me that you have any thing to fear from any of the divisions of the army of Portugal going near Almaraz. Of course you will not march till you shall hear farther from me.

On the 30th he was directed to be prepared, and by the end of the first week in May would have marched on, but his progress was impeded by the delay arising from the timber supplied being too small for the repair of the bridge at Merida. The work itself was commenced in ample time, and Sir Rowland reported to Lord Wellington that Major Squire and another engineer had been there to make every arrangement.

They remained three days, and returned, saying that all the materials were to be ready on the following Monday. Every assistance required by the engineers was given, and 400 men sent to Merida.

They had to send for more timber to Badajos, so that a considerable delay arose, giving much uneasiness to all parties; and Sir Rowland wrote as follows to Lord Wellington:—

Almandralejo, May 10. 1812, 6 p.m.
My dear Lord, "Last night I received your letter of the 7th. Your Lordship will have been informed before this of our delay, in consequence of the bridge at Merida not being repaired. If, however, we take into consideration the advantage of having given Dickson's train one day's halt, not more than twenty-four hours will have been lost. That, however, may be of consequence, but I trust it will not; and your Lordship may depend on celerity and exertion when we do start. The engineers reported to me three days ago, that the bridge would be ready

on the evening of the 12th. I am, however, in hopes it will be passable tomorrow evening, or early on the 12th. In either of the latter cases, I will march tomorrow, so as to be able to make a march on the other side of Merida by the 12th. At present I am sure no one here has the least idea of our destination. It is generally supposed that Dickson is coming to this side of the Guadiana with the intention of our attacking Bella Casa. I have the honour to enclose some papers just received. Penne Villemur's account of Soult is rather contradictory.

I have, &c.

R. Hill.

General the Earl of Wellington, K. B.,
&c. &c. &c.

On receiving this intelligence Lord Wellington remarked to Sir Thomas Graham, "I am very much afraid Hill will be late." But on the 13th he heard that Marmont's troops had not yet moved into Estremadura, and observed, "If this is the case, Hill will be yet in time." He was in time for his chieftain's project and his own fame. Ere sunset on the 12th all the troops destined for this service had filed over the bridge and assembled in the town. By the 15th he reached Truxillo, and caused skilful feints to be made for deceiving the enemy. Foy was completely taken in, and by the morning of the 16th Sir Rowland was at Jaraicejo. From this place to Almaraz there are two leagues of majestic scenery. The descent from a high ridge to the Tagus has on its right broken masses of wild mountains, and deep beneath their rugged bases lie vales of a fertility and a verdure, mingled with romantic glens, such as Spain alone can exhibit, and which might make her the envy of the world.

At Jaraicejo the troops were formed into three columns, and a night march was undertaken with a view to attack at the same instant the bridge of Almaraz, with its forts, the tower of Mirabete, and a fortified house in the pass. Never was a movement better arranged; but the column destined to descend from the Sierra, by the pass of Cueva, on Almaraz, had not come down half way from the rugged mountain ere daylight unveiled its approach; and the other two found both the Castle of Mirabete and the pass of Mirabete so defended by the enemy that, under the circumstances of the moment, it would have been madness to attack. The only course was to bivouac on the mountain; and the 17th and 18th were spent in reconnoitring: but there seemed not a ray of hope of forcing the pass, or of discovering a single spot on the wild ridge where artillery could either proceed or be let down. Many a man would have given up the attempt in despair, but the genius of our hero shone forth more conspicuously in the gloom of disappointment.

At nine o'clock in the evening of the 19th he led a brigade down the mountain by a goat's path, and by the morning's dawn had halted it in concealment on the left bank of the river, about 800 yards from a fort called Napoléon. By eight the rear came up and the troops were formed; but the hills hid them from the French, who had no conception that they were at hand. First there was a feint made upon Mirabete; and the enemy's soldiers crowded on the parapet of their work to look at this attack. Then rushed the assailants in earnest on Fort Napoléon, which covered the bridge of Almaraz. Its defenders never dreamed of an attack till the sight of the ladders, still stained with the blood of Badajos, and the opening of the fire, roused them into a sense of their danger, which they made instant efforts to avert. But they were all in vain: the parapet was soon mounted by the British soldiery; resistance in the interior was quickly suppressed; the defenders gave way, and leaving the tower and entrenchment, fled to the *tête de pont*. Their entrance into this work, and that of their pursuers, were simultaneous.

The confusion was tremendous; and all hope of escape being destroyed by the removal of the boats by the first of those who fled, numbers fell into the river and were drowned, while about 250 were taken prisoners. The guns of Fort Napoléon were soon pointed by the victors against Fort Ragusa, on the other side of the river, and quickly ejected its commandant. Attention was now turned to the passage of the river, and some of them leaped in, swam over, and brought back the boats. Two grenadiers, James Gould and Walter Somerville, led the way; and their gratified general presented them each with a handsome sum of gold, when they returned with the boats from their perilous adventure. The river was immediately passed. Then followed a rapid destruction of the towers, the stores, the ammunition, and at last of the boats; and at night the successful troops reascended the Sierra, bearing the enemy's colours in triumph, and with them more than 250 prisoners, including one commandant and sixteen inferior officers.

The entire loss of the British amounted to fifteen officers and 162 privates, killed or wounded. One officer perished by the explosion of his own mine, designed for the destruction of the tower; and the brave

Captain Chandler, as he was leading his men up the ladders, had his head severed from his body by a cannon shot.

This rapid and masterly enterprise cut the works of Mirabete off entirely from the right bank of the Tagus, and preparation was made by Sir Rowland Hill to reduce them with his heavy artillery; but in consequence of a report from Sir William Erskine, that Soult was in Estremadura with his whole army, he obeyed his instructions and retired to Merida, which place he reached on the 26th. It was a groundless alarm, and Mirabete was left unattempted. Major Currie was sent to Lord Wellington with the news, and the colour taken from the enemy. He went afterwards to England with the official despatches, and a recommendation to the government for his own well-merited promotion.

General Hill's despatch is already published in the ninth volume of Colonel Gurwood's work. One sentence, however, is too characteristic of the writer to be omitted here. Alluding to the diversion against Mirabete by General Chowne, he observed:

> I regret much that the peculiar situation of Mirabete, should have prevented my allowing the gallant corps under his orders to follow up an operation which they had commenced with much spirit, and were so anxious to complete; *but the possession of these forts would not have made amends for the valuable blood which must have been shed in taking them.*

This was the spirit of Hill: the comforts of his men and their lives were as dear to him as his own. Lord Wellington, with his peculiar keenness, marked some parts of this despatch not to be published, feeling convinced that the French themselves would evacuate Mirabete, unless they imagined that the British entertained a formidable opinion of its strength. As soon as Sir Rowland arrived at Merida he wrote to Lord Wellington:—

Merida, May 26. 1812.

My dear Lord,

I arrived here about an hour ago, and had the pleasure to receive your Lordship's letter of the 23rd, for which I beg you to accept my best thanks. Sir W. Erskine's information, which I received when I was on the bridge at Almaraz, certainly made me a little anxious to get out of the difficult country I was in at that moment. I did not, however, move from thence until the morning of the 20th, consequently had nearly twenty-four hours to destroy the place. I eerily believe that the destruction of every thing was completely effected in every respect, with the exception of the parapets of the redoubts, which were not entirely levelled. The guns were rendered useless by firing one against the other, and were afterwards thrown into the deepest part of the river; the masonry towers were entirely levelled, and every piece of timber connected with the works, buildings, and bridge was totally consumed,—indeed, I do not think there was a single thing left that could be of any service to the enemy.

With respect to Mirabete, I certainly should have been very glad to have got hold of the place, but it appeared impossible to get guns to bear upon it in any reasonable time, and to have attempted to assault it would in all probability have cost us very dear indeed. I at one time had an idea of blockading Mirabete, but ascertaining they had provisions in the place for six weeks I did not think it was right for me to delay my return, particularly as Foy and Drouet both appeared to be in motion.

I feel much obliged to your Lordship tor your intention of sending Major Currie to England. I fear you will have considered my official report too long. If any apology is necessary on the occasion, it is to be found in the conduct of those whose merit I thought it my duty to bring to your notice, aware that I could offer no greater stimulus to their future exertions.

I have, &c.,

R. Hill.

General the Earl of Wellington, K.B.,
&c. &c. &c.

No man was ever more anxious than Sir Rowland Hill to do justice to those under his command; and Lord Wellington on this occasion expressed his concurrence in all he said in their praise, while his own share in the exploit called forth new admiration, and opened the way into Spain.

CHAPTER 8

Sir Rowland Marches to Join Lord Wellington

Major Currie was received at headquarters with a hearty welcome, as the messenger of the tidings from Almaraz. His own letter to Sir Rowland Hill will convey the best idea of the impression made by the services he had to report.

Fuente Guinaldo, May 23. 1812.

My dear Sir,

I arrived here at five o'clock yesterday afternoon, after very great fatigue and exertion. Lord Wellington expressed the greatest joy and satisfaction at what had been done: in a word, he seems fully to appreciate the merits of the troops and every body connected with the expedition. Foy, he says, has been prettily humbugged, and must now go round by Toledo. When I mentioned our small loss, and the extent of the enemy's establishments at Almaraz, he said, 'Yes, Hill has done it well and ably: and I will send you to England; it will give you a step.' From letters which he received last night from Sir W. Erskine, and which he did not seem altogether pleased with, he said, 'he was afraid you would be hurried back to stop Drouet before you had completed the destruction of everything at Almaraz.'

Half-past nine o'clock.

Lord W. has just repeated before his staff that he will send me to England, and that I had better stop here until the arrival of your despatch. The marshal and every body offer a thousand congratulations; and they are known to attach a great deal of consequence to your late services, and particularly to the manner in which, according to Lord W.'s own words, things have been uniformly managed.

I have no time to say a word more, as the post is just going off, and I waited till the last moment for his Lordship's commands. Ten thousand thanks for the very kind and considerate manner in which you have put me in a fair way of promotion. I can never forget your brother's kindness neither. My dear Sir,

Ever yours most faithfully,

E. Currie.

P. S. Lord W. asked me how I thought the garrison of Mirabete would get away. Could it not be starved out? and would it not have been well to have left something to blockade it? I mentioned the guerilla force in the neighbourhood.

From Niza, on his way to England, Major Currie wrote again,—

Niza, May 28. 1812, 5 o'clock p. m.

My dear Sir,

Yesterday, after dinner. Lord Wellington took me on one side, and told me that he had received your despatch, and that every thing had been done that he could possibly have wished for, and that too in the most able manner. He had just received the account of Mr. Perceval's untimely end, and appeared happy that he had something to send home to occupy the public mind. He added, however, that it was necessary to make the most of every thing in England, and that he would not send off the despatch before Friday or Saturday, in hopes of hearing something satisfactory respecting Mirabete.

The despatches are to be sent to me, open, at Mr. Stewart's; and his Lordship has cautioned me against the unfair questions which are put to people who go home in my situation. I left headquarters last night at seven o'clock, and arrived here an hour ago (26 leagues). I am consequently very much fatigued, and am going to rest for a few hours before I set out for Gavião. Your horse I have just seen; he looks as sleek and as fat as ever; and a Mr. Commissary Griffiths will deliver him to you about the 2nd or 3rd of June.

I am not able to write to Clement for your commissions in London. In haste, my dear Sir,

Your ever faithful servant,

E. Currie.

P. S. I presume Lord W. rested his hopes of the fall of Mirabete upon what you stated in your despatch, for I never held out any such expectation to his Lordship. I said last night that I trusted my verbal report corresponded with your despatch in all the essential points; and he said, 'Most perfectly so.'

The reception of the news of this victory in England was highly flattering to Sir Rowland Hill, as were the commendations of the Prince Regent, the Commander-in-Chief, and the Government. Lord Bathurst's letter to Lord Wellington contained the following direction:—

Your Lordship will have the goodness to take the earliest opportunity of conveying to Sir Rowland Hill his Royal Highness's approbation of the distinguished skill, decision, and vigour displayed by Sir Rowland Hill on this occasion, and of the firmness and intrepidity so eminently manifested in the reduction of the redoubt of Fort Napoléon by Major-General Howard, and the officers and troops under his command. I am commanded by His Royal Highness to mark his satisfaction of the loss of officers and men being, comparatively speaking, so small, more especially as it appears that it is in a great measure owing to the judicious arrangements made by Sir Rowland Hill previous to his making the attack.

The Spanish and Portuguese authorities, the latter of which had conferred on him the Grand Cross of the Tower and Sword a few months previously, also expressed their admiration and gratitude.

This event at Almaraz put all the hostile army in motion. On the 25th Foy was at Truxillo, and sent a captain, named Guingret, with letters and money for the prisoners. In his letter to Sir Rowland, there is a passage which shows how annoyed the French were by the guerillas. He wrote,—

M. le Capitaine Guingret se rend aux avant-postes de l'armée Anglaise avec 50 chevaux. Je lui ai donné une escorte si considérable contre l'usage établi pour les parlementaires, parce-qu'il pourrait rencontrer en chemin des partis Espagnols peu familiarisés avec les coutumes et les lois de la guerre.

Foy's design was to succour Mirabete; and he was vigilantly watched by Hill, whose consummate prudence, with regard to him, appears in his communication from Merida, on the 28th of May, to

Lord Wellington. He says:

> I am inclined to think Foy will not remain long where he is. The enclosed Spanish paper, written by an intelligent man in observation, confirms my opinion respecting Foy's intention to return to the other side of the Tagus by Arzobispo. I am also inclined to think the enemy will abandon Mirabete. I could easily oblige Foy to go off from Truxillo, but under present circumstances I do not think it would be advisable for me to go so far to my left; and on the other hand, adverting to Foy's situation, I do not like to take all my force so far to the right as Almandralejo. Therefore, for a day or two, I will halt here, which will give my troops a little rest, and time to mend their shoes, &c.; and in the meanwhile, probably, I shall hear from your Lordship.

Lord Wellington did not answer this letter, "thinking it probable that Foy would move off again immediately," and gave this as a reason for not writing. Foy retired, but Drouet was at hand with instructions, if strong enough, to cut his way through Hill, to cross the Tagus, and to occupy Foy's position. This became known to Lord Wellington by means of an intercepted letter from Joseph to Drouet, a copy of which was immediately forwarded to Sir Rowland.

Madrid, 31 Mai, 1812.

M. le Comte D'Erlon,
Vouz auriez su la marche du corps du Général Hill sur Almaraz, et sa retraite au-delà de Truxillo, ou le Général Foy était encore le 26me Mai.

Le Duc de Raguse me mande qu'il paraît hors de doute que le mouvement de l'armée Anglaise se promena vers le Nord, ainsi il rappelle à lui la division Foy.

Si vous êtes assez fort pour combattre Hill, marchez-lui sur le corps, et venez passer le Tage au front de l'Arzobispo. Si vous ne vous jugez pas en état de le battre, accompagnez le sur la rive gauche.

Si le Général Hill vous évite, et va passer le Tage, soit à Alcantara, soit a Mecas, pour joindre Lord Wellington, prenez, sans hésiter, la route la plus courte sur l'Arzobispo, et passez le Tage.

Instruisez-moi de votre marche, et pensez. Monsieur le Comte, que de l'exécution de ces dispositions dépend le sort des affaires en Espagne.
M. le Duc de Dalmatie en est instrult, mais dans tous les cas n'attendez

pas ses ordres pour vous confirmer à ces dispositions.
Votre affectionné,

Joseph.

Drouet's designs gave little alarm to our general, who observed to Lord Wellington on the 3rd of June:

> If Drouet is not supported it will not be difficult for me to disturb him in his present position, and probably to destroy some of his magazines and fortified posts. On the other hand, if Soult keeps within reach of him, it will not probably be advisable for me to adventure far.

In a postscript to the letter, from which this is an extract, he further developed his plans:—

> Two deserters are come in from Drouet's corps, stating that the enemy are about to advance. I cannot, however, think it likely; nevertheless I shall be prepared, and have my corps collected in the following cantonments:—Almandralejo, Ribera, V. Franca, Fuente del Maestre, Los Santos, Penne Villemur at Zafra.

On the 4th intelligence was brought that Mirabete had been relieved with about 300 men, and that the peasants were engaged in carrying water up to the fort. By the 7th he had moved his headquarters to Fuente del Maestre, where he received instructions to occupy the position of Albuera in the first instance, if Soult should move into Estremadura in force. This Lord Wellington thought it probable he would do, with a view to move upon Sir Rowland as soon as his Lordship's own march was known; and he accordingly supplied reinforcements, with which Sir Rowland advanced to Zafra when Drouet fell back. Penne Villemur's horse were detached from Llerena on the right flank, and General Slade, with some British cavalry from Llera, on the left. Sir Rowland Hill, in his report to Lord Wellington says:

> The count, having expressed a wish to make a reconnaissance from Llerena towards Azuaga, with a view of inducing the enemy to retire, in order that he might establish his advanced posts at those places, and requesting me to cover his left, I ordered General Slade to advance for that purpose by Llera, with instructions in writing not to commit himself in any affair of consequence, and to keep in constant communication with the Count."

Lallemand happening to come forward with some horse, Slade, contrary to instructions, dashed furiously at them, and having gained a slight advantage, pursued them through a pass into a plain, where the hostile reserves made him pay dearly for his well-meant indiscretion. Lieutenant Strenuwitz, however, effected the recovery of some of the prisoners, under the direction of Sir Rowland Hill.

Soult having reinforced Drouet, Sir Rowland retired on the 18th of June, and took up his position at Albuera, where the bones of many a fallen soldier were seen still bleaching in the sun. The opposing armies now gazed on each other, as if pondering which should give the first blow. The English and French generals had both been directed to use their own judgment; and Sir Rowland Hill exercised a discretion which proved that he could calculate and refrain as well as dare and achieve. He seriously weighed all the circumstances of the case, and particularly their effects on the ulterior projects of Lord Wellington, to whom he sent a masterly letter, written on the 25th of June in the wood near Albuera, where he had posted his men, quite prepared for an attack if deemed expedient. Lord Wellington replied on the 28th:

> Fall upon the enemy if you can with advantage. I should prefer a partial affair to a general one; but risk a general affair, keeping always a very large body in reserve, particularly of cavalry, rather than allow Drouet to remain in possession of Estremadura and keep you in check.

On the receipt of this letter Sir Rowland proposed at once to advance against the enemy on the 2nd of July. The French made a strong reconnaissance on the 1st, and drove in his outposts. The Conde de Penne Villemur was rather rash with his cavalry, and would have been overpowered, had not he been supported by a squadron of the 3rd Dragoon Guards. Sir Rowland's subsequent movements are described in a letter to Lord Wellington after he left Albuera.

> Los Santos, July 4. 1812, 9 p. m.
>
> My dear Lord,
> Early in the morning of the 2nd I marched from the camp at Albuera to Santa Martha, where I learnt that Drouet had the main part of his army collected at Villa Franca and Fuente del Maestre, occupying Azauchal, Villa Alba, and Almandralejo with the greater part of his cavalry. Yesterday morning I moved forward towards Feria in two columns, the right and principal column marching by the great road near the mountain; the left, under Sir W. Erskine, consisting of the light cavalry and horse

artillery, and one brigade of British and one of Portuguese infantry, marched upon Azauchal and Villa Alba, at which place he fell in with three regiments of the enemy's cavalry, and after skirmishing with their rear guard, they fell back into the plain towards Villa Franca, where they remained till dark. In this affair Sir William took four prisoners and killed seven horses, and wounded a few men; our loss being one man of the Hussars killed.

This morning I found the enemy occupied a strong post near Fuente del Maestre, with General Barrois's division of infantry, and having the whole of his cavalry in the plain; I therefore determined to make a march upon this place by the great road, which had the immediate effect of making the enemy abandon Fuente del Maestre. Drouet's infantry at the same time retired from Villa Franca, taking the road through Ribera. I was on a height about a league and a half from Villa Franca; at sunset I saw the whole in march. I shall move forward in the morning. Several deserters have come in: I think we cannot have had less than thirty in the course of the last week.

I have, &c.

R. Hill.

General the Earl of Wellington, K.B.,
&c. &c. &c.

At daylight the next morning he marched in two columns, the right upon Usagre, and the left on Bienvenida. Soult remained at Usagre until he came up; and he saw him pass about three o'clock. On the 9th Sir Rowland was at Llerena, whence he despatched an interesting and important communication to Lord Wellington.

Llerena, 9th July, 1812, 9 a. m.

My dear Lord,

Yesterday a courier arrived from Cadiz with a despatch for your Lordship from Mr. Wellesley, dated the 2nd instant. Mr. W. was good enough to leave the despatch open for my perusal, with a request that the courier should not be detained. He accordingly set out about three yesterday evening. I think it likely, however, that he will not reach your headquarters so soon as this letter; I therefore beg to mention to you that the principal contents of the despatch were respecting Ballesteros. It appears that he was near Gibraltar, with about 400 cavalry and 5000 infantry, and that he did not consider himself in sufficient force to make a diversion upon Seville, but that he would make some movements which would have the same effect, of drawing the enemy's attention from Estremadura. It also appears that the Regency had prepared to embark Ballesteros, and send him and his troops round by Ayamonte. Mr. W. did not think this measure advisable, and Ballesteros remains near Gibraltar.

Mr. W. sends intelligence from Seville, which agrees with what I had received. He also sends two intercepted letters from Soult to the French Government, the most interesting part of which is in cipher. Your Lordship will of course have received the intercepted letter of Joseph to Drouet, a copy of which I send. The intelligence I have received of the enemy's movements of the last ten days, indicates his intention of carrying Joseph's instructions into execution. I have officers in observation at different points, and expect hourly more positive information on this head, and shall act accordingly, keeping a look-out towards Cordova and Seville, as it appears to me that Ballesteros, in his present weak state, will not be sufficient to prevent Soult from sending considerable reinforcements to this quarter, should he feel inclined.

I have, &c.

R. Hill.

P. S. I have just received intelligence, which I believe to be true, that Drouet was yesterday with his headquarters at Zalamea, with the main body, having sent some troops by Berlanga and Assuagar. I shall move immediately in the direction of Zalamea.

General the Earl of Wellington, K.B.,
&c. &c. &c.

Lord Wellington replied in the following terms:—

Rueda, July 13. 1812, 1 p.m.

My dear Hill,

I have received your letter of the 9th inst., 9 a.m., and you'll have observed from my letter of yesterday that I had anticipated the report expected from you, that Drouet would march in this direction. The king, from accounts received last night, appears to be collecting a large force at Madrid, particularly in cavalry;

and I am apprehensive after all the enemy will be too strong for us. But we'll see.

Don't let any time be unnecessarily lost.

Ever yours most sincerely,

Wellington.

Lieut.-General Sir Rowland Hill, K.B.

The French, however, did not move; and Sir Rowland Hill apprised Lord Wellington that he thought Drouet would retire into the mountains if pursued, and that it did not seem advisable to go further forward. He also stated that he had obliged Soult to withdraw his cavalry from Berlanga, and two other places which were occupied by the British advanced posts, while the principal part of the infantry were cantoned in Llerena. When Lord Wellington heard that the enemy were not carrying into effect Joseph's orders to cross the Tagus, he expressed to Sir Rowland his hope that he had not detached the troops according to previous directions; the answer to which was, that the steps taken were in entire accordance with his expectation. Sir Rowland's next position was at Zafra, where he moved in consequence of intelligence contained in three intercepted letters, that he might be in a better condition to act if attempts should be made to carry Joseph's instructions into effect.

The letter he wrote to Hawkstone from Zafra describes his anxieties at this time, and shows his readiness to oblige a courteous enemy:—

Zafra, July 28. 1812.

My dear Sister

I thank you for your letters which you have been kind enough to write me. I hope Clement keeps you informed of what is passing in Estremadura; if he does, you will see we are not idle in this quarter. At this moment we are anxious to know what is going on with Lord Wellington's main army. We have not heard from thence for these last four days, and when the accounts came away the two armies were pretty near each other. During the operations in the North, Soult is giving us all the trouble he can. He has reinforced the Count d'Erlon's corps; and there is seldom a day we do not see some of his troops. Four days ago my cavalry gained an advantage over some of his. I think he must have lost about forty; our loss not more than eight or ten.

> The accompanying letter is from the first *aide-de-camp* of Count d'Erlon, Colonel Salaignac, to his brother, who is a prisoner at Whitchurch. Will you have the goodness to send him the letter; and if he wishes to send an answer back, I will forward it to Count d'Erlon's headquarters. Colonel Salaignac is reckoned a very good sort of man, and liked by the Spaniards much better than Frenchmen in general are. He has shown great attention to some of *our* prisoners; and I should have no objection to show some little attention to his brother, if circumstances would admit of it. I have had a letter from Monsieur Salaignac, by which I see he writes and understands English perfectly well. It appears by the papers, that some of the French prisoners in England have behaved very ill; I therefore conclude Salaignac and others at Whitchurch are pretty closely watched: I will, however, forward a letter for him if he wishes it. Kind remembrance to all.
>
> Yours ever,
>
> R. H.

From Zafra he moved to Villa Franca, where he received from Lord Wellington the intelligence of his victory over Marmont at Salamanca. On this success he offered the victor his congratulations, while he pursued his own course with consummate prudence and skill.

Drouet occupied the whole length of the Sierra near Hornachos, an exceedingly strong post; and Sir Rowland thus expressed his reasons to Lord Wellington, for not attempting to drive him from it:—

> Considering that the enemy's force does not at present appear to be such as ought to keep me in check, I have felt anxious to dislodge them from this line; but there are objections to so doing which have hitherto prevented my making any movement with that view. I do not think it would be advisable to make a forward movement without taking into consideration the prospect of my being able to hold the country I should gain; and the enemy having already some force on the high Seville road, with 3000 or 4000 men in Seville, and which might at any time threaten my right and rear, this would be very doubtful.
>
> The enemy has a retreat open to him either on La Mancha or Cordova, so that I could not, by moving round either flank of the Sierra, hope to cut him off, or even to distress him, if he chooses to fall back; nor am I sufficiently positive as to his ac-

tual force to feel certain, in the event of taking up a favourable position, that I should be able to gain any important advantage over him. Therefore, for the present, I propose keeping the troops in cantonments, with as much reference as possible to their health and convenience, and shall watch for a favourable opportunity of acting. The Count D'Erlon's headquarters being at Hornachos would rather indicate a forward movement on their part, and I shall be prepared accordingly. I am disposed to think, however, *he has no such intention*, but that his object is only to keep us in view.

In the same letter he gave an account of a little skirmish between the outposts. A few days previously he had reported what Lord Wellington called "a very handsome affair" with the enemy's horse, on the 24th of July, by the division of cavalry under Sir W. Erskine. His time was so fully occupied that he had little leisure to write to his relatives in England; but this brief note from Zafra contains much in a few words:—

Zafra, Aug. 4. 1812.

My dear Sister,
I wrote the accompanying letter last post-day; but owing to my being obliged to go out in a hurry, the letter was not sent. It is of little moment whether you receive it or not; it shall, however, go by this day's post. Since I wrote it we have received accounts of the defeat of Marmont's army near Salamanca. It has been a most glorious event, and I trust its consequences will be most advantageous to the cause. It appears, however, to have had very little effect on my immediate opponents. Count D'Erlon continues in a strong situation In my front, and Soult remains at Seville with about 4000, and more at no great distance ready to move upon me should I follow Drouet.

Therefore for the present I shall remain where I am, and watch for a favourable opportunity of acting. Lord Wellington still continues advancing; and if he is able to keep his forward position, Soult will be ordered to reinforce the king. Indeed, I think Soult must quit this part of the country entirely if matters do not mend with them. Everything looks well at present. The last accounts from the North of Europe are of the greatest consequence to us.

Yours ever most affectionately,

R. Hill.

Clement writes a *letter* by this post: you will consider this as a *mere memorandum.*

The movements of Drouet were still closely watched by Sir Rowland, and regularly reported to headquarters.

Zafra, Aug. 12. (noon) 1812.

My dear Lord,

Drouet has withdrawn his troops from Guerena; but he still occupies Hornachos, keeping the troops and baggage out of the town every night. I hope your Lordship has received the intercepted letter I sent on the 8th, from Drouet to Jourdan, by which we see that on the 6th the former had received no official account of Marmont's defeat. We also see that Soult expected the king in Andalusia. The late glorious event must, however, frustrate all his intentions. Your Lordship will see by your returns that we continue very healthy. There was a little fever in the 50th. I have in consequence moved that regiment to Feira, which is reckoned a remarkably healthy place.

I have, &c.

R. Hill..

P. S. I have not heard from Seville or Ballesteros since my last.
General the Earl of Wellington, K.B.,
&c. &c. &c.

On the 13th Lord Wellington entered the capital of Spain, welcomed by tears of joy as the friend of the oppressed inhabitants, who hailed him as their deliverer; but they were so dispirited by their sufferings, that no heart remained in them for tumultuous exultation. From this scene of one of the purest triumphs ever resulting from arms, his active mind took a survey of the whole condition of the afflicted country. He first directed the blockade of Cadiz to be raised, expecting this would enable him to relieve Ballesteros and Sir Rowland Hill. Soon after, in consequence of the retreat of Joseph into Valencia, and the certainty that it was not intended to join the troops under Drouet to the army of the centre, while reinforcements under General Maitland had landed at Alicante, he ordered Sir Rowland to move on Drouet, to drive him out of Estremadura, if possible, and to threaten to enter Andalusia. At the time of receiving these instructions Sir Rowland informed his friends privately:

Soult is evidently a good deal alarmed, and is certainly about to move, and it is generally supposed he will retire by Granada. We are ready for a start whenever the period shall arrive for us to advance.

On the 19th the enemy made a strong reconnaissance with nearly the whole of his cavalry, but only drove in some picquets, and then retired at a trot towards Llerena. Sir Rowland observed to Lord Wellington, that his own proceedings ought to depend, in a great degree, on those of Soult:

> If Soult gets rid of his encumbrances, and remains at or near Seville in force, it will not, I should think, be advisable for me to follow Drouet far. I shall, however, give him every annoyance I can, and if circumstances permit I shall make a direct movement upon him tomorrow.[5] It was my intention to have surprised the post of Hornachos, but I find the troops which are there in the day, march out and bivouac at least one league from the town on the road. Therefore to have attempted to have surprised that place would, in my mind, have harassed my troops, and have been attended with no advantage.

His further movements are thus detailed in a letter to England, dated Berlanga, August 31st:—

> On the 27th my corps broke up from its cantonments at Zafra, and reached Assuaga and this place yesterday. The Count D'Erlon has evacuated Estremadura, and is in full march upon Cordova, at which place there is every appearance of a general union of the army of the South. I propose making an immediate movement to my left to the Guadiana, from which point I shall be in the way to make a movement to the Tagus, should it be necessary to form a junction with Lord Wellington. The joy of the people at this moment is great indeed, and I trust it will have the best effect.

By a letter of the same date, sent by a trusty peasant in duplicate on account of the slowness and uncertainty of the post, he acquainted Lord Wellington that Soult, with his whole army, was making "a rapid and decided movement upon Cordova, with a view, probably, of uniting with the king." He therefore proceeded towards Medellin, Truxillo, and Almaraz, where he crossed the Tagus. As he passed the famous

---
5. August 26th.

fortress of Mirabete, now evacuated by the French, he had the satisfaction to find that it would have been impossible to have escaladed it, for besides the outworks, it consisted of an enormous circular tower, the door of which was halfway up, entirely beyond the reach of any ladder. The great commander of the army, now deservedly raised to the rank of Marquis, said:

> Hill's corps will soon be across the Tagus, and I shall have the whole army together, or in close communication. The blockade of Cadiz is raised, Seville evacuated, and Soult retiring through Andalusia.

Sir Rowland moved on by Naval Moral, Oropesa, and Talavera, and Major-General Charles Alten was placed under his command. On his route he despatched the following account to Hawkstone:—

> Carpio, Sept. 28. 1812,
>
> My dear Sister,
> Soult left Granada on the 15th, and Ballesteros entered it on the 17th. Soult has taken the direction of Guadin to Caravaca. Before evacuating Granada and Jaen, the works and guns were destroyed by the French. Joseph is still at Valencia, but *it is said* he is going off to France. The castle of Consuegra has surrendered to General Elio. It was an important post for the enemy to occupy; and if it had not fallen I should have attacked it. The whole of my corps is on its march towards Toledo and Aranjuez: the head of my column will be at the former town tomorrow. The enemy has evacuated the town of Burgos, and Lord Wellington has carried some of the outworks before the place; the castle, however, still holds out. Tom is at Burgos; he was quite well a few days ago, since the storming of the fort at Burgos. I thank you for your letter of the 25th of last month. Kind remembrances to all.
>
> Yours most affectionately,
>
> R. H.

He reached Toledo at the time he expected, and received a report from General Alten, who wrote as follows:—

> Madrid, Sept. 29. 1812.
>
> My dear General,
> I have the honour to transmit to you the enclosed, received from Don Carlos d'España, and from a gentleman who has

been long employed by the Marquis of Wellington for the purpose of obtaining information. I also received yesterday, from an officer of the 1st Hussars, whom I had sent in front, a letter dated Genesta, 25th instant, informing me that on the 23rd instant King Joseph and Suchet had joined at Almanza, after having made some demonstrations towards Alicante, and on the 24th had advanced as far as Villar and Bonete towards Albacete. This officer also says that the advanced guard of Marshal Soult was, on the 14th instant, at Hellin, and that it was expected he would form a junction with Suchet on the 27th or 28th instant. I have the honour to be,

   My dear General,
     Your very obedient and faithful servant,
       Chas. Alten, M.-General.

Lieut.-General Sir R. Hill, K.B.
&c., &c.

The same information was sent to headquarters, but Lord Wellington remarked on it to Sir Rowland, "The movements and intentions of Soult and the king do not yet appear to me to be quite clear." He also expressed his fears of not being able to take the castle of Burgos.

Sir Rowland's own impressions were given as usual in his family correspondence. He said, in writing on the 12th from Aranjuez, where he had advanced from Toledo:

> The castle of Burgos was not taken when the last accounts came away. Lord Wellington tells me it is the most difficult job he ever had in hand. Tom has his share of the fatigue, and was quite well when I heard from him on the 6th. In my last I told you that the armies of Joseph, Soult, and Suchet were united in Murcia and Valencia; they have approached a little nearer to Madrid, their advance being at Albacete. If they do advance upon Madrid I think they will run great risks, though at the same time it does not seem very unlikely that they may attempt it, either with the view of bringing Lord Wellington back from Burgos, or in hopes of getting hold of the capital again.
> If these three armies do not advance with their whole force they can do nothing; and if they do bring the whole they must abandon their possessions in Valencia, and will be followed by General Maitland, who is at Alicante, and Ballesteros, who is coming up by Granada from Seville. I wish we had possession

of Burgos, and hope you will hear of its surrender by the time you receive this. I rode over to Madrid a few days ago: it is a beautiful city. You will see by the map that this place is on the Tagus, where I am tolerably well posted to stop King *Joe* should he try to return to his capital.

Lord Wellington's views and those of Sir Rowland Hill coincided in every particular: and though his Lordship sent him directions, he observed:

> I write all this, as I always do, to provide for every event, not believing that these instructions are at all necessary.

Nor were they; for in almost every instance he had anticipated his commander's intention; and whenever the peculiarities of his situation led him to deviate from the strict letter of his orders, that deviation was acknowledged to have been an improvement.

By the 18th of October he had sufficient intelligence of the proceedings of the enemy to be able to say in a private letter:

> The king, Soult, and Suchet, having united their armies, are on the frontiers of Murcia and Valencia, and appear to be moving this way. It is certain that a considerable force is advancing towards Madrid; but I think it very doubtful whether they will attempt to force their way to the capital.

This he also made known to Lord Wellington, who commenced his famous retreat from Burgos, the siege of which place he raised on the 21st. Sir Rowland retired from the Tagus in order to join his Lordship, and on the 30th moved from the position of the Jarama and destroyed the bridge of Aranjuez. How he proceeded may be gathered from his correspondence with Lord Wellington:—

> Aravaca, October 31st, Noon.
>
> My dear Lord,
>
> I have just received your letter of the 29th. We commenced our retreat yesterday, and it was my intention to have moved every thing off by daybreak in the morning, but the failure of the mine at the Puente Largo obliged me to keep the troops at that point until after dark, when they also commenced their retreat; and I have reason to think, that until daylight this morning the enemy was ignorant of our movement. It appears to have been the enemy's intention to have gained the bridge yesterday, as

they had collected a considerable force in front of it; and after they discovered the failure of the mine they made a vigorous attempt to get possession of it, but were repulsed in a very handsome manner by the 47th regiment and a detachment of the 95th, under Colonel Skerrett, placed there by Lieutenant-General Cole, who had charge of the rear-guard. The conduct of Colonel Skerrett and the detachment of the 95th was very conspicuous on this occasion. I am sorry to say they suffered some loss.

A great part of the infantry will reach the Escurial this night, and I shall endeavour to have others forward agreeably to your Lordship's expectations.

I communicated your wishes to General Elio, and have received no answer to them; but General Alten tells me he believes it to be his intention to head the Tagus and pass by the enemy's rear.

I have, &c.

R. Hill.

General the Marquis of Wellington, K.B.,
&c. &c. &c.

The next morning found him at the Escurial, pressing on to join Lord Wellington, who congratulated himself on having "got clear in a handsome manner of the worst scrape he ever was in." Sir Rowland sent an express, at ten o'clock, to headquarters, to say he had heard that four squadrons of the enemy had entered Valde Moro on the previous day. At night a report arrived from the officer in observation, that the advance of the French had entered Madrid; but at five o'clock the next morning it was signified that a Spanish officer, leaving that city at the same hour the evening before, had not seen them there. In the front of Lord Wellington they were very quiet, but had sent to Toro to repair the bridge destroyed by the British, and orders were given to Sir Rowland to send an officer into the valley of the Tagus to observe their movements.

He next ascended the Sierra de Guadarama, over which the passage was rendered easy by the excellence of the royal road. The scene was magnificent—column defiling after column, all in sight of each other, through the road winding along the brown rocky mountain, studded here and there with thick coverts of fir-trees, or patches of the greenest herbage blending with silvery torrents darting down their beds, while below lay the wide plains of Old Castile, covered with towns, villages, and well-cultivated farms. Into these they descended, followed by the enemy, of which Sir Rowland immediately sent tidings to Lord Wellington.

> Villa Neuva, Nov. 4. 2 p. m.
>
> My dear Lord,
> I have this instant received the enclosed report, by which it appears that four regiments of the enemy's cavalry and two regiments of infantry, were advancing this morning up the pass of Guadarama at eight o'clock.
> I have no information of what may be moving in their rear.
> I shall continue my march, as far as the encumbrances of the sick and baggage will permit me, to Fontiveros, about which place I hope to have every thing collected tomorrow.
>
> I have, &c.
>
> R. Hill.
>
> General the Marquis of Wellington, K.B.,
> &c. &c. &c.

The reply to this was that his Lordship did not think the enemy were following him in force, but had merely sent out these regiments to see what he was doing. From Fontiveros, which Sir Rowland reached on the 5th, he reported—

> The enemy's column, which I mentioned to your Lordship by Lieutenant Hay, advanced this morning at nine o'clock. I could see them descend the heights, and I do not think the number which descended the hill could exceed from 8000 to 10,000 men; but there were other troops in their rear. When I came away, at half-past two, about three regiments of cavalry advanced as far as Blasco Sancho, the remaining infantry halting about the bridge of Almaza.

It turned out that the hostile cavalry which had shown itself was nearly 3000 strong; and Sir William Erskine had withdrawn General Alten's horse from the Adaga, and brought them nearer to Fontiveros, Sir Rowland also thought of falling back, as the ground he occupied afforded no good position. His instructions were:

> Do not allow the enemy to come too near you with a small advanced guard. Move upon them immediately, and make them keep a proper distance.

This, he said, he was quite ready to do. Sir Rowland was now in close communication with Lord Wellington, who was retiring on Salamanca, followed by Clausel, and he proceeded to Alba de Tormes. On the 9th at two o'clock a.m. his Lordship wrote to him from Salamanca—

> I think you will do well to move in the morning to your left to Machaon with the second division, excepting one British brigade, leaving Hamilton's division and that brigade at Alba. Take Slade's brigade and the Spanish troops and Portuguese cavalry with you, leaving Long's brigade looking out in front of Alba. Have a good garrison in the Castle of Alba. You should not load the mine of the bridge, because we must keep a communication with the garrison. If the enemy should attempt to cross either of the fords of Huesta, fall upon the first who cross.

His answer was speedily sent: it was a crisis of no ordinary interest.

Alba de Tormes, Nov. 9 half-past 10 a. m.
My dear Lord,
Your Lordship's letter of two a. m. reached me about nine. The second division will commence its march as soon as possible, and proceed according to your directions. General Howard's brigade remains here with General Hamilton. Captain Goldfinch is now employed in repairing the front of the lowest work of the castle, which had been destroyed by the Spaniards, and a garrison will be put into it. I do not know whether your Lordship has been at this place; I therefore think it right to mention that the castle, with only a small garrison without artillery, would but imperfectly cover the bridge, unless the town was held also, which would require a considerable force.
I have, &c.
R. Hill.
General the Marquis of Wellington, K.B.,
&c. &c. &c.

At four o'clock on the same day he reported the advance of the enemy towards the River Tormes. By a quarter before six Lord Wellington replied that he had never been at Alba, and asked for correct information respecting the garrison and castle. Almost at the same time Sir Rowland transmitted to him the news that the enemy threatened the place. He added, "The mine is all ready, and the powder on the spot, if your Lordship should think fit to give directions about it." He said, too, that he had seen "large bodies of cavalry and infantry moving over the heights towards the village of Babalfuente." Lord Wellington's opinion was that the French could not take the town of Alba—nor did they; for when they made the attempt on the 10th, they were most gallantly repulsed by the troops under General Hamilton. Sir Rowland was himself on that day at Calvarassa de Abaxo, and continued to watch and report all the manoeuvres of the great force now threatening the allies.

While proceeding to effect this junction with Lord Wellington, Sir Rowland received the flattering intelligence that he had been elected member of Parliament for Shrewsbury. This caused him to write home.

Rolleda, near Ciudad Rodrigo,
Nov. 25. 1812, 8 a. m.

My dear Sister,

Last night three packets arrived at my headquarters, two of which have been wandering about the country for some time. They contain all your interesting letters, and my father's, as well as the papers relative to the late election at Shrewsbury. It is my intention to answer the whole of them this evening, and to write to you more fully on all subjects, and send my letters by the post. This I send by a private hand, which sometimes travels quicker, but is often more uncertain than the post.

The public despatches will have informed you of the late events in this country. You may imagine that I have had my share of anxiety on the occasion.

The overwhelming force which the enemy had collected made it necessary for Lord Wellington to retire, and for him to send me orders to the same effect. Thank God, I completed my junction with his Lordship at Salamanca without any material loss, though pressed by a very superior force.

Lord W., I believe, would have made a stand on his old ground near Salamanca, but the enemy declined a contest *there*, and obliged Lord Wellington to quit it by marching round our right and towards our rear. The enemy's force collected is so superior to ours, being, it is supposed, near 90,000 men, with 200 pieces of artillery, that Lord W. thought it advisable to continue his retreat to this strong frontier, where we are now cantoned, and where I think the enemy will not follow us, at least at present. The last five days they have done nothing. The dreadful weather we have had has been very much against us, and our army has, I am sorry to say, suffered a good deal, particularly our cavalry and horses. Clement is quite recovered. Tom was with us a few days ago; he wrote to you from Alba de Tormes: and if you receive this before the post, tell Sir John and my brother I write to them by that conveyance. In haste,

   Yours ever,

               R. Hill.

The incessant occupations of this eventful march prevented his writing the letters he proposed until he reached Coria, where his whole corps was directed to proceed on the 28th. The scenery of his route was grand in the extreme; and as he passed the lofty Sierra de Gata, and descended by the rugged road to the plain, the sun chased away the mountain mist, and displayed the lovely plains below. Sir Rowland's headquarters were in the small town of Coria, beautifully seated on the River Alagon, having a cathedral and some interesting remains of a Moorish tower and castle.

At this place he did every thing in his power to make the winter quarters of his officers and troops comfortable, after their late privations and fatigues. He now found time to write the promised letter to his father:—

             Coria, Nov. 30. 1812.

My dear Father,

I enclose a few lines to the electors of Shrewsbury, expressive of my thanks for the honour they have done me in electing me one of their representatives in Parliament, which I request you will take the earliest opportunity of communicating to them.

"My present occupations have prevented me from addressing the electors at that length which I otherwise might have wished, and the same cause precludes me from addressing myself individually to Mr. Edward Burton and other gentlemen amongst the electors, who have most particularly exerted themselves to procure my return. I am not, however, the less sensible of their kindness, and must beg of you or my brother to take an opportunity of personally assuring them of my gratitude.

I beg you will accept my warmest thanks for your kindness and

exertions on this occasion, and believe me to be, my dear Sir,
Your ever dutiful son,

Rowland Hill.

Sir John Hill, Bart.

"I think," he said in another letter, "we shall be quiet here for some time." Lord Wellington had, in fact, disposed his whole army in cantonments, waiting only for the burst of spring and its supply of green forage, to take the held again with the largest and most efficient body of troops he could collect.

CHAPTER 9

Battle of Vittoria

The army had scarcely settled in winter quarters in 1812, before the appearance of Lord Wellington's memorable circular, relative to its discipline and its moral condition, created extreme sensation. There were many who felt it the more deeply, because conscious that the sweeping charges of irregularity it contained, were not applicable to their conduct. The troops under Sir Rowland Hill were restrained by his influence, from the excesses so feelingly deplored by the commander of the whole. If compared also with French soldiers, the patience of the English under privations may be said to have been exemplary; though, as their wants pressed and temptations offered, they were led away into occasional irregularities.

Whatever Sir Rowland Hill may have thought of these proceedings at the period referred to, it is certain he never offered any opposition to them; and his own troops were under a discipline marvellously efficacious, considering the sufferings they endured and the triumphs they won. No general ever used less severity, yet the fear of offending *him* acted on the minds of his soldiers far more effectually than the dread of punishment, which was recklessly braved when unsparingly administered. An officer of his division wrote of him thus eloquently and justly in a recent letter:—

> The great foundation of all his popularity with the troops was his sterling personal worth, and his heroic spirit; but his popularity was increased and strengthened as soon as he was seen. He was the very picture of an English country gentleman. To those soldiers who came from the rural districts of Old England, *he represented home*—his fresh complexion, placid face, kind eyes, kind voice, the total absence of all parade or noise in his habits, delighted them. The displeasure of Sir Rowland Hill was worse

to them than the loudest anger of other generals; and when they saw anxiety in his face that all should be right, they doubly wished it themselves; and when they saw his countenance bright with the expression that all was right, why, they were glad for him as well as for themselves.

Again, the large towns and manufacturing districts furnished a considerable body of men to the army. Now these soldiers were many of them familiar with the name and character and labours of his pious and devoted uncle, Rowland Hill, who was, perhaps, of all the preachers of the Gospel in the past century, *the one* best known, best loved, and most talked about amongst the common people all over England. His sincerity, his boldness, and his many strange sayings and doings, were known and reported in the ranks; and the men did not like Sir Rowland the less, for being the nephew of this celebrated and benevolent individual.

Also his kind attention to all the wants and comforts of his men, his visits to the sick in hospital, his vigilant protection of the poor country people, his just severity to marauders, his generous and humane treatment of such prisoners and wounded as at times fell into his hands—all consistent actings of a virtuous and noble spirit—made for him a place in the hearts of the soldiery; and wherever the few survivors of that army may now be scattered, in their hearts assuredly his name and image are dearly cherished still.

Coria, where Sir Rowland's winter quarters were established, was a favourite place with the officers, who passed their leisure time in coursing, shooting, and a variety of amusements which he liberally promoted. Lord Wellington's departure on business of importance to Cadiz left him in a most responsible situation. He says in one of his communications to his relatives:

> Lord Wellington, having set off for Cadiz, the command of the armies is left in my hands. It is not his Lordship's intention to be absent more than a month. In the meanwhile there does not appear any great likelihood of active operations. The enemy, however, are at no great distance, and it is possible we may have something to do.

Sir Rowland also mentioned in the same letter, dated December 15., the appointment of his Lordship to be *Generalissimo* of the Spanish armies, which he considered "as likely to have the best effect, notwithstanding Ballesteros's *opposition* to it." He further observed:

> That general's conduct has been rather extraordinary. I have many letters from him, and indeed I have received one this day (of the 26th of October), expressing his anxious desire to comply with *my wishes* and Lord Wellington's, in which I believe him to have been sincere. But subsequently finding from his own government that Lord Wellington was *to command him*, Ballesteros said *no*.

On the 12th of January Sir Rowland wrote again:

> I do not wish to be too sanguine, but there is every appearance of the enemy's army in this country being on the point of making a general move to the rear. They seem to be fully aware that things are not going on well with them in Russia; but the troops in general are kept in ignorance as to the real state of affairs there. I have, however, endeavoured to set them right, and to let them know how matters stand, by sending to their outposts some copies of Lord Cathcart's late despatches. For some time past the enemy have been sending off their sick and raising immense contributions—measures which indicate retrograde movement.

Seven days later he stated:

> The troops that were nearest to us marched off about a week ago, and appeared to be going to their rear; they have, however, taken the direction of Toledo, and been replaced in our front by troops from Astorga and Leon, the whole of that country having been evacuated by the enemy. Upon the whole, it appears that the French in this country have collected the greater part of their force in the centre of Spain. I do not mean to say that they have brought troops forward from their rear, but have closed those on their flanks more to the centre. This may be an arrangement preparatory to retiring, or a measure of precaution; but I cannot conceive that it means anything offensive on their part at present.

The movements of the hostile forces at this time were viewed with great anxiety by the British officers; and it may be interesting to see a report at such a juncture sent to Sir Rowland Hill from officers in observation.

> *First Officer.* It is incalculable (what) the enemy are levying in all the villages. On the 7th 3500 men entered Madrid; the 8th they marched out for France. They took with them a convoy of 300 carts, and many persons made prisoners. In the hospitals at Madrid they have 756 sick; and they have given orders for a quantity of biscuit to be baked; it is not known for what purpose.
>
> *Second Officer.* On the 5th 1000 Polish cavalry marched from Madrid for France; on the 7th 4000 to 5000 infantry marched also from Madrid for France; on the 8th 400 cavalry marched for France; on the 9th also left Madrid some troops of the Confederation of the Rhine. Joseph has dismissed many domestics of the palace, and it is said he is going to Guadalaxaran. On the 11th 800 men left Madrid for France. Count D'Erlon is at Agreda, Soult's headquarters at Toledo, with 4000 men. The enemy continue their exactions of enormous contributions.
> On the 21st everything was quiet at Talavera, when in the night an officer arrived, which produced a great bustle. An embargo was laid on all transports, and all the posts were called in. The idea amongst the people at Talavera and the French troops was, that they were going to retire in consequence of the accounts from the North of Europe.

These reports, when they were found to have come from the enemy. Sir Rowland treated with due suspicion. He made a tour of inspection to his own posts northward, and found them generally healthy and in a satisfactory state. Measures also were taken by him to prevent the French from plundering Placentia, where the inhabitants were in great terror from rumours of their approach. He next had what he called "a little affair, which he had no doubt would be magnified in England." This happened at Bejar, and he gave his own version of it thus:—

> The enemy have for some time been plundering the neighbouring country in a most shameful manner; and in order to protect some of the towns, I moved troops forward, and placed two regiments in Bejar, a large town, the most advanced. On the night of the 19th the enemy collected about 12,000, and made a night march upon Bejar, in hopes of surprising the gar-

rison. Our troops were, however, on the alert, and repulsed the enemy.

On this occasion he reported with great pleasure to Marshal Beresford, the gallant conduct of the Portuguese.

About this time Sir Rowland added to his staff an officer who was destined to be his companion, secretary, confidant, and friend to the last moment of his public life. This estimable man was Captain Egerton[1], of the well-known and respected Cheshire family of the same name. Sir Rowland had by the permission of Lord Wellington taken him as extra *aide-de-camp*, and thereby contributed to the happiness of his circle at Coria, as well as to the advantage of the public service. As spring advanced, the chieftains of the British army glowed with anticipations of their coming successes, and collected the most accurate accounts they could obtain of the enemy's force and proceedings. A letter from Sir Rowland Hill to his father shows what intelligence they had obtained.

Coria, March 23. 1813.

My dear Father,

Yesterday Captain Erskine came over here, and left your letter of the 28th of January. What you have said to Lord Erskine on the subject of Lord Buchan's attention to me is perfectly correct, and I trust I need not say that I shall on every account he glad to show his son any attention in my power.

The enemy have withdrawn their troops from La Mancha, and I am inclined to think they are about to evacuate Madrid, perhaps not with the intention of quitting Spain altogether, but more with the view of concentrating their troops in the direction of Valladolid. They continue to exact enormous contributions in every part of Spain they occupy; and I have been kept a little on the alert of late, in order to preserve the neighbouring country from being plundered by them.

I believe I have got pretty correct returns of some of the French armies; and as I know you are much interested in all military matters, I annex a memorandum from them for the private information of the Hawkstone family:—

The army of Portugal, *as it is called*, is commanded by the Comte de Reille, *aide-de-camp* to the emperor, and consists of 8 divisions; 8 generals of divisions; 11 generals of brigade; 31 regi-

---
1. Later Colonel Egerton, of Eaton Banks, near Tarporley.

ments of infantry, amounting to 31,256 infantry.

Cavalry.—1 general of division; 2 of brigade; 9 regiments, amounting to 3256 men. Artillery, 1775 men.

The above army is cantoned in Avila, Valladolid, Toro, and Salamanca.

The army of the South, lately commanded by Soult, is now commanded by the Comte de Gazan, and consists of 8 divisions of infantry, amounting to 30,785 men; 3880 cavalry; and 500 artillery.

This army has its headquarters at Toledo, and is immediately in front of my corps.

The army of the Centre is commanded by the Comte D'Erlon, Drouet, has its headquarters at Madrid, and amounts to 7081 infantry, and 4022 cavalry, besides artillery.

The army in Valencia, from 13,000 to 14,000, is commanded by Suchet.

The army of the North, I believe, does not exceed 12,000.

The above includes all the sick, and was made out before Marshal Soult left the army for France, taking with him the selected officers and men to complete the imperial guards. I do not know the exact number he took with him, probably eight or ten thousand.

With respect to our army, I believe it is very effective. The second division of infantry never was so strong in the field as we are at present, and the cavalry are recovering from their weak state. I am induced to think the enemy have sent *no* reinforcements into Spain.[2]

The British forces at this time were in a state of great efficiency, and Sir Robert Chambre Hill, the brother of Sir Rowland, was highly commended by Lord Wellington for his efforts in the household brigade of cavalry, which he commanded. As the month of April was drawing to a close, Sir Rowland sent word to his friends:

> All our troops in the rear are closing up to be more *à portée* to the movements we may have to make, and I imagine by the time you receive this that the whole will be moving forward.
>
> If it was the enemy's intention to quit this country as we advance, they would be taking the steps they are now adopting. It is, however, possible they may make a stand; but I do not think

---

2. This letter, like some others, had no signature.

it will be before we get to the Douro or the Ebro. Our army is now in very fine order, and never was more effective since we have been in the Peninsula. That of the enemy cannot be so strong as it was; for although they have received about 7000 recruits, they have of late sent to France upwards of 20,000 of their best men, and a great number of officers.

In the long marches which Sir Rowland's troops had now to make, and during the various halts which occurred, he endeavoured to afford them all the relief in his power from the monotony of a camp life. The whole corps was concentrated at Galisteo on the 4th of May, where it remained till the 21st. While here the 28th Regiment, which had signalised itself in Albuera, determined, on the 16th, the second anniversary of that battle, to give a dinner to Sir Rowland and the Staff of the second division. But they had neither tables nor chairs. This did not deter them from their purpose, and ingenuity, never wanting where there is inclination, soon invented a mode of giving a banquet *al fresco*. Lieutenant Irwin selected the softest and most even piece of turf he could find, on which he marked out the due length and breadth of a table for no less than one hundred guests.

The turf was carefully pared off, and a trench was dug round it large enough for all the company. The table was formed in the centre of the sods and mould, duly levelled, and excavated to give ample room for the legs, and then the green turf was once more gently laid on, and supplied the place of a table-cloth. Each officer invited was desired to bring his own knife, fork, and plate, and not to be particular about having them changed.

The cookery was of the substantial order, the heavy artillery of field *cuisine*. There were ponderous joints roasted and ponderous joints boiled; there was soup in abundance, in which the shreds of meat gave assurance that it was, at least, unsparingly concocted; there were pies baked in camp-kettles turned upside down, of dimensions and quality Friar Tuck would not have disdained. Then came the cordial welcome of the chief guest, the man who never had an enemy but on public grounds, whose bland smile set the company at ease, while his genuine dignity prevented in his presence every word and every act that did not perfectly become it.

It was nearly the end of May before Sir Rowland's corps arrived at Salamanca. As they crossed the plains that lay in their road, the officers let loose their greyhounds to course the hares along the columns, and many of them were killed in the midst of the marching ranks. By the

4th of June they were near Burgos. On the 12th, at five o'clock in the morning. Sir Rowland's corps moved forward in two columns, the right on Celada, the left on Hornillo. The enemy, after skirmishing a little to favour the retreat of the main body of their rear-guard, retired up the heights above Hornillo. There, for a time, they presented a front to the pursuing British; but, at length, being alarmed, they passed the River Arlanzon, and joined Reille, the entire body taking the road towards Burgos. At early dawn on the 13th the picquets left on the heights saw the distant castle of Burgos enveloped in a thick white smoke, followed by a tremendous sound. The French themselves were destroying the fortress which baffled the genius of Wellington, and resisted his victorious army. In a few minutes more came a second explosion; shortly all was again clear, and the yawning ruins told their own tale.

At length King Joseph brought his army and all its appurtenances into the basin of Vittoria. In that direction Sir Rowland's troops passed on with the rest, and no particular event interrupted their march. The Asturian mountains were on their left. The scenery on their route was worthy of the season and of Spain. One portion of it is beautifully described by Major Moyle Sherer. He says:

> On the 16th we descended by a steep and rocky road into a low secluded valley, through which the Ebro, here narrow and inconsiderable, winds its way, and crossing the river by a stone bridge of five arches, turned to the left, and followed a road running for nearly two miles along the bank of the Ebro, and almost on a level with its waters. The view of this valley on your descent to it, the vale itself, and the singularly picturesque road by which you pass out from it, are amongst the most enchanting scenes it has ever fallen to my lot to contemplate. Here you may imagine yourself transported to the happy retreat described in Rasselas. On every side mountains enclose and shelter this favoured spot; all the passes leading to and from it are concealed from you; the fields all teem with cultivation, and the orchards all blush with fruit.
>
> The ash, the beech, and the poplar, the woodbine, the rose, and a thousand shrubs shade and adorn the rural dwellings. The narrow wheel tract by which you leave this Elysium runs curving at the foot of impending precipices, so bold and varied in their forms and the character of their beauties, that no pen could describe them justly. Here they are clothed with rich and

shaggy brushwood; there naked to their blue or grey summits, which frown above you: and here, again, from the rude clefts and fissures of the rock grow solitary trees and plants, where no hand can ever reach them, while in some places thick wreaths of ivy half cover the projecting crags.

The river brawls along between these cliffs, often impeded by huge masses of mountain stone, which have fallen in some wintry storm, or been detached by some violent convulsion of nature, and now form islands in its bed. In a scene so lovely, soldiers seemed quite misplaced, and the glittering of arms, the trampling of horses, and the loud voices of the men, appeared to insult its cheerfulness.

The bivouacs here for the next three days were delightful beyond all conception, and those that had food were cheerful and contented. But the poor Portuguese were, by reason of the negligence of those appointed to supply them with provisions, in a starving condition; so that, notwithstanding the stern but just command of Lord Wellington that they should look to their legitimate sources for their support, Sir Rowland could not refrain from addressing him on their deplorable state.

Barquiseda, June 20.

My dear Lord,

I am sorry to have occasion to address your Lordship again on the subject of provisioning the Portuguese division under my orders, after the instructions which I have received from you; but they are at present in so destitute a state that I feel it my duty to make your Lordship acquainted with it. They for some days have been on very reduced rations.

The day before yesterday they had only three quarters of a pound of meat, and yesterday nothing, and have no prospects for this day. To give them bread I am aware is out of the question, but I beg to know whether your Lordship will permit me to give them some meat?

I have, &c.

R. Hill.

Marquis of Wellington, &c. &c.

This application was irresistible, and elicited the following reply:—

June 20. 1813, half-past 1 p.m.

My dear Hill,

I have just received your note of this morning. You may assist the Conde d'Amarante as you please, but let the Conde know that it is an exception to a rule to which I am determined to adhere, and that he must make his commissaries exert themselves.

Ever yours most faithfully,

Wellington.

Lieut.-General Sir R. Hill, K.B., &c.

On the morning of the 21st hints from staff-officers, bustle in the bivouacs, the saddling of Sir Rowland's black charger, and other significant proceedings, indicated that something was expected to occur beyond the ordinary events of a march. The moving masses of our general's division were excited about nine o'clock by some skirmishing in the mountain, and a league farther on, the defile formed by the high lands and the river opened to their view the splendid sight of the hostile army, all in battle array, with the spire of Vittoria in their rear. There were 70,000 fighting men and 100 pieces of artillery opposed to the advancing allies, who were disposed by Lord Wellington in three corps.

The right was commanded by Sir Rowland Hill; two columns in the centre received orders from the chief himself; and the left was placed under Sir Thomas Graham. Sir Rowland commenced the work of victory; and the first fruits of his exertions were the heights of La Puebla, gained to him by Spaniards well led by Murillo. This advantage was maintained in spite of great efforts on the part of the enemy, but at the cost of the life of the brave Cadogan, when the British soldiers were brought into the fray. The possession of the important village of Subijana de Alava next rewarded the skill and efforts of our general. The hostile troops filled the ravines in the heights above, and a wood on the left, and struggled, with no ordinary fury, to recover the ground they had lost.

The allies in front of the wood suffered greatly, till the head of a column sent by Sir Rowland along the lofty ridge which ran from the Puebla Mountain, came irresistibly upon the flank of the French. Coincident with this skilful movement, were the energetic operations of Cole, Picton, and Dalhousie. At length the four divisions formed quickly on the left of the Zadarra, and advanced against the right and centre of the enemy. Their left gave way under the successful flank attack of Hill, who followed up the retreat with his customary vigour and decision. At last the entire French army was driven back by the allies in one helpless confused mass, flying like a frightened mob, and leaving their cannon, with all the rich, curious, and ill-gotten spoil of the usurper Joseph. Nothing was wanting to the most decisive victory even Wellington had then ever gained, except more prisoners; but they fled so fast. King, marshals, generals, and men, that the allies, who had been sixteen hours under arms, and had marched three leagues since the day dawned, had no chance of overtaking them.

Many, also, could not resist the temptation of stopping to revel in the unprotected treasures of the fugitives which covered the ground—a heterogeneous wreck of hoarded plunder. Some soldiers, and the followers of the army in general, thickened upon the spoil like bees upon the honeycomb of some prostrate hive, and seized it with tumultuous exultation. They hung in clusters on the cars, waggons, and carriages, scrambled for the money scattered from the chests, searched the gilded coaches of the court, and drew forth, with shouts, robes, uniforms, court dresses, stars, jewels, plate, pictures, once the pride of the grandees and hierarchy of Spain. One solitary gun, and one howitzer, were all that were carried away in the headlong scamper of the overthrown army. Even the baton of Marshal Jourdan was left on the field, for which the champion who laid it at the feet of his prince, received that of England in exchange.

Lord Wellington had foreseen this great victory, and kept the secret in his own breast. While near Medina, four days before the battle, Captain Clement Hill observed, in writing to his friends:

> England will, I think, be a little astonished at our rapid march. The whole of our army got over the Ebro yesterday, and continues to advance. What Lord Wellington's plans are, I believe nobody knows but himself. We all feel confident of great success, and you may expect to hear of the French being fairly *turned* out of Spain. We have driven them so far almost without the loss of a man, and they find themselves completely outmanoeuvred. After they destroyed the Castle of Burgos, we did not venture to march in the line by which they retired; but, by rapid marches to our left by a difficult road which they could not have expected us to attempt, we crossed the Ebro before them, and expect to continue moving, and get between them

and their communication with France, which will *bother* them a good deal.

The forces of Reille, which rallied on the 22nd at Salvatierra, soon found the pursuers were approaching; and the next day Captain Clement Hill wrote to Hawkstone:—

> Salvatierra, 23rd June,
> On the road from Vittoria to Pampeluna.
>
> I hope you will receive this in good time to assure you of the safety of the four brothers after the Battle of Vittoria. We are all at this moment together in the same room, and in perfect health. I have not time now to send you an account of all that happened during the action. Never was an army more completely routed and defeated than the French. Rowland's corps were principally engaged during the first part of the action, and have suffered more than any other. The Blues were in the fire, but not engaged. Tom had a good deal to do, which was well done.

The next duty on which Sir Rowland was employed was the blockade of Pampeluna. He received a letter of concise and able directions from Lord Wellington.

> Caseda, June 28. 1813, 8 p.m.
>
> My dear Hill,
>
> I am anxious that some measures should be adopted for the more close and strict blockade of Pampeluna, and I suggest the following for your consideration.
>
> First, that the water which supplies the town by the aqueduct should be cut off. It will not be difficult to effect this object without mischief to the country, by cutting the aqueduct at any place at which there may be a channel through which the water might run.
>
> Secondly, in order to complete the annoyance of this measure, it will be necessary to establish posts upon the river, and fire day and night at any persons who may approach for water. These posts should be covered by a trench; a redoubt should likewise be constructed at the distance of musket shot from each of the bridges; each to hold a sufficient number of men to support the posts on the river, in case the enemy should make a sortie upon them. There should be a gun or two in each of these redoubts,

which we can bring from Vittoria.

Thirdly, there is a wood to the westward of the place, on the same side of the river, and that should be examined, and if possible an abattis should be formed in it to protect the blockade on that side, which should be brought as close as possible.

Fourthly, the remainder might be occupied by pickets at the usual distance communicating well with each other, having support at hand in redoubts armed with artillery.

Fifthly, measures should be taken without loss of time to cut and carry away, or if that cannot be done, to burn the corn between the posts and the place. These measures must be well considered, and must not be allowed to fail.

I beg that all this may be done without loss of time, and the sooner it is done the sooner I shall be able to relieve your troops entirely from this blockade, and give it in charge to the Spaniards.

I don't think we shall be able to do much against Clausel. He has passed Tudela on his march to Saragossa. I propose to try him on the road to Jaca.

   Ever yours most sincerely,

              Wellington.

The four gallant brothers were now constantly meeting each other, and one or other of them was deputed to convey tidings of events to their family. From Orcoyen, two miles from Pampeluna, July 1st, 1813, Mr. Clement Hill wrote:—

We have been four days investing Pampeluna with Rowland's corps, which we expected to have had the siege of had there been one, but I believe it is determined only to blockade the place, and I am not sorry we are relieved from that tiresome duty by other divisions. Tomorrow we push on towards the frontier, and I hope in a few days to write *from France*. We move towards San Estevan: General Graham is also in that direction. Lord Wellington will be near here today, but we imagine will not remain long, and leave the blockade to the Spaniards. The army we so gloriously beat at Vittoria has been in France some days. They ran so fast, having lost every encumbrance, even their last gun, that we made but few prisoners on their retreat.

Lord Wellington, with four divisions, has been some days in chase of a French corps under General Clausel, which was pre-

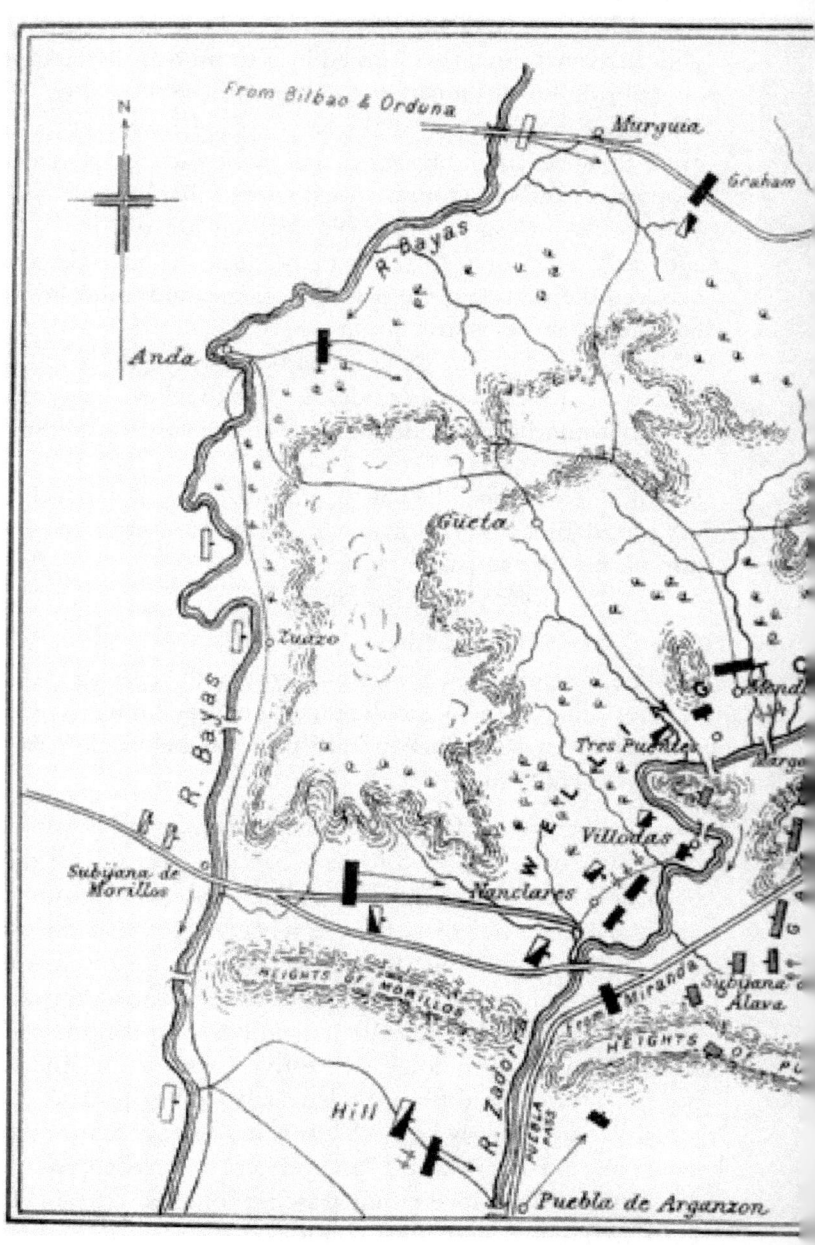

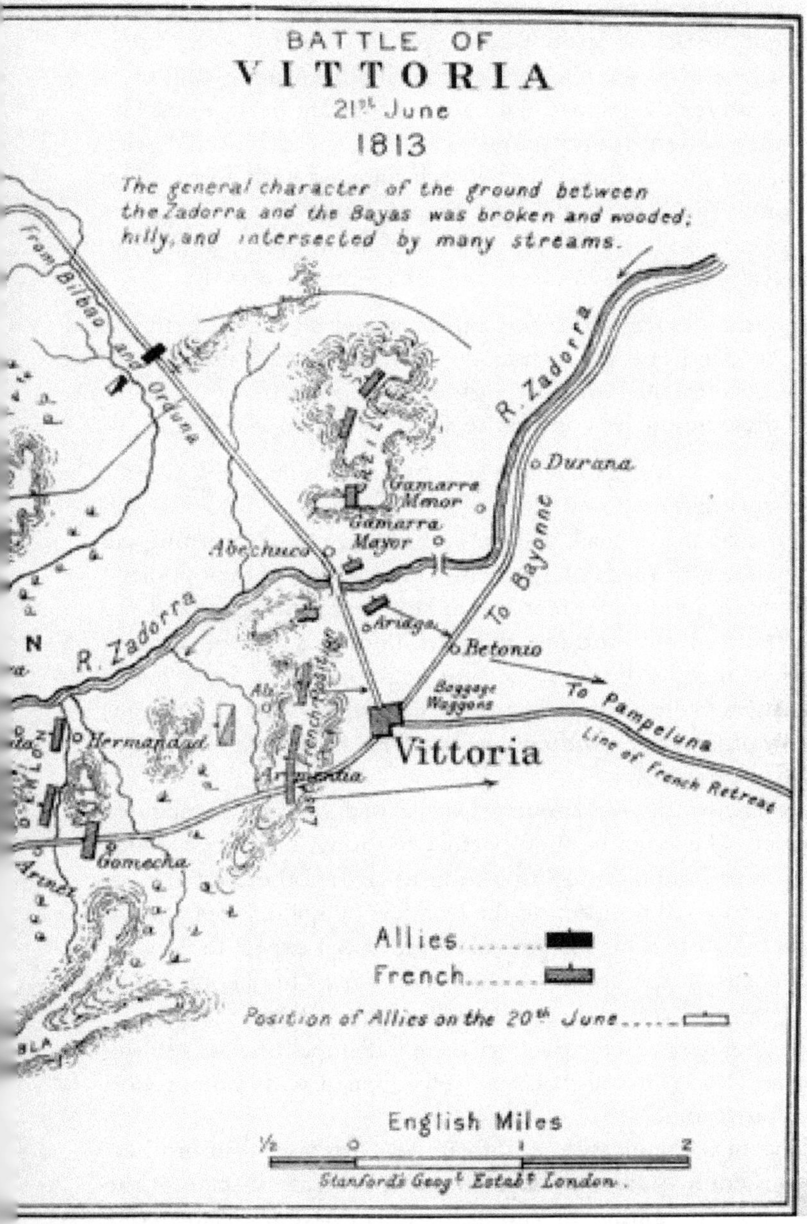

BATTLE OF
VITTORIA
21st June
1813
The general character of the ground between the Zadorra and the Bayas was broken and wooded; hilly, and intersected by many streams.
from Bilbao and Orduna
R. Zadorra
Durana
Gamarre Menor
Gamarra Mayor
Abechuco
To Bayonne
Aríaga
Betonio
Baggage Waggons
To Pampeluna
Line of French Retreat
Vittoria
Hermandad
Gomecha
Allies
French
Position of Allies on the 20th June
English Miles
½
0
1
2
Stanford's Geogl. Estabt. London.

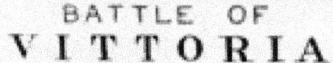

vented joining the main army in time for the Battle of Vittoria. He could not catch them, and retires from the pursuit today. They will probably join Suchet's army. We are in the most delightful part of Spain I have ever seen for summer; but it must be bad in winter. The weather has been quite cold even now, and for the last fortnight almost constant heavy rains. The country is very mountainous, with fine valleys covered with corn and good villages. We get well supplied with every thing: amongst the *luxuries*, excellent French butter. The Blues are at Logrono on the Ebro, and I fancy will not move up at present, as cavalry are not of much use in the country we are in.

From the day on which this letter is dated till the sixth, the corps of Sir Rowland Hill was constantly skirmishing with the enemy, but always drove them from their various positions. Still he found time, amidst these mountain conflicts, to write hastily to Hawkstone.

Lanz, three leagues from France, July 3. 1813.

My dear Sister,

I am told that a mail will be despatched in the morning *via* Santander, for England, I therefore avail myself of the opportunity of sending you a few lines. The public despatches and the letters from my brothers, will have informed you of our late proceedings in this country. Nothing could have been better managed and executed than our recent operations, and there is every prospect of our doing well, provided matters go on tolerably in Germany.

The enemy in this country have halted on the frontiers of France. The country they occupy is strong, but they do not appear to have taken up a position to risk another battle. If we can get a good position on the frontiers of Spain, I imagine we shall be satisfied for the present. Tomorrow I expect to be with my corps on the borders of France. Some of my people are at this moment at Arriège, which village is in France.

The enemy have left a good garrison in Pampeluna: it is a strong fortress, and *it is said* that it is well supplied with ammunition and provisions.

I have now the pleasure to inform you, that your four brothers in this country are well. Tom, as usual, has had his share of the fatigues and fighting; he and his regiment have invariably conducted themselves well. Clement is with me, and he tells me he wrote to Hawkstone two days ago; he is not looking very stout, but is well. Robert, whom I saw about a week ago, is in perfect health. Lord Wellington is much pleased with the conduct and appearance of the Blues. This not being a cavalry country, Robert and his brigade are, I believe, to remain, for the present, in the neighbourhood of Vittoria.

Ever yours, most affectionately,

R. H.

On the sixth of July the French ascended the mountain which forms the key of the entrance into the valley of Bastan, and took possession of it. The next day Sir Rowland first encountered the lofty steeps of the Pyrenees, and was met by Lord Wellington. They had been reconnoitring together the previous evening, and orders had been issued for dislodging the French from their several positions; but on this occasion a dense fog veiled the enemy from their view, and they spent the night amidst the mountain mist, sharing the fatigues and privations of the men. From the pinnacles of this range of mountains Wellington exhibited to Europe the full grandeur of his plans; and Sir Rowland Hill, who gave the first check to the French cavalry in Egypt, had now the honour of first driving the soldiers of Bonaparte from Spain. This he accomplished on the 8th of July, and took possession of the various passes of the Puerta de Maya. Often have these achievements been acknowledged and commended; but I believe they will yet be enhanced in public opinion by the simple unaffected way in which they were announced by his brother, to those who anxiously awaited news from the Pyrenees at home. On the 9th of July he wrote from Elizondo:—

> We have gone through a very interesting part of the campaign, having completely driven that part of the French army to which we were opposed over the Pyrenees. Great part of Rowland's corps being detached from him, his force has been inferior to the enemy's, and they have always had the advantage of strong positions. The troops have been engaged, more or less, with some hard fighting every day, for the last five days; but I do not think, during that time, we have lost more than one hundred men. The last position they took was in the pass of Maya, which is very strong. We were to have attacked them yesterday morning. However, at daylight, we saw the last of them move from the pass. Our troops pursued them, and we had the pleasure of

seeing them driven out of Spam.

We have been marching constantly over mountains rising amidst some of the finest valleys I ever saw, with good towns; and the people in no part of Spain have appeared more happy to see the English. I think we had one of the finest sights yesterday I ever saw, on arriving on a high hill, from which, for the first time, we had an extensive view into France, and saw the French driven into it.

All the officers of merit in Sir Rowland's corps experienced almost equal joy with his own brother, at the honour thus gained by their General; and such regard for him was his just due, for he had looked upon their reputation as his own. There exist two letters written at this time, so illustrative of his consideration towards them, that I cannot refrain from inserting them. The first was written to a distinguished general officer on Lord Wellington's staff, who had made a complaint, the nature of which will be sufficiently apparent in the letter itself.

Elizondo, July 9. 1813.

My dear General,

I have received your letter of yesterday relative to the orders given for the march of the *Caçadores*, and on the subject of the interference which you say you have experienced from my ———— and ————. The order given by yesterday, for the march of the whole of the *Caçadores*, instead of part of that corps as previously ordered by me, was in consequence of information he had received, of which he was before ignorant. His having done so, which he reported to me immediately afterwards, met my entire approbation. Having spoken to ———— on the subject, he begs me to explain to you that the circumstance of his not having communicated the order for the march of the *Caçadores* direct to you, proceeded entirely from a wish to execute the order with as little delay as possible, not knowing that you had returned to your quarters, and a desire to lose as little time as possible in carrying into effect the movement of the *Caçadores*, which, from the report he received, was certainly required.

With regard to the interference of the two staff officers above mentioned, in general, I cannot say that I am aware of its having ever been improperly exercised, or of inconvenience having arisen to the service from it. I certainly by no means wish the staff officers attached to me to be giving orders to their superiors in their own name, but there are times when the superior staff officers who are acquainted with my views and intentions may, with advantage to the service, give orders in my name, and they have my authority to do so, acquainting me, of course, by the earliest opportunities of their having done so, and being responsible to me for the same.

Indeed, I am sure if staff officers were to be only the mere messengers of my orders, they would be of little advantage to me. By the situations they hold, I consider them to be officers of discretion, and, as far as I am at present aware, I think you will find that the same degree of interference which is exercised by them, is exercised by the officers at the heads of their departments in this and most other armies. In saying these staff officers are not to give orders in their own name, I must make an exception. With what concerns the details of their own department they are responsible for those details, and I conceive they may communicate in what manner they please with the officers acting under them. I write this in ignorance of the particular instances of the interference of my ——— and ——— which have led to your complaint. I beg leave to assure you, however, that I shall be ready to attend to any further representations you may have to make on this or any other subject.

I have, &c.
R. Hill.

The next letter was addressed to Lord Wellington himself, in defence of an officer of lower rank, who imagined he had fallen under his Lordship's displeasure.

Elizondo, July 10. 1813.

My dear Lord,

I only yesterday received the enclosed letter from ——— and although it did not appear to me from the conversation which I had the honour to hold with your Lordship on the subject, that you felt any displeasure towards ——— on the occasion alluded to by him, I think it my duty in justice to that officer to state, that the very moment your instructions for the closer investment of Pampeluna were received, he proceeded to make the necessary examination of the ground, and reported to me without loss of time. And if there was any improper delay in carrying your Lordship's wishes into effect, it rested entirely with me, and I feel myself fully satisfied with ———'s desire to exert himself on that occasion, and should be sorry if your Lordship thought otherwise.

I have, &c.

R. Hill.

Marquis of Wellington,
&c. &c. &c.

The perusal of these letters will be the best possible clue to the sentiments entertained towards one, who was looked upon as the friend of his officers and the father of his troops.

On the 11th Lord Wellington, having reason to think that the whole army of the South between Ainhou and Urdax was in Sir Rowland's front, instructed him to examine the passes of the hill from the high road, and to open a way for the artillery along the height to the post which had, on the 7th, been occupied by General William Stewart. His actual situation and proceedings are stated in his reply to his Lordship:—

Elizondo, July 12. 1813.

My dear Lord,

Yesterday I had the honour to receive your letter of the 11th, 6 a.m. The enemy are certainly in force in front of the Maya pass; but it did not appear yesterday that it had been increased since the day your Lordship saw them from the heights.

The peasants say the king arrived at Ainhou yesterday. I have directed all the roads and communications mentioned in your letter to be examined and repaired without loss of time.

I have, &c.

R. Hill.

Marquis of Wellington.

On the very day this letter was penned, Soult took command of the three armies now organised into one body, and called *The Army of Spain*. Lord Wellington two days after was at San Estevan, whence he thus addressed Sir Rowland Hill relative to his movements and designs:—

St. Estevan, July 14. 1813, 7 p.m.

My dear Hill,

I arrived here this afternoon, and have opened your letter to

Murray.

It would appear that the enemy have reinforced their left towards St. Jean de Pied de Port; and I should besides conclude that Clausel, who was in the valley of Anso on the 9th, has by this time passed on to Oleron, and is in communication with St. Jean de Pied de Port.

I ordered General Clinton two days ago to march to Lanz with the 6th division, where I believe he has arrived this day; and I have ordered Sir Lowry Cole with the 4th division, to move from the blockade upon the road towards Roncesvalles. He may march to-morrow, but probably not till next day. Sir Thomas Picton likewise, with the 3rd division, will march to Olagre, on the road to Lanz, and to Ugui as soon as he will be relieved in the blockade by the corps under General O'Donnell, which is at Puerta la Regna, three leagues from Pampeluna, and is ordered to take the blockade.

The truth is, that having two objects in hand, *viz.* the siege of St. Sebastian and the blockade of Pampeluna, we arc not so strong on any point as we ought to be. These movements, when effected, will render us full strong enough for anything.

I shall not complete the movement upon Vera tomorrow, unless I should be able to see well, however necessary it may be to complete the siege of St. Sebastian, that we should have the command there. Considering how ticklish our affairs are to the right, I think you had better not yourself quit Elizondo; and endeavour to have an early communication with Campbell and Byng; and let me hear from you by Echelar. I shall be with the light division in the morning, but think that my quarters will be tomorrow at Sambilla, or perhaps here.

I write to General Clinton at Lanz to desire him to endeavour to find a road to Ugui from Lanz on to Roncesvalles. I know that he can go to the former from Olagre.

If you should find that Byng is attacked, order General Clinton to move upon Roncesvalles by Ugui and Espinal.

Ever yours most faithfully,
Wellington.

For some time after the receipt of this letter, but few movements of importance were made by the enemy, within the observation of Sir Rowland, who remained at Elizondo. A portion of his troops were in the mountains, where, for several days, no sounds reached their ears but the rush of falling waters and the scream of eagles, emblems of the fury and swiftness of the attacks which awaited them. On the 25th, at Lingoen and at Maya, the enemy made tremendous onslaughts, disastrous to the allies and to the French themselves. On these occasions, Napier well observes, the stern valour of some of our troops would have graced Thermopylæ. The advantage gained by the Count D'Erlon cost him 1500 men and a general. The loss inflicted on our ranks at Maya amounted to 1400 soldiers and four guns. Although the overwhelming force of the assailants obliged the defenders of the pass to fall back, Sir Rowland Hill recovered the key of the position in the pass before nightfall. General Byng was attacked with prodigious impetuosity, and though he resisted with all the energy of his distinguished valour, he was unable to stand against the overpowering weight of numbers, and was forced up the mountain. His letter to Sir Rowland Hill, on the following day, gives a most correct account of the affair:—

Lingoen, July 26. 1813.

Dear Sir Rowland,

Enclosed with this I send you a copy of my report to Sir Lowry Cole, of what occurred yesterday. I cannot express the regret I feel in having been obliged to retire from the passes entrusted to my defence. I trust you will have the goodness to inquire into particulars from Sir Lowry Cole, and that inquiry will satisfy you that no blame attaches to myself or the troops I commanded; that for nine hours we maintained our position against five times a superior force to ourselves; that when we did retire, it was done in good order; that we had not a man taken prisoner, except those whose wounds were such that it would have endangered their lives to remove them—all that could be removed were brought away; and, lastly, we occasioned the enemy so severe a loss, that he neither ventured an attack on our second position, nor to molest us in our retreat. These, Sir, I assure you, are facts which any inquiry will corroborate.

Believe me,
   Respectfully and truly yours,
             J. Byng.

I really believe the force of the enemy opposed to me was little short of 20,000 men, and that opposed to Sir Lowry Cole's division 12,000.

J. B.

In his report to Sir Lowry Cole, General Byng said:—

> An officer who was prisoner to us, but who was too dangerously wounded to bring off, stated that the enemy had increased their force at St. Jean de Pied de Port the preceding day by every possible means; that he knew their force was full 22,000 men, and believed it to be more; that Marshal Soult was expected there that morning, but was uncertain if he was in the field; that General Moncey commanded the troops to which I was opposed.

The general ere long made ample reprisals.

The only retrograde movement of Sir Rowland in consequence of these checks in the passes was a withdrawal on the 25th; and we have seen that he recovered the important position before night. All the other movements made were dependent on those of the corps on his right flank, and were *by order*. They were not in any degree forced on him by the enemy in his immediate front. The withdrawal in consequence of the attacks was considered eminently skilful; and Lord Wellington, in his despatch to Lord Bathurst, observed:

> I beg to draw your Lordship's attention to the valuable assistance I received throughout these operations from Lieutenant-General Sir Rowland Hill.

On the 29th Soult, who had been foiled in his attempts against the allied position the two previous days, decided to try the relief of Pampeluna by an attack on Sir Rowland Hill, which was destined to turn the left of the allies. All these efforts were effectually repulsed, and severe losses were inflicted on the enemy. Sir Rowland took advantage of a movement of Count D'Erlon to place his troops on a mountain ridge, about a mile in his rear, where he kept his ground the whole day with a coolness never surpassed. The French, thoroughly discomfited, were compelled to retire in the night, and were followed the next morning. In the pursuit the allies came in contact with two hostile divisions, in the pass of Donna Maria. They were quickly dislodged by the joint efforts of our general and Lord Dalhousie. General Byng, also, now triumphed over his late opponents by capturing a large convoy in the town of Elizondo. On the first of August the pursuers followed the retreating French into the vale of the Bidassoa, and took many prisoners, as well as a great quantity of baggage. The evening of this day found the army posted on the frontier, in nearly the same positions as they occupied on the 28th of July. Thus ended the often recounted conflicts of the Pyrenees.

Sir Rowland Hill immediately assured Lord Wellington, that though not present at the action in the Maya pass, he was:

> Thoroughly satisfied that every exertion was made for the defence of the post, and that it was only abandoned when the superiority of the enemy's force would have rendered it impossible to have maintained it longer.

To General Stewart, who was wounded on the 25th in this pass, he wrote thus:—

> Arizain, August 4.
>
> My dear General,
>
> Having been much occupied during the last two days, must plead my excuse for not having written to you sooner, to thank you for your gallant exertions and zeal during our late operations, and to express my regret at being deprived of your services. I am, however, glad to find that your wounds are not of a dangerous nature, and request you will not again think of taking the field until you are perfectly recovered.
>
> I am, &c
>
> R. Hill.
>
> Lieutenant-General Stewart.

He also assured General Byng of his entire satisfaction, and that he should take the first opportunity of speaking to Lord Wellington of his gallantry in the mountains, and of his valuable services in the Battle of Vittoria. Nor did he forget his *aides-de-camp,* Captains Egerton and Churchill, on both of whom he passed, in recommending them for promotion, the most distinguished encomiums. The former he described as "a very active and zealous officer of fifteen years' standing in the army—nine of them as captain," by whose promotion he should be particularly obliged. Thus he encouraged and endeavoured to reward all his gallant friends; but they were never admitted into that favoured circle unless the privilege was well deserved.

The British of all grades, as if inspired with the romance as well as peril of their wild position on the mountains, performed marvels of strength and daring in these contests. The Rev. Charles Frith, chaplain of the brigade composed of the 28th, 34th, and 39th Regiments, during the conflict of Maya, actually carried three or four wounded officers down the rugged steeps into the village, a distance of a mile and a half, at separate times, and gently deposited his gallant burdens where they were secure. The loss of the enemy was probably 15,000 men.

In the beginning of August, Lord Wellington deemed it expedient that Sir Rowland Hill should be on the extreme right of the army. He accordingly encamped near Roncesvalles; and towards the middle of the month, found leisure to tell his friends at home what difficulties he had encountered in the Pyrenees.

Camp near Roncesvalles,
August 17. 1813

My dear Sister,.

Before this time, I imagine, the Prince of Orange will have reached England with the accounts of Soult's attempt to relieve Pampeluna, the action near that place, and the retreat of Soult again to the frontiers of France. During the whole of these operations you will observe that *we* had a good deal of fag and fighting; and although the small force I had with me was not, at all times, able to withstand the overwhelming numbers that were brought against us, yet I am sure we contributed very essentially to the glorious result of the business.

The fact is. Lord Wellington found it necessary to desire me to send from my corps to the main army, the divisions of Morillo and the brigades of Generals Campbell and Byng, amounting to about 7000 men, leaving me with not more than 5000 to occupy a very extensive line of country, which was liable to be attacked in any point by a superior force. In this situation the whole army of the centre, commanded by the Count D'Erlon, consisting of at least 17,000 men, attacked one of my posts, while Soult, with his main army, moved by this road towards Pampeluna. The public despatches will have given you details of all these events; and I shall merely add that, during the whole of the above-mentioned operations, the entire corps of the Count D'Erlon was employed against my 5000 men, which circumstance made a considerable diversion in favour of the battle near Pampeluna.

We have again taken up a position on the frontiers of France, and I am on the right, having the whole of my corps with me.

The country I have to defend is strong, but the position is very extensive. Soult must have lost a very considerable number of men during the last three weeks. I think it cannot be less than 15,000. One would imagine he cannot be in a state to act offensively, but he is near his resources, and it is possible he may make another effort to relieve Pampeluna and St. Sebastian. The former, I am told, may hold out till the beginning of October; the latter may be expected to fall sooner. The French officers talk very much of a general peace, which they seem very anxiously to wish for.

Clement is quite well. Robert and Thomas, I believe, are also well. I have to thank you for your letters of the 7th of July, and remain

    Yours very affectionately,

             R H.

The terms "fag and fighting," were evidently suggested by his gallant friend Sir Thomas Graham, who had written to him a few days before from the vicinity of San Sebastian.

        Ozarzun, August 12. 1813.

My dear Hill,

I profit by Dr. Ferguson's passing here in his way to the second division to send you two lines. You have had a great deal of fag and fighting of late, which I was glad to hear you had escaped safe from. We are waiting for ordnance ships to bring ammunition and more guns, to enable us to renew the attack against St. Sebastian, which we tried to storm unsuccessfully on the 25th *ult*. But the defences were untouched, and the enemy made too good use of them against our column of attack, confined to a very narrow front between the river and the foot of the left line wall, where it was left dry by the falling of the tide. *Adieu*.

I hope you received the box sent by Lieutenant-Col. Colburn of the 52nd safe, with the coffee essence from Lord Mulgrave, in the top of which I sent an old map of yours which has been travelling about with me for years, in order to be returned.

    Ever faithfully yours,

            Tho. Graham.

Remember me to Currie. I have been suffering again a good deal from my eye and stomach.

Sir Noel Hill was engaged in the siege of San Sebastian, and was by no means delighted with his post, he said:

We are still detained here by this abominable place; but as another battering train is arrived from England, the siege will now be carried on with *some* prospect of success.

When the town did fall at last, he was reported for distinguished services.

Soult, after his repulse, had resumed his former position, and the work of fortifying it was carried on with much assiduity. During September and October Sir Rowland occupied the camp near Roncesvalles, and kept up a constant observation of the proceedings of the hostile army. Every clear day he was actively employed with a glass in endeavouring to make out their plans and intentions; nor was he less attentive to his own defences. On October the 8th, Lord Wellington attacked the enemy's right, "with the view of obliging them to go a little farther back on that side." Pampeluna still held out; but Sir Rowland felt persuaded that it could not stand much longer. O'Donnell, Conde de l'Abispal, who had been stationed near that place, and cooperated with him during the battles of the Pyrenees, was gone; but his Andalusians and Don Carlos D'España had blockaded the place till the middle of September;—still it was not till October that the surrender was made, under pressure of intolerable disease and misery. The Conde was always looking out for some opportunity of distinction. On one occasion in the Pyrenees, when Sir Rowland had obtained an advantage, O'Donnell became exceedingly angry at not having been called out into a more effective position, and considered himself deprived of the glory he should certainly have acquired.

"O'Donnell is in such a rage," said Sir Rowland quietly to Lord Wellington.

"Never mind, I'll find plenty for him to do another day," was his Lordship's reply. The day came; he was put forward with his troops in a ravine; the French enfiladed them; O'Donnell did not flinch, but was angry no more.

"From that day," Lord Hill used to say, "I never saw him nor heard from him."

About the middle of October, it was suggested from home that Sir Rowland should go and take the command of the armies of Catalonia. With regard to this proposition he remarked, "Lord Wellington expressed a wish to the contrary; consequently I remain here, which

I am glad of." At the end of the month he thus described his situation to Sir George Murray:—

Roncesvalles, Oct. 29. 10 a.m.

My dear General,

We have had a great fall of snow yesterday and this day, and from what I have heard this morning, I fear it will be impossible to keep our troops on the height, at least while the snow continues to fall, for it drifts to such a degree as to endanger their being buried. Indeed I understand that three men are missing this morning. I send this in the hope of its being able to reach you, which I think by no means certain. I have desired General Pringle to report to you also the state of the country in his neighbourhood. I expect General Byng down from the mountains; I shall then be able to judge what is best to be done.

I have, &c.

R. Hill.

Sir Geo. Murray,
to be read by Gen. Pringle.

To a friend he also wrote:

Dreadful weather for the troops on the mountains; snow, rain, and such tremendous winds that no tents can be used.

Lord Wellington proposed shortly after this time to confer with him, and desired both Marshal Beresford and Sir George Murray to inform him of his intention, and to appoint the spot where they should meet. His answer to the latter shows the difficulties he had to contend with:—

Roncesvalles, Nov. 5. 1813. (Noon.)

My dear General,

I have received your letter of yesterday in duplicate. The road from hence to Alduides is still bad, but I believe there is no doubt as to its practicability for the troops and baggage and commissariat. Our movements will therefore commence tomorrow as directed. I have no doubt we shall be collected in the valley of Maya on the day following. I go myself to Elizondo tomorrow, and will meet Lord Wellington at noon on the 7th, at the place pointed out, 'Colonel Browne's quarters in front of Urdax.' In a letter I wrote to you a few days ago, I mentioned that we had buried three of Captain Maxwell's guns on the mountains, owing to the impossibility of withdrawing them on account of the snow. I am happy to say that we have, by the great exertions of the artillery and troops, been able to extricate them.

I have, &c.,

R, Hill.

Sir George Murray.

Lord Wellington was now preparing for the Battle of the Nivelle, where Sir Rowland established new claims upon the gratitude of his country.

CHAPTER 10

Abdication of Bonaparte

The French spared no pains in fortifying their position. In front of St. Jean de Luz their right rested on the sea, and their line covered the town, stretching from the shore twelve miles inland, crossing the Nivelle, and ending behind the village of Ainhoue. The approach to their left was protected by works on a mountain fronting that village, and their centre was on the left of the river, which takes a sinuous course northwards. The bridges above and below Ascain were strongly defended, as was the space enclosed by the curve of the river. On a range of elevated ground behind Sarre was the grand defence of the centre, strengthened by two redoubts, and by a mountain called La Petite la Rhune, which had been retrenched.

Nature and art combined to afford security to the enemy, but Lord Wellington had decided, in defiance of both, to force their centre and turn their right. Before one o'clock on the morning of the 10th of November, the allies descended from the mountains by moonlight. Sir Rowland Hill commanded the right wing, which emerged from the rocky passes, and arrived within reach of the French about seven o'clock. While victory was being achieved by our other gallant officers, Sir Rowland moved against the heights of Ainhoue, and cleared the nearest redoubt. He afterwards led two divisions on Espelette, forced the enemy from the works in front of Ainhoue, and obliged them to retreat.

The combined successes of the allies at length established them in the rear of the enemy's right, and ere sunset terminated the dread fight of the Nivelle. Soult was completely manoeuvred out of the designs of his long labours. Though his numbers were seventy thousand, and he had every advantage that mountains, whose intricacies were well known to him, could afford, fifty guns and fifteen hundred prisoners were taken from him as the spoils of the day.

Four days after the Battle of the Nivelle, Sir Rowland was at St. Pé. He sent a hurried letter home, which he wrote while Lord Worcester and Lord Fitzroy Somerset were in the room.

> I do not see any prospect of our having another fight. The glorious news from the North, I trust, will ere long settle Napoleon. The people in France receive us well. I never met with so much attention. The mayor of Ustaritz prepared an excellent dinner for me yesterday; and the people run out of their houses to give our people wine.

On the 27th of November, he observed, in writing to his brother,—

> Our future operations, I imagine, will depend a good deal upon what is going on in other quarters. We are perfectly prepared to act on the offensive; and if the allies on the Rhine continue to do so, we shall not be idle. On the other hand, if Bonaparte is not kept well occupied either by internal commotions, or by our northern friends, perhaps it may be well for us to maintain a safe and threatening position. This latter situation we have at present. At the same time, we are very much cramped; and although we may be able to get our men under cover, the total want of forage for the animals is a serious inconvenience. If you look at the map you will see our present position. My right is on the mountains to the right of this place; my left at Cambo. Marshal Beresford is at Ustaritz and down the Nive to within about a league of Bayonne, from which point, to the sea. Sir John Hope has his corps. The rains which fell about a fortnight ago rendered the River Nive a formidable barrier: the last week's fine weather has, however, made the river fordable in many parts, in consequence of which both parties are kept on the alert. The enemy, notwithstanding, has much more to fear than we have. The inhabitants, certainly, are not unfriendly to us; and many are daily returning to their homes, finding they are well treated by the British and Portuguese. The main body of our cavalry is kept in the rear at present.

About the period of this letter, a correspondence passed between Lord Wellington and Sir Rowland Hill relative to the passage of the Nive, and considerable discretionary power was placed by his Lordship in his hands. The second week in December, Marshal Beresford apprised him that it was considered probable an attack would be made upon him.

Arouritz, 11th Dec. 1813, 7 a. m.

My dear Hill,

I have here, on my way to the outposts, received a letter from Lord Wellington. He says the enemy made no progress yesterday beyond driving in the outposts and pickets, and he does not think he will renew the attack. The prisoners in general say that only one division (of Paris) retired towards St. Jean de Pied de Port; one prisoner said two divisions. It appears all the rest of this army came through Bayonne for the attack yesterday. Lord W. says we must not be surprised if he should turn his attack against you, in which case the 6th division, now at Ustaritz, will pass over to your support; and, at all events, if you want it send for it, and Sir W. Clinton has directions to conform to your wishes. Lord W. says the enemy yesterday brought from your side three, some say four, divisions; and it is not quite certain if one division was not left in their entrenched camp on your side.

Yours most sincerely,

W. C. Beresford.

Lt.-General Sir Rowland Hill.

The expected attack was made on the 13th; and the same day, "at noon," Lord Wellington had the satisfaction of writing to Sir John Hope, "I have the pleasure to inform you that Hill has beat them completely ;" and also to Sir J. Kennedy, "Sir R. Hill has given the enemy a terrible beating." To General Castanos he wrote:

> *Vous serez bien-aise de savoir que le Général Hill battit l'ennemi terriblement avanthier. Il y a long temps que je n'ai pas vu tant de morts sur le champ de bataille. J'ai ma droite sur l'Adour, de laquelle la communication est coupée pour l'ennemi.*

This great service was thus performed by Sir Rowland. The enemy, who had failed in all their attempts with their whole force upon Lord Wellington's left, withdrew to their entrenchments on the night of December 12th, and passed a large body of troops through the town of Bayonne. With these, on the morning of the 13th, they made a desperate attack on Sir Rowland Hill. This, as has appeared, was not unexpected; and Lord Wellington had placed at his disposal not only the sixth division, but the fourth division, and two brigades of the third. Soult's objects were to gain the position of St. Pierre, to make himself master of the road to St. Jean Pied de Port, and to break through the allies. For these purposes he put forth his whole strength, and was completely vanquished. Even before the sixth division arrived.

Sir Rowland had repulsed him with prodigious loss; and although he skilfully availed himself of a high ground in retreating, he could not stand against the famous charge of General Byng, and was entirely defeated. It was a battle fought and won by the corps of Sir Rowland Hill alone and unaided. At the instant of victory Lord Wellington came up, and in the ecstasy of the moment of triumph caught him by the hand and said, "Hill, the day is your own." Such were his successes at the battle of the Nive. His gallant brother. Major Clement Hill, was again sent to England with the news. It was incorrectly reported that he had returned to Passages from stress of weather, which is alluded to in Sir Rowland's next letter.

Vieux Mauguerre, Dec. 31. 1813, 10 p. m.

My dear Clement,

By this time I hope you have reached London in safety. You must have had tremendous weather about the 20th. It was a great satisfaction to us to hear of your getting back to Passages. Soult has not shown any disposition to disturb us in this quarter; he has moved about six divisions out of the town of Bayonne, placing two opposite to Urt, the others further up the Adour, and on this side towards St. Palais. With respect to our future operations, nothing, as far as I know, is yet determined upon, though we are looking for the best communications for our pontoons towards the Adour. I enclose you a letter from Egerton, who no doubt sends you all the family anecdotes and events. Should it appear that the year 1814 is likely to turn out another year of campaigning in this country for us, I think you will do well to bring out some canteen dishes, &c., a complete set of saddlery for two or three horses, with cloths, rollers, &c., and any thing else you know will be acceptable.

Jan. 1. 5 p.m.

It was my intention to have finished this letter this morning, but I have been prevented in consequence of a little expedition on my part to the island opposite to Urt, with the view of preventing the enemy from constructing works upon it.

Lord Wellington at the beginning of the new year disposed his forces so as to be in readiness on any emergency; and Sir Rowland Hill was busily engaged in adopting measures to prevent the enemy's boats from navigating the Adour. Finding musketry ineffectual, he proposed to try rockets, which he thought would, at least, confuse the boatmen; but Lord Wellington considered that if the French found them almost harmless, they would after the first alarm cease to regard them. At length he sent for some heavy guns. In a note to General Fane respecting them, he mentioned the detriment to the service which arose out of the intimacy of the French and his own soldiers:

> You did perfectly right in receiving the flag of truce addressed to me. The intercourse, however, going on between our soldiers and the French has increased to such an extent, that I have been under the necessity of giving out another order upon the subject.

The fact was, the officers had become quite intimate with each other, and the men carried on a regular traffic upon a rivulet running between the two armies. A great stone was placed in the stream, and on it a canteen was put containing money. After a time this was found filled with brandy. One evening the French sentry failed to supply the brandy to a man named Patten, who was, as he supposed, tricked out of his liquor. He dashed across the stream in the morning, seized the French sentry, stripped him, and carried his accoutrements in triumph to the picket house. A flag of truce soon afterwards appeared, and the French captain who came with it begged hard for the return of the things taken from the sentry, on the ground that if they were retained, his own commission and the sentry's life would be undoubtedly forfeited. "I have got them in pawn," said Patten, "for a canteen of brandy;" but he gave them up, and refused to accept money offered him by the officer. Still, poor Patten was sentenced to receive 300 lashes. Sir Rowland had the delinquent led out with great parade, as if to undergo this severe punishment, and addressed a remonstrance to all the regiments on the indiscretion and probable consequences of such conduct. But, at length, he unexpectedly enumerated many acts of gallantry performed by the prisoner, and, in the midst of faces beaming with admiration, remitted the sentence.

The enemy's boats still persisted in navigating the Adour. Sir George

Murray was consequently directed by Lord Wellington to desire Sir Rowland to fire red-hot shot against them, both from the heavy guns and the four-pounders. Sir George likewise said:

> It might be expedient to fire some of these shot across the river, in situations where the enemy may be made aware of our using them, as their knowledge of our doing so may be an additional means of deterring their boatmen from the service. Lieutenant-Colonel Dickenson will be directed to send you some rockets, that you may make use of them whenever circumstances appear favourable.

These precautions enabled Sir Rowland on the 21st to report—

> I do not believe that any boats have passed Urt since the night of the 16th, when, as Colonel Jackson will have informed you, three went down the Adour. General Fane has fitted out two boats, and has selected for each ten or twelve men from General Barnes's brigade, and given charge of each of them to Lieutenant Law, of the 71st, who was formerly in the navy. He is an active intelligent officer; and I am inclined to think that if any of the enemy's boats attempt to pass, he is very likely to get hold of them. The Portuguese officer on picket duty yesterday reports, that in the evening about 3000 men passed over the bridge of Bayonne from the town to the right bank of the river.

All the reports at this time were of an exciting nature. On the 25th, 5 p. m.. General Fane reported—

> It seems the opinion of the people about here that something is intended against our posts tomorrow. It is said that a number of conscripts have joined, and that biscuit and spirits were today given to the troops."

On the 26th, General Byng reported—

> Two regiments marched into Bayonne between twelve and one last night. In the night a large boat made an attempt to get up the river, which our picket was able to prevent, and she now lies opposite. Two smaller boats did pass.

On hearing this. Sir Rowland took instant measures, and no more boats appeared; but the French retaliated by attacking his pickets near Urt. The object of Soult seemed to be to throw the allies on the defensive. He also sounded Morillo on the possibility of gaining over the Spaniards. Morillo sent Sir Rowland some curious documents on this subject, including a letter from General Paris stating that he had orders not to attack the Spanish troops. These papers were immediately forwarded to headquarters.

In February the weather was such as to enable Lord Wellington to commence a series of manoeuvres, to draw Soult from his line of defence on the Adour, and important instructions, too technical for insertion here, were sent to Sir Rowland Hill. It was in consequence of these that he was enabled to tell his friends that he was again in motion.

Marshal Beresford's House, Ustaritz,
Feb. 12. 1814.

My dear Sister

I have the satisfaction to inform you that we are again in motion, with every fair prospect of success. The weather has improved, and the state of our commissariat is such that I hope we have nothing to fear with regard to our supplies. It appears that my troops are to commence the operations, for which purpose we are this day collecting in the neighbourhood of Hasparren, with the view of moving towards Pau. In addition to my troops I shall have Sir Thomas Picton's division with me. The enemy have some force in my front, but I do not expect any serious resistance. I trust you will receive good accounts of our proceedings.

I have received your letter of the 21st of last month, and the Shrewsbury papers up to that period. I perfectly agree with you that the Salopians not only deserve my grateful thanks for the manner in which they are manifesting their regard towards me, but I feel I never can use expressions sufficiently strong to convey my sense of their kindness on the occasion.

With respect to the handsome present of beef, I am sorry to say it has not yet reached Passages. Immediately on my receiving your letter on the subject, I sent Robert Sharp to inquire about it. He is returned without it. I do, however, hope the next packet will bring this present.

It is said the French princes at St. Jean de Luz have been waited upon in a private manner by many respectable people, and have received assurances of support *when the moment shall arrive*. This is indeed a most interesting time, and a few weeks will in all likelihood produce great events. God grant they may be for the best.   Yours most affectionately.

Sir Rowland marched with the right of the army on the 14th. He soon came upon the French pickets on the Joyeuse River, and drove them in. He then advanced against Harispe, whom he obliged to retreat, with some loss, towards St. Martin. The next day he pursued the enemy in the direction of Garis, where Harispe had been joined by Paris, and by troops from the centre. Towards sunset, after a fatiguing march, the soldiers of his division were excited by the sounds of skirmishing, which made "the men as fresh as when they started." They proceeded from the Spaniards under Morillo, who were assailing the outposts of a strong French position on a height. It was nearly dusk when Sir Rowland arrived at the foot of the hill, but he gave instant orders for an attack. Sir William Stewart led the gallant second division up the steep, dislodged the enemy, and dispersed them in all directions, though they fought most valiantly.

In the night they passed over the river at St. Palais, destroying the bridges. These, however, were speedily repaired, so that Sir Rowland crossed on the 16th. The day following, the French were driven across the Gave de Mauleon, and meant to destroy the bridge at Arriverete, but were prevented. In the night the fugitives retired across the Gave d'Oleron, and proceeded to Sauveterre, where they were joined by other troops. On the 18th the allies were established on the Gave d'Oleron, where Sir Rowland had to await the arrival of the pontoon train before he could cross the river. These operations with the right of the army entirely concealed from Soult the design of Lord Wellington to cross the Adour below Bayonne with his left.

While Sir Rowland was waiting for the pontoons, the French took possession of a building called the "Red House." Lord Wellington refers to it in the following letter:—

Garis, 6 a.m. Feb. 19. 1814.

My dear Hill,
Churchill has just left me. If you can retake the Red House in the manner you took it yesterday morning, it is desirable to have it; but I should think the enemy would have covered themselves during the night from the effect of the fire of your artillery, and it will not be very easy then to dislodge them, or to prevent them from working at the *tête de pont*, as it is most

probable that our guns in the wood would be under the fire of theirs from the right bank of the river.

If you cannot take the Red House, you had better hold the village of Arriverete, as a *tête de pont*; the village on the right of the same river where the Barca was, in the same manner, in order to secure the passages, and St. Gloire, Barrante, &c. as advanced posts from them,

Your position, in this case, would be on the heights on the left of the Gave de Mauleon, and it is a very good one.

Morillo would occupy the upper fords and bridges in the same manner.

I think you had better leave the third division where they are; those at St. Palais cover you from any movement by Mauleon, and the others your left; however, you will move them if you think proper.

I mention all this in case the enemy should undertake any enterprise against you, which is not very probable.

Ever yours most sincerely,

Wellington.

Lieut.-General Sir Rowland Hill, K.B.

In the position above mentioned, concealing your troops, and not making any movement of large bodies in sight of the enemy, you will be able to reconnoitre all the passages of the river within your reach.

In the midst of these engagements Sir Rowland wrote briefly to his sister:

St. Palais, Feb. 20. 1814.

My dear Sister,

I feel thankful for the further success which has attended my troops in our operations during the last week.

Lord Wellington was witness on these occasions to our proceedings, and, I have no doubt, was perfectly satisfied with the conduct of all. This is the first day that I have sat down in a house for the last week, and I have now not many minutes to write, but I cannot resist sending you a line to tell you that I am well. I do not see any immediate prospect of my being engaged with the enemy; indeed we are in hourly expectation of hearing of peace, as it appears that the Congress has been sitting for some days, and it also appeal's that the ministers assembled at it are on good terms. This is a fine country, and the inhabitants extremely civil. Kind remembrance to Sir John and all at home. Yours very affectionately.

On the 24th the Gave d'Oleron was crossed at Villeneuve, and the enemy evacuated Sauveterre, retiring upon Orthez. They were speedily followed, and the Gave de Pau was passed on the evening of the 26th without opposition, though the whole French army was in front of Orthez. On the same day Sir Rowland was thus instructed:—

Sauveterre, 26th Feb. 1814.

My dear Sir Rowland,

I conclude the detachment of pontoons ordered to join you will have arrived tonight. If so, Lord Wellington wishes you to endeavour to establish a bridge near Orthez, as early as you can in the morning. I beg you will send a report to the left in the morning of the appearance of things in your front. I expect we shall hear from you that the enemy have retreated.

Believe me faithfully yours,

G. Murray, Q. M. G.

If we get into Orthez every exertion should be made to repair the bridge, that our pontoons may become again disposable for other service, for which they will be immediately wanted.

G. M.

The troops of Sir Rowland Hill occupied the heights opposite Orthez and the road leading to Sauveterre. On the 27th, after the sixth and light divisions had crossed the river, they found the French in strength, and determined to oppose the passage of Sir Rowland. Lord Wellington himself reconnoitred the enemy's disposition for battle. He took his survey from a spot once the site of a Roman encampment; and without the slightest disturbance of the calm intelligence of his clear and piercing eye, beheld the two divisions which had crossed coming up from the river. They were impeded by the rocks, and the point of junction with the third division, to which they tended, was in dangerous proximity to the French.

When that point was reached, he connected his wings, formed a central reserve, and deliberately arranged his plans. Though even Picton was agitated, Wellington was apparently unmoved. Finding, however, that unexpected difficulties arose, and that at one moment success seemed to declare in favour of the enemy, he suddenly changed his method of attack. He successfully availed himself of a narrow

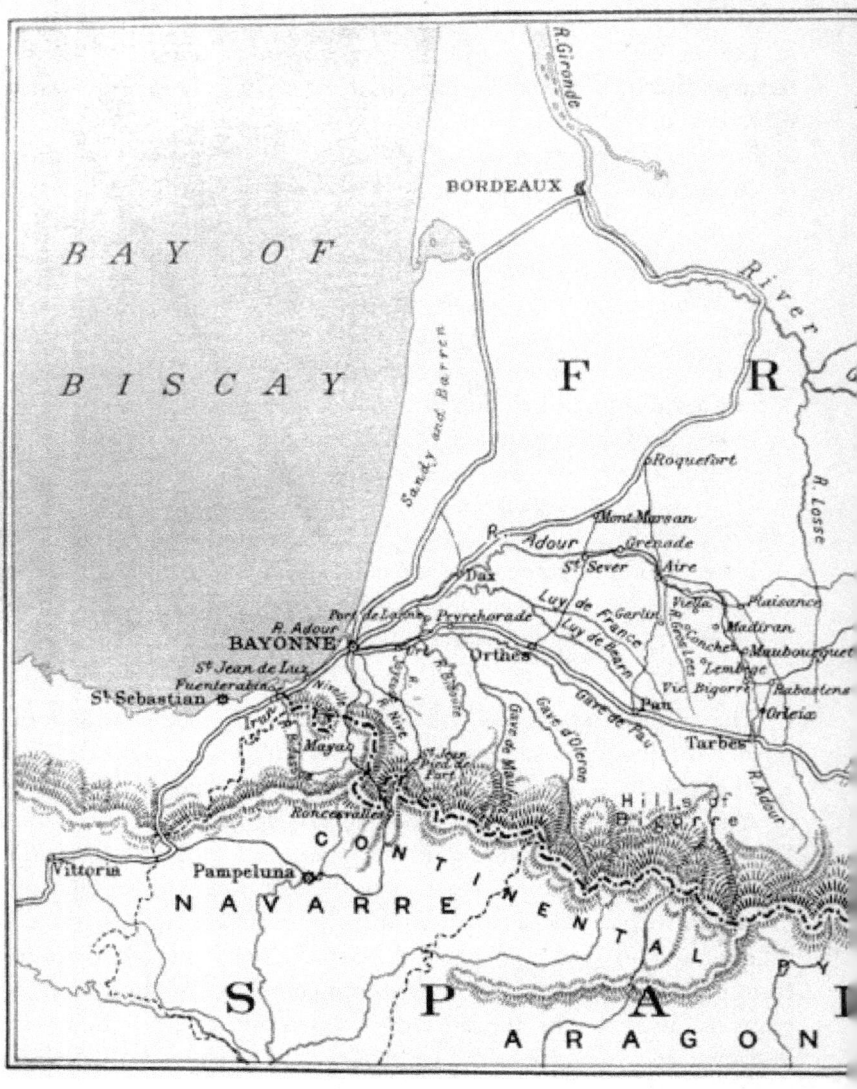

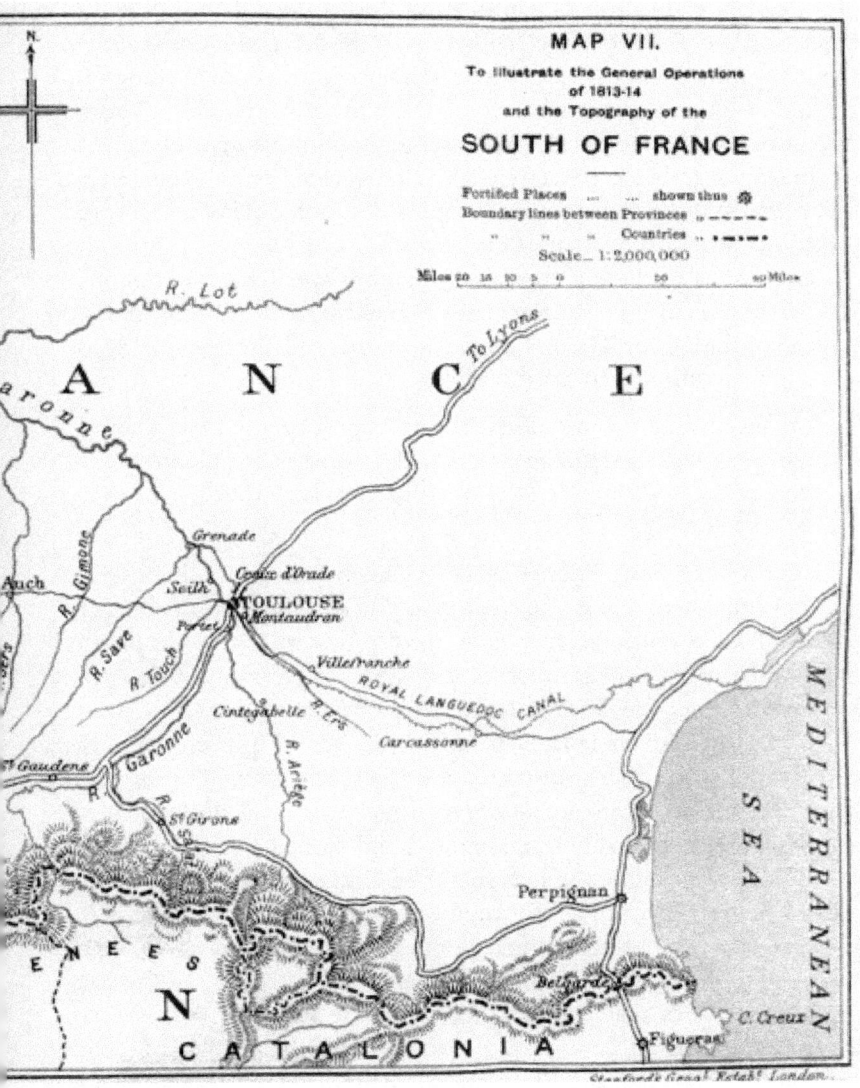

pass behind the village of St. Boes, hitherto deemed impracticable, got through his infantry, cavalry, and artillery, spread his front on the other side, and secured a victory. Two thirds only of the army had been engaged. Sir Rowland, with twelve thousand men, was before the bridge of Orthez, and at the critical instant of Lord Wellington's change of plan was ordered to force the passage of the Gave. This he effected above Orthez, and made a subsequent movement of a nature so threatening, that it determined the retreat of Soult. "This retreat, first made in order, became," said Lord Wellington, "at last a flight, and the troops were in the utmost confusion."

The results of these victorious operations were the investment of Bayonne, St. Jean Pied de Port, and Navarrens, and the long-desired passage of the Adour, The names of Beresford, Hill, Hope, and Cotton were thus mentioned in Lord Wellington's despatch:—

> It is impossible for me sufficiently to express my sense of their merits, or of the degree in which the country is indebted to their zeal and abilities for the situation in which the army now finds itself.

After a very short interval. Lord Wellington had to acknowledge another important service on the part of Sir Rowland Hill. A corps of the enemy was collected near Aire, "probably with a view to protect the evacuation of a magazine they had at that place." In this direction he advanced on the 2nd of March. The French occupied a strong ridge of hills, with their right flank on the Adour, thus covering the road to the town. It was about two o'clock when Sir Rowland approached, and gave immediate orders for an attack. Sir William Stewart, with the second division, assaulted and gained possession of the enemy's extreme right, while General La Costa moved up the heights against their centre; but his Portuguese troops were repulsed. Sir William Stewart promptly repaired the ill effects of this disaster, by sending a strong force under General Barnes to the assistance of the Portuguese, and they made such a charge on the French as threw them into utter confusion.

Still they rallied again. But General Byng came up with a brigade, and Harispe and Villette, the French generals, were completely driven off, the former towards the River Luz, the latter through Aire into the space formed by two branches of the stream. They suffered a great loss in killed and wounded, besides more than 100 prisoners. The troops that fled in the direction of Pau threw away their arms. It was in all respects a signal victory; "affording," to use the words of Lord Wellington, "another instance of the conduct and gallantry of the troops under" Sir Rowland's command.

In the midst of these successes he was yet a mourner. Coincident with this victory was the announcement from home of the death of his eldest brother, Colonel Hill, beloved by his relatives, the favourite of all the county to which he belonged, courteous, mild, benevolent, dignified, and the father of a young and promising family. It was from Aire, the scene of his victory, and on the very day when he was obliged to write his official despatch, that he thus addressed his sister on this painful topic:—

Aire, 3rd March, 1814.

My dear Sister,

No event ever occurred to me that shocked me so much as the receipt of your second letter, on the subject of the decease of our dear brother. I do not know which of us has most reason to regret the sad event. He was beloved by all of us. His amiable wife is greatly to be pitied. Her kindness to our family can never be forgotten, and it will be my most anxious wish, as well as my duty, to do all in my power towards her. If I had ever so much time I could not express my real feelings on this melancholy occasion, but under present circumstances I am sure you will not expect me to say much. I am only this moment come into this town, and I understand Lord Wellington will send his despatches off early tomorrow morning.

You will see that in the midst of my affliction, I have had to attend to important military matters. Scarcely a day has passed without our being in the presence and in contact with the enemy: all our operations have been attended with success, and the enemy are now retreating towards Toulouse. Surely Bonaparte cannot hold out much longer. If I have time, I will, in the course of the day, write to you again, but in case I should not, I send this off. I must, however, beg to be kindly remembered to Sir John and Mrs. Hill, and do most sincerely condole with all at home on the late afflicting event which has taken place at Hawkstone.

Yours, my dear Sister, most affectionately.

Two mails missing!

Major Clement Hill, who had arrived at Hawkstone, reported to Sir

Rowland the resignation with which his family submitted to their loss. To this he adverted in a letter addressed to one of the mourners:—

> Garlin, four leagues from Pau, March 13. 1814.
> I have received Clement's letter of the 12th February, by which I am truly happy to hear so good an account of all my friends at Hawkstone, after the melancholy event which has taken place there. Indeed, the more I think of it, the more I lament it. We all, however, must expect death, and ought to keep prepared for it.
> I imagine Major Fremantle has reached London by this time with accounts of our operations up to the 2nd of this month, on which day you will see I had a little affair of my own, and which, owing to the bad conduct of some Portuguese, was the most critical I had ever to do with. The gallant conduct, however, of a few British soon put matters to rights, and the result was most fortunate for us
> Soult's army is about four or five leagues from hence, and our main force is halting while Marshal Beresford is marching with two divisions to Bourdeaux, where it is supposed he will be well received by the people. It is a cruel situation for the people. I am sure they would be glad to get rid of Bonaparte, and wish well to Louis, but are given to understand that the allies are treating for peace with Bonaparte; consequently it would be madness in them, and cruel in us to expect them to hoist the white cockade at this moment.

On the 18th, by break of day, the whole army was in motion, and Sir Rowland's corps formed the right, marching from Garlin upon Conchez. Sir Rowland, after a severe skirmish, drove back the French outposts upon Lambège; then came the combat of Vic Bigorre, and on the 20th the Battle of Tarbes. To the last-named place the enemy retired in the night, and in the morning were seen by the allies with the advanced posts of their left in the town, and their right upon the heights, near a neighbouring windmill. Their centre and left were retired; the latter in an elevated situation. On Sir Rowland devolved the attack on Tarbes, which was made by the high road from Vic Bigorre. He moved through the town, and the French fled in all directions with considerable loss. Sir Henry Clinton drove them through the village of Dours, and Baron Alten from the heights above Orleix. In the evening Soult retired by St. Gaudens on Toulouse, the hills blazing with fires for guidance.

On the 21st Sir Rowland's directions were:

> Lord Wellington desires that you will be so good as to put the troops under your immediate orders in motion to-morrow morning, and advance by the great road as far as Monrejau, rendering a part of your cavalry more forward, and pushing your *patroles* as far as you can upon the Toulouse road by St. Gaudens. It is desirable to keep up the appearance of the enemy being followed by the army in that direction.

On the 22nd the instructions were:

> The left and centre of the army are to be thrown in the direction of the great road which leads from Auch to Toulouse, pointing in that direction either upon l'Isle en Jourdain or upon Gimont. We shall therefore be in a sort of *échellon*, of which the left will be towards one or other of the places above named (l'Isle en Jourdain or Gimont), and the right upon the great road by St. Gaudens to Toulouse. It is probable that as the left and centre move on, the left of your corps will be directed to conform to their movement; but it will be necessary that part of your right should be always in a situation to keep a force upon the great road by St. Gaudens to Toulouse.

At length the pontoons arrived, and the following plan was drawn out:—

> Portet, March 27 1814, 3 p.m.
> Arrangement for the Passage of the Garonne.
>
> Sir R. Hill will be so good as to cause the pontoon-bridge to be thrown across the river at Portet this night. He will commence passing the troops under his immediate command, beginning with the infantry, as soon as the bridge is laid. The troops of the centre and left of the army will be moved at daybreak towards Portet, and will pass the river after the right column has crossed. Sir Rowland Hill will establish himself in strength as soon as possible upon the heights on the right bank of the Garonne, forming a front towards Toulouse and towards the great road which runs from Toulouse by Castanet towards Castelnadaury. The position of the army will be further extended in proportion as more troops pass over.
>
> Sir R. Hill will be so good as to establish as direct a communi-

cation as he can with headquarters this afternoon, and apprise the quartermaster-general of the line of communication established. Sir Rowland will be so good as to order reports to be sent to headquarters of the progress made in the establishment of the bridge, as also when the troops begin to pass. A communication is also to be established with Plaisance.

The passage of the Garonne was found impracticable, and Sir Rowland's troops were withdrawn to St. Roques. In the night of the 30th a new bridge was laid near Pensaguel, and he passed with two divisions of infantry. He used sometimes in conversation to mention the great trouble these bridges cost him, he would say:

> For instance, at a point where all seemed most promising, I found we had not enough to cross by exactly *one* boat, and we had all our work to do over again at a narrower place.

I shall never forget the coolness with which he mentioned this provoking circumstance; and some person present remarked, that he was no doubt just as cool when it happened.

By the 3rd of April he had advanced to Toulouse, and his officers occupied the beautiful villas of the suburbs. On the 3rd Lord Wellington thought Sir Rowland would probably be attacked the next day, and instructed him, if there seemed to be any risk in attempting to maintain the position opposite Toulouse, to fall back first behind the Touch river. If he deemed it expedient to retire still farther, he was to do so by the Auch road behind the rivulet between Colomiers and Lequenin. In case the enemy's force moved to his right to oppose the passage of the river, Lord Wellington wished him to make a show of attacking the suburb, and to be informed of it, that he might know the cause of the firing. No movement, however, took place, and a corps was thrown over the right of the Garonne on the 4th. At 10 p.m. on the 9th, Sir Rowland was informed:

> It is intended to move against the enemy's position on this side of the river, tomorrow morning soon after daybreak. Lord Wellingtons wishes therefore that you should make such arrangements, threatening the suburb of Toulouse on the left bank of the river, as circumstances admit of, in order to draw a part of the attention and force of the enemy to that side. You will be able to see the commencement and progress of the operations on this side, and you will be good enough to regulate yours accordingly.

The next morning, Easter Sunday, came the Battle of Toulouse. While the other operations of Lord Wellington were proceeding, Sir Rowland performed the task allotted to him with his usual vigour and success. He drove the French within the ancient wall, from their exterior works in the suburb on the left of the Garonne. It was a desecration of the Sabbath in every way to be lamented; for Napoleon had previously abdicated his throne.

On the 12th Lord Wellington entered Toulouse, and Sir Rowland was directed to move through the town, and to continue his march along the Carcassonne road. It was a moment of anxiety. Lord Wellington's message to him was:

> It is impossible to say until Colonel Cook's return, whether we are to be at war or at peace with Marshal Soult.

In the meantime he was desired to make his cavalry keep sight of the enemy, but not to move his infantry unless the cavalry required support. The arrival of Colonel Cook was joyfully announced by Sir Rowland to his family.

> Near Toulouse, April 13. 1814.
>
> I do most sincerely congratulate you and all my friends upon the glorious event which has just been made known to us. Colonel Cook arrived this morning from Paris with the account of the abdication of Bonaparte. The colonel is gone in to Marshal Soult, and I have no doubt an immediate cessation of hostilities will take place, though at this moment there is some little firing at the outposts. Should matters be settled so soon as there is every reason to suppose they will, I may hope ere long to have the happiness of seeing you all. It is indeed most gratifying to find that we have got rid of Bonaparte; the more so as, only a few days ago, we had every reason to think that a peace would be made with *him!* The papers will give you an account of our late operations.
>
> You will see that my troops had not much fighting at the battle near Toulouse, though we had our share of fatigue and anxiety during the period we were about that place. The joy and enthusiasm of the people of Toulouse when we entered, was, to all appearance, more sincere than anything of the kind I ever witnessed. Robert is at Toulouse: I have not yet seen him. I have this instant a message from my outposts to inform me a flag of truce is there; no doubt upon the subject of Colonel

Cook's mission. I will let you know the result tomorrow, but send this off in case Lord Wellington's despatches should go off this evening,

Yours, my dear Sister,
Very affectionately.

Soult, upon the receipt of the important information from Paris, proposed an armistice, to gain time for further tidings, to which Lord Wellington declined to accede. On the 16th it was officially stated to Sir Rowland,—

> It is Lord Wellington's intention that no unnecessary or partial hostilities should take place previously to the army being closed up. His Lordship will then see whether it is necessary to press Marshal Soult further.

Two days afterwards they heard as follows:—

Toulouse, 18th April, 1814,

My dear Sir Rowland,

The terms of an armistice have been agreed upon, and as soon as Marshal Soult has signified his assent to them the business will be completed. The armistice includes the allied troops in Catalonia and those under Marshal Suchet, as well as the armies in this quarter, and the fortresses and the troops before them. The army will therefore not make any movement today, and headquarters will be at Toulouse. It is probable that the greater part of the troops will be drawn further back tomorrow, to be cantoned, or encamped in more convenient situations.

I beg you will be so good as to let the contents of this letter be communicated to Sir Lowry Cole, and also to the other general officers, whose troops are in communication with those under your own immediate command.

Believe me, my dear Sir Rowland,
Very faithfully yours,

G. Murray, Q. M. G.

On the 21st Sir Rowland had the pleasure of writing,—

> Soult has acknowledged the present change of affairs; and we are at peace with him.
>
> I have just left Robert at a ball given by the inhabitants to *us*.

The joy of the people at having got rid of Bonaparte is beyond anything of the kind I ever witnessed.

Lord Castlereagh soon summoned the Commander of the Forces to meet him in Paris. He kindly undertook to be the bearer of a letter from Sir Rowland.

Toulouse, April 30. 1814.

My dear Sister,

Lord Wellington sets out this day for Paris, and has desired me to remain in command of the army. His Lordship talks of returning in a few days; but I imagine arrangements will be made in England to get the troops home with as little delay as possible, and that he will scarcely have time to come back.

The Duc d'Angoulême's reception here has been most gratifying. Several French generals have been to wait upon him. Marshal Suchet came last night. Soult is, I believe, gone to Paris.

A part of this army is ordered to be in readiness to embark on an expedition—I suppose, for America. The general officer commanding it is not named, but should it be offered to me, I shall not accept it. Indeed I am, as you may imagine, truly anxious to get home, and as soon as I can with propriety, I shall be with you.

I send these hasty lines by Lord W., who is just going off. Kind remembrance to all.

Yours most affectionately.

A few days afterwards he wrote,—

I am just sending off despatches to Lord Wellington at Paris, and by the same opportunity I forward to you a few lines. No instructions have yet arrived for our quitting this country, though I am in hourly expectation of hearing from England on the subject. Every thing is going on extremely well in this part of the country. The joy of the people is not at all abated. The Duc d'Angoulême is gone to visit the French armies. I have not heard how he has been received by them; but as Marshal Suchet and several of the French officers have been in here to wait upon his Royal Highness, I have no doubt they will in return pay every respect to him. We have had rather a curious meeting with the French officers of late. Two days ago three of their general officers dined with me; and as they have been my opponents for many years, we had an opportunity of talking over, in *the most friendly manner,* events which have occurred in our late campaign.

Sir Rowland Hill was at this time anxious to return to his family, and declined a lucrative post offered him by Lord Wellington, that he might attend to the comfort of his late brother's widow, and the interests of her children. The Duke of Wellington, now raised to that illustrious rank, soon returned to Toulouse. Peerages were conferred on five of his generals; in which honoured list appeared the name of Sir Rowland, as Lord Hill of Almaraz and of Hawkstone.

Chapter 11

Lord Hill Arrives in London

Lord Hill quitted Toulouse sooner than he expected, and reached London on the 27th of May, 1814. His arrival was thus hastily made known to his sister:—

Devonshire Place, 27th May, 1814,
Half-past five p. m.

My dear Sister,

I have just time to send you a line to inform you of my arrival here. In a letter I wrote to you some time ago from Toulouse, I mentioned that I should not accept the command of the troops going to America. Since then I was told that it was the *particular wish* of government that I should go. I therefore thought it right to come here to know the real sentiments of government on the subject. I cannot now enter into particulars, not having seen Lord Bathurst, nor have I time; but I beg to tell you *in secret*, which I have from *good authority*, that I shall not be called upon to go out, though it will be politic to keep up the idea of a large force going to America. Mr. and Mrs. Tudway[1] are now at dinner waiting for me. You shall hear from me tomorrow.

Yours,
R H.

The next letter stated:

I have seen Lord Bathurst this morning, and have the pleasure to inform you, that I am not likely to be called upon to go out

---

1. Mr. Tudway was member for Wells, in Somersetshire, and for several years was father of the House of Commons. He was Lord Hill's uncle by marriage. He received Lord Hill as his guest on his Lordship's arrival in London.

to America for some few weeks. In the meantime I shall have the happiness of seeing you, and *some changes may take place.*

Lord Hill in a few days removed to the Hanover Hotel, and I well remember being taken by his uncle, the Reverend Rowland Hill, to call upon him there. We went early, and found him at breakfast with several officers. He received us with a kindness of manner and gentle tone of voice peculiar to himself; yet his quiet step across the room to meet his uncle, and the beaming of his eye, showed the happiness he felt at seeing his zealous and devoted relative. The conversation at the breakfast table was extremely animated, and amongst other topics Lord Hill's *share of the spoils* of Vittoria was mentioned. This seemed odd enough, for he prided himself on never having acquired a single item of booty in all his campaigns, save one plain china drinking cup. But his man, looking well out for *provant,* had managed to appropriate some dried hams and tongues, which he vowed were from King Joseph's own larder.

They added, however, on that day only to the burthens of the mules, for never did his Lordship and staff fare worse during the whole Peninsular campaign, than after the Battle of Vittoria. With the treasures of Spain scattered around them by their own victory, the conquerors had not necessary refreshment. After breakfast, Lord Hill went with Mr. Rowland Hill, to see the picture by Heaphy of the heroes of the Peninsula; and I shall never forget the kind way in which he described to myself, then a boy, the various personages of whom that group was composed. He thought all the portraits excellent; but said the Duke of Wellington should not have been painted in a blue frock coat, but a grey one, that being the dress in which he was constantly seen in Spain.

On the 1st of June Lord Hill took his seat in the House of Lords. In the midst of all the gaieties consequent on the presence of the illustrious strangers in London, he wrote home:

> It is not for pleasure I remain here, but I am told it is quite right that I should attend some of the intended fetes, particularly the prince's. His Royal Highness was very gracious, and inquired after Sir John. I believe I shall receive my sword on Saturday.

The sword here alluded to was voted to him by the city of London. On the day of presentation, Mr. Rowland Hill arrived at Guildhall a little before the time appointed, and was cordially welcomed by the worthy Chamberlain. In the course of conversation, reference was made to the motto on the arms of Lord Nelson. The Chamberlain observed:

> There are not many people who know that this motto is a specimen of the good taste and accuracy of the king.[2] It was originally shown to him in these terms, '*palmam quam meruit ferat.*' His Majesty said 'No; let it be *palmam qui meruit ferat.*'

At length those who had the privilege of admission arrived in quick succession, and presently the cheering of the crowd in the street announced the approach of some person of distinction. It was Lord Beresford, who was most enthusiastically greeted. Shortly after the same sounds of welcome were heard, and Lord Hill came in, shaking hands with every one within his reach. The Lord Mayor and the civic authorities then proceeded, with their gallant guests, to the place appointed for the ceremony. Two swords were placed before the Chamberlain, with a gold box containing the freedom of the Corporation, long previously voted to Lord Beresford.

The Chamberlain addressed Lord Hill in a most appropriate manner, neatly alluding to the fact that his ancestor, of the same name, was the first Protestant Lord Mayor of the city of London. He then presented the sword, and Lord Hill was completely overcome in endeavouring to return thanks. Lord Beresford next received his sword and the box before mentioned. No sooner were these ceremonies over, than all present crowded round both the heroes, and a hearty shaking of hands took place, such as has not been witnessed since those days of joy at our deliverance from a long and awful war. It was carried to such an extent, that old Blücher one day, lifting up his aching arm, exclaimed, "*Me shake at hands none more.*"

Wherever Lord Hill appeared in the metropolis he met with a similar reception, till at length he quitted the fetes of London for the romantic scenes and beauteous woodlands of Hawkstone. His arrival was the signal for a general burst of rapturous welcome; and all the principal towns through which he passed showed him some token of respect. At Birmingham he was presented with a sword in these terms: "*Take it, my Lord, and it will not fail you.*" "*Trust it to me,*" was his reply, "*and I will not disgrace it.*"

His Lordship's visit to Shrewsbury was a triumph. The streets were filled with thousands who came pouring in from every quarter. The trees on the road by which he entered were adorned with flowers,

---
2. George III.

and the very road itself actually strewed with them. Thirteen hundred children of the charity and Sunday schools, were so placed as to be amongst the first whose shouts should hail him as their benefactor and friend. The yeomanry came out to be reviewed by him on his way, and formed part of the procession which accompanied him into the town. Lord Kenyon rode next Lord Hill, who was attended by his gallant brothers and *aides-de-camp*. Out of respect to the memory of the late Colonel Hill, the trappings of Lord Hill's horse were of black, a marked contrast to the uniforms of fourteen troops of cavalry that followed in his train. The decorated fronts of the houses were occupied by ladies, whose handkerchiefs waved over the heads of the cheering multitude beneath them.

A splendid dinner was given at the Guildhall, where the venerable lather of Lord Hill was an object of universal interest. He appeared fresh, vigorous, and animated as the youngest of the guests at that festive board, until he rose amidst the plaudits of the company to return thanks for the honours of the day. Then the tears rolled down his aged cheeks; but at length his manly spirit conquered all emotions, and he expressed in a few brief words his sense of the reception of his name by the Salopians. Amongst those assembled on the proud occasion was India's future bishop, the devoted Heber, who spoke with all the elegance and fervour of his chaste and poetic mind. Nor was the worthy Major Egerton forgotten: loud and long were the cheers that followed the mention of his name, and well did he deserve them.

There seemed to be no end to the festivities, and the eagerness of the people was every moment on the increase. The freedom of the Corporation was voted to Lord Hill and his gallant brothers; and, in order to gratify the populace, it was determined that the presentation should take place in the beautiful garden of Mr. Rocke, facing the quarry—a romantic promenade belonging to the town, where a prodigious concourse had gathered. When the ceremony was over, his Lordship addressed the crowd from the back of a sunk fence between the garden and the quarry. But this was not enough. The shaking-hand mania of the capital had reached the provinces. Hundreds of hands were extended over the bank, so he good-naturedly knelt upon the top of the fence, and shook heartily as many as he could reach. In the afternoon there was a profusion of tea and cake provided for the women and children.

Lord Hill, who dined at Mr. Rocke's, every now and then appeared on the terrace; but the people were determined to have him out. An escort of gentlemen was formed to attend him; but, seeing the immense throng, he at first declined going into the quarry. He, however, yielded and went; but was obliged to retreat, such was the overwhelming rush to get near him. A *diversion* was tried. "That's Lord Hill," said one of the escort, pointing to another gentleman. Away went some of the multitude who had not seen him; and the subject of the ruse was obliged to make his escape as fast as he could. Lord Hill acknowledged that he now certainly did run away for the first time—not from his enemies, but from his friends, he said, laughing:

> I never did fly from the *fury* of my enemies; but I have been now obliged to do so from the *kindness* of my friends.

The Salopians did not suffer these and other transient honours to be all they offered. A splendid column was erected near Shrewsbury, which is one of the noblest Doric pillars in Europe. A vignette in the title-page of this volume correctly represents it. It is called Lord Hill's Column, and has been conveyed to his family.

While Shropshire gave this distinguished reception to Lord Hill, Cheshire also determined to do honour to Lord Combermere,[3] and the former was earnestly requested to participate in the festivities. Nor did Chester forget that Lord Hill had been a schoolboy within her ancient walls.

The two gallant heroes entered the city in a triumphal procession, and were welcomed with enthusiasm. As they passed along the crowded streets, Lord Hill was perceived to wave his hand with great emotion towards a window filled with ladies, and pointing to one whom his quick eye had caught, he exclaimed, "I shall be with you at breakfast tomorrow." All wondered who this could be. It was the lady of his former tutor, Mrs. Winfield.

When all these festivities had terminated, the only drawback to the happiness of his family was the fear that he might be called upon to go out to America. In August, a letter from Lord Bathurst put an end to their anxiety:—

> Downing Street, August 10. 1814.
>
> My dear Lord,
> Since I had the pleasure of seeing your Lordship, the information I have received has given me reason to believe that great

---

3. *The Golden Lion*, Wellington's intelligent and flamboyant cavalry commander, by Mary Combermere, W. W. Knollys & Alexander Innes Shand, is also published by Leonaur.

difficulties would arise from the extended scale of the expedition, which I found would not be less than one hundred sail. If we succeed, it must be undertaken more in the shape of surprise, the place presenting no *great* obstacles, the country and shores *many* in proportion to the extent of force brought against it. Sir Alexander Cochrane's letter received yesterday confirms me in this opinion; as he proposes an attack at a different point, but in fact with the same object, with a force very inferior to any in contemplation when I proposed the expedition to you.

I find also that the collecting such a force as would be fit for your Lordship to command, is attended with much more difficulty than I had imagined, having a regard to the great demand for troops to be stationed in Ireland.

Under all these circumstances I am inclined to give up the thoughts of availing myself of your Lordship's zeal to serve in an expedition, which, I am afraid, would have exposed your health more, than, from the little opposition to be expected, it would have added to your glory; and I shall, probably, do nothing more than detach a very small force, to be placed under the command of Major-General Ross, now in America. I take the first moment to communicate to you this change; at the same time, I hope you will allow me to consider your services as available, should any occasion happen which would be judged worthy of your Lordship's assistance. I have the honour to be, my dear Lord,

With great respect,
Your faithful servant,

Bathurst.

In September, Lord Hill was offered the command in Scotland. The proposal was made by an autograph letter from his Royal Highness the Commander-in-Chief:—

Brighthelmstone, September 12. 1814.

My dear Lord,

The command in Scotland having become vacant, in consequence of its having been determined that Lord Cathcart should remain as ambassador at Petersburgh, both from duty and inclination, I wish to offer the situation to your Lordship, and shall feel much obliged to you if you will communicate to me your wishes on the subject at your early convenience.

Believe me to be,
>My dear Lord,
>>Yours most sincerely,
>>>Frederick.

The Rt. Hon. Lieut.-General Lord Hill, K.B.

Lord Hill declined this appointment, and remained in the midst of his family during the autumn and winter.

Early in the spring of 1815, he said one day to his sister,[4] "Come, now let us go to London, and enjoy ourselves," little thinking of the return of Bonaparte from Elba, and all its consequences. In the autumn of 1842, I happened to be talking with his Lordship alone one evening, when some reference was made to that estimable diplomatist Monsieur Dedel, the Dutch ambassador, on whom he passed a high eulogium. This led to his mentioning the Prince of Orange; and he then said:

> I will tell you something that few persons know. When Bonaparte came back from Elba, I was in London. One day I was sent for suddenly to the Cabinet. They told me there was a fear of an action being risked on the frontier of the Netherlands, that might prove disastrous. 'We think,' they said, 'your influence would operate to prevent it—will you go?' I answered, 'Yes.' 'When? Tonight?' 'No; not tonight; tomorrow morning.' I went home, got ready, and set off; and was able to keep all right till the arrival of the Duke of Wellington. This, I believe, is not generally known.

When this conversation was told to his sister, she said she remembered that the evening before his sudden departure, he was to have gone to the opera. At dinner, he quietly remarked, "I cannot go with you this evening; I am. off tomorrow morning;" but the cause of his rapid movement was not mentioned. He went, leaving his attached *aide-de-camp*, Major Egerton, to arrange his affairs, and follow him as soon as possible.

Amongst his papers I have found the correspondence on this important mission. It was towards the end of March that he left England. The first note was the summons:—

>Tuesday morning, 8 o'clock.

My dear Lord,
Two gentlemen arrived last night from Ostend. Their account

---
4. Miss Emma Hill.

is very bad. The King of France has lost Lille, &c., and is *in Ostend*. Bonaparte is on the frontier, but no large body of his troops yet arrived. Government is anxious you should go out *immediately*, as it is of the greatest importance that you should prevent any rash action, and also that you should persuade Louis to retreat upon Holland, rather than come to England. Pray call in Downing Street at three o'clock.

Yours very truly,

H. E. Bunbury.

As we have seen, Lord Hill lost no time in going out. He was charged to recommend to the Prince of Orange the "utmost caution on the part of the forces under his command;" and to assure him that it was deemed of the greatest importance that his Royal Highness's "army should be preserved in an efficient state, until a greater mass of force could be brought forward." It was also to be urged, that it was not desirable:

> To maintain too advanced a position; and that it was more creditable, as well as more secure, to withdraw before the enemy had assembled such a force as would compel a retreat, rather than to risk the being obliged by their activity and numbers, to retire in such a manner as might produce an unfavourable effect upon the public mind.

Also, it was to be conveyed to him, as the pleasure of the prince regent:

> That the army under his command should avoid any serious engagement, and should withdraw into more retired positions, which should be closer, with a view both to covering Antwerp and the Dutch frontier, and also to preserving a ready communication with the Prussian forces.

These were the principal points in the instructions Lord Hill was charged with to his Royal Highness the Prince of Orange, for whom he entertained the highest personal respect and esteem. Lord Bathurst further explained the tenor of his mission:—

Downing Street, March 29. 1815.

My dear Lord,
In delivering to you a duplicate of my instructions of yesterday's date, I think it will be satisfactory to you that I should put down

in writing the substance of the explanations with which I have accompanied it.

Your Lordship is aware that the instruction not to maintain so advanced a position is peremptory; but you know also that it was given under the impression that Bonaparte was collecting a force on the frontier. In the event of no such force being in progress, the obedience to the instructions becomes less urgent, if any positive advantage be derived from maintaining that position longer; but even on this supposition that no force is collecting, the measures for commencing a retrograde movement must be taken, so as to be able to execute it at any time.

If a force be collecting, but no great progress made in it, the obedience to the instruction may be more gradual, but the commencement should not so depend; first, because the enemy has means of collecting a sufficient force to advance; and, secondly, because the change of position will be made with more advantage every way, when it appears to be, and in truth is, voluntary. The object of the instruction being not to risk an action, but not to risk, if it can be helped, the change of position with an enemy in force near you. I am,

  My dear Lord,
    Yours very sincerely,
        Bathurst.

The next day Lord Hill was on board His Majesty's ship *Rosario*, and arrived at Brussels on the evening of the 1st of April. He lost no time in seeing the Prince of Orange; and communicated to Lord Bathurst the result of his interview with that gallant personage in the following terms:—

> I beg to acquaint your Lordship that I arrived here yesterday evening, and immediately waited on the Prince of Orange, and had a long conversation with His Royal Highness, on the subject of the instructions which I received from your Lordship.
> It appears that the army under the prince is stationed as follows: Headquarters at Brussels, the Dutch troops coming up towards Genappe, and the British and Hanoverians at Tournay, Ath, &c. It also appears that the troops at and about the two last-mentioned places have orders to retire in case of being attacked. Conceiving, however, that the British and Hanoverians are too far advanced, I did not fail to refer His Royal Highness to the

late instructions, and to explain to him the conversation I had with your Lordship on the subject; in consequence of which, the prince has ordered the main body of the troops on the advanced line of Tournay to fall back tomorrow to Enghien, keeping their advance at Leuze and Lens, and occupying Tournay and Mons with garrisons, if they are considered tenable.

This arrangement seems good for tomorrow; but if the intelligence from the frontier is in any way threatening, I hope the prince will lose no time in bringing the troops further back.

The prince informs me that he does not think the enemy are collecting in force on the frontier, and he does not seem to expect any attack. Your Lordship is aware that the King of the Netherlands is here; and, from what I can learn, it is the anxious wish of His Majesty to preserve this place—a circumstance, no doubt, very desirable; at the same time, it ought not to be considered if it is to be effected by force. Indeed, I am not aware that the prince has now any intention of making a stand to cover Brussels; and I shall do what I can to prevent our coming in contact with the enemy in any way until we are in a better state to do so.

By accounts from Vienna, I am told we have reason to expect and hope that the Duke of Wellington will be here in the course of a day or two.

The Prince of Orange begs me to mention, in case I should write to your Lordship, though he will no doubt write himself, that he never had any intention of fighting a battle on the frontiers near Tournay."

3rd April.

Since writing the accompanying letter, the quartermaster-general has informed me that the movement on Enghien, alluded to in my letter of yesterday, did not take place this day, but is ordered for tomorrow.

Thus Lord Hill's sudden mission terminated most satisfactorily to all parties, and was particularly acceptable to the Prince of Orange, who always showed marked attention to his views, as well as friendship for his person. To the great joy of all parties, the Duke of Wellington arrived at Brussels on the 4th of April in the night, and the influence of his command was quickly diffused over the whole scene of action.

Lord Hill was placed at Grammont, where, by a curious combination of circumstances, he found himself opposite his old opponent, Girard, whom he surprised at Arroyo de Molinos, and close to the chateau of the Prince d'Aremberg, whom he took prisoner on that occasion, and who had been on his parole at Shrewsbury. Lord Hill's pay, at this time, was not sufficient to cover his expenses. The Duke of Wellington said to Lord Bathurst:

> He is again at the head of what is really an army, composed of troops of different nations, with a large staff attached to him, and great expenses to be incurred, and he is paid only as a lieutenant-general, of whom he has several under his command.

His Grace proposed the augmentation of his means; and it was ordered that he should receive the pay and allowances of a general on the staff. But for this, he would have been impoverished by his services.

On the 15th of May he wrote to his sister, Miss Emma Hill, whom he had taken with him to enjoy the pleasures of London:—

> Grammont, May 15. 1815.
>
> My dear Emma,
>
> I have received your last letter. The collection of French troops on the frontier mentioned in my last, appears to have been in consequence of an apprehension on the part of the French that we were about to attack them. Matters are now nearly in the same state as they have been for some time; the allies are coming up, and in the course of another fortnight, I imagine will be in a state to move forward.
>
> The only unpleasant circumstance which has occurred, has been amongst the Saxon troops attached to Blücher's army: nearly the whole of them, about 30,000, declared the other day in favour of Bonaparte, and it was with some difficulty that old Blücher made his escape from them. They have been discovered, and the ringleaders have been shot.
>
> Love to all, from your ever affectionate brother,
>
> Hill.

The troops of Prince Frederick of the Netherlands were sent over to Lord Hill, and his anxiety for the comfort of the men appears in a letter he addressed to his Royal Highness:—

Grammont, May 17. 1815.

Sir,

Your Royal Highness having been pleased to say that you would allow me to see your corps, I shall be happy to have that honour whenever it may be convenient to your Royal Highness for me to do so.

Considering that your corps is rather dispersed, it is by no means my wish to give the troops a long march, for the purpose of collecting at any particular point. I can ride to their several cantonments, and see them in brigades or divisions, or in any manner you may be pleased to fix. I have only to request that your Royal Highness will have the goodness to let me know the arrangements you make on the occasion, in order that I may be punctual to the time, and not keep the troops waiting.

I have the honour to be,
Your Royal Highness's very obedient
and faithful servant,

Hill.

H. R,. Highness Prince Frederick of the Netherlands,
&c. &c. &c.

His great consideration for the soldiers made Lord Hill exceedingly beloved by them. I remember a private of his corps telling me that, on a very hot day, at a review, he was overheard saying to an officer, "Let us shorten these manoeuvres; it is very hot: you must not fatigue your men." A whisper ran through the ranks, "Bless him! there he is: Father Hill again!"

On the 22nd of May Lord Hill thus expressed himself, in writing to his brother Sir Francis Hill, then in England:—

> I returned late last night from an inspection of our frontier. Everything here is much in the same state as it has been for some time. Bonaparte is busy in France, and the allies are coming forward, but I imagine it will take a few weeks yet before the latter can be well up. By all accounts, Paris is in a very unsettled state. Many deserters come to this country, but in general they are soldiers of the last conscriptions. General Latour came into Mons yesterday while I was there. He has served a long tune with Bonaparte, and is considered a distinguished officer: he is a native of this country. He left Paris two days ago, and confirms the accounts of the capital being in a very disturbed state. If you

have nothing better to do, I think you could spend a short time in this country very pleasantly: you could consider my house as your headquarters.

Sir Francis Hill and the Honourable Charles Shore, now Lord Teignmouth, paid Lord Hill a visit at Grammont, where they found an agreeable sojourn until the approach of the French, and the certainty of a battle, caused Lord Hill to recommend their departure to Antwerp.

Lord Hill was in the constant receipt of information respecting the movements of the enemy, which he communicated to the Duke of Wellington at Brussels. On the 13th of June he was informed that, at one o'clock in the morning, the French outposts and pickets all fell back towards Maubeuge, and that it was generally believed that an attack was intended on the 15th. Marshals Soult and Drouet, it was added, were in command of nearly 120,000 picked troops; but Bonaparte had not yet come down from Paris, and the National Guards were in full march to the frontier. On the afternoon of the 15th information was sent to Lord Hill from the Duke of Wellington that, in consequence of an attack made upon the Prussian posts on the River Sambre in the morning, his Grace had ordered the army to be collected that night. The movements of the army were notified, and Lord Hill sent his instructions to Prince Frederick:—

June 16. 1815, 3 a. m.

Sir,

I have this moment received orders from the Duke of Wellington to move the troops under my command, and his Grace requests that your Royal Highness will occupy Oudenarde with 500 men, and collect the first division of the army of the Low Countries and the Hanoverian brigade at Sotteghen. These movements to take place without delay.

I have, &c.

Hill.

His Royal Highness Prince Frederick of Orange.

All the orders of the duke addressed to Lord Hill were executed with his accustomed judgment. His whole mind was filled with the momentous interest of the coming struggle for the destinies of Europe. The history of the fight at Quatre Bras, and the retreat to Waterloo, belongs not to this memoir. Nor need any allusion be made to the ball at Brussels, from which the chieftains were summoned to the field, further than to say that Lord Hill was not there. He was at his post, attending to the movements of the enemy and his own duties.

The night previous to the Battle of Waterloo was spent by Lord Hill and his staff, in a small house by the side of the road leading from Brussels to the field. At the commencement of the day, his corps was on the slope of Merke Braine to the right of the Nivelle road, covering the right wing of the general line. Later in the day it advanced, and added greatly to the decisive issue. As the whole army moved to the left, the divisions of Lord Hill's force came up, and were engaged in the thickest of the battle. His Lordship's own station was on a spot where a little rise enabled him to see the enemy's movements.

It was a post of great danger from its exposure to the shot, which flew about him in every direction; but he remained there, coolly marking all that he deemed of importance, and only leaving it occasionally to animate by his presence any faltering portion of the line. He manifested the same energy as at Arroyo de Molinos. His usual gentle and reserved demeanour was exchanged for a decisive and spirited air of command, regulated by most consummate prudence. He had foreseen the dreadful attack made by the Imperial Guards; and, having placed himself at the head of a brigade, contributed greatly to the last decisive repulse of the choicest troops of Napoleon. Lord Hill was following this advantage with his customary ardour, when the duke ordered the advance of the whole army. Cordial as were his Grace's acknowledgments of the services rendered by his Lordship at Waterloo, the full extent of them never seems to have been known to the public.(See note following).

✶✶✶✶✶✶

Note:—To show how Lord Hill's corps was engaged, I give a memorandum placed recently in my hands by his Lordship's aide-de-camp:—

Lord Hill's Corps engaged at Waterloo.

Sir F. Adam's Brigade.					1st Brigade, K.G.L.					
	K.		W.		M.		K.		W.	M.
52d —	16	—	174	—	0	1st —	22	—	69	— 17
71st —	24	—	160	—	3	2d —	18	—	79	— 7
95th —	20	—	124	—	0	3d —	17	—	93	— 31
						4th —	13	—	77	— 14
Colonel Mitchell.						Hanoverians 70			318	69
23d —	11	—	78	—	0	British 87			577	3
51st —	9	—	20	—	0	Total, exclusive of officers	157		895	72
14th —	7	—	21	—	0					
British 87			577		3					

★★★★★★

Sir Digby Mackworth, who was on the staff of Lord Hill, has kindly communicated what lie witnessed of his General's efforts at the grand crisis of the day. Sir Digby states:

> He placed himself at the head of his Light Brigade, 52nd, 71st, and 95th, and charged the flank of the Imperial Guard, as they were advancing against our Guards. The Light Brigade was lying under the brow of the hill, and gave and received volleys within half pistol shot distance. Here Lord Hill's horse was shot under him, and, as he ascertained the next morning, was shot in five places. The general was rolled over and severely bruised, but in the *mêlée* this was unknown to us for about half an hour. We knew not what was become of him: we feared he had been killed; and none can tell you the heartfelt joy which we felt when he rejoined us, not seriously hurt.

When the tremendous day was over. Lord Hill and his staff again reoccupied the little cottage they left in the morning. His two gallant brothers. Sir Robert Hill and Colonel Clement Hill, had been removed wounded to Brussels; the party was, nevertheless, nine in number. A soup made by Lord Hill's servant from two fowls was all their refreshment, after hours of desperate fighting without a morsel of food. Lord Hill himself was bruised and full of pain. All night long, the groans and shrieks of sufferers were the chief sounds that met their ears. It was to them all a night of the greatest misery. The men whom the nations of Europe were about to welcome with acclamations, and to entertain in palaces, could only exchange sigh for sigh with each other in a wretched cottage. Such is war even to the winners.

Sir Digby Mackworth, fatigued as he was, had the resolution to record the proceedings of the past day. His memorandum, kindly sent for the service of this volume, bears date "June 18th, 11 p.m., Waterloo." After describing certain well-known circumstances, he proceeded:—

> The cavalry and infantry repeatedly charged in masses, under cover of a tremendous fire from 240 pieces of artillery. Four times were our guns in possession of their cavalry, and as often did the bayonets of our infantry rescue them. For upwards of an hour our little squares were surrounded by the *élite* of the French cavaliers: they gallantly stood within forty paces of us,

unable to leap over the bristling line of bayonets, unwilling to retire, and determined never to surrender. Hundreds of them were dropping in all directions from our murderous fire, yet as fast as they dropped, others came up to supply their places. Finding at last that it was in vain to attempt to break our determined ranks, they swept round our rear, and rushing into the Nivelles road attempted to cut their way back to their own lines; but the whole road was lined with our infantry on both sides, and at the advanced part of it was an almost impassable *barricado* of felled trees.

Here fell the remainder of these gallant *cuirassiers*, of whom not one was taken without a wound. The cannonade continued without intermission; and about six o'clock we saw heavy columns of infantry supported by dragoons returning for a fresh attack. It was evident it would be a desperate, and we thought probably a decisive, one. Everyone felt how much depended on this terrible moment. A black mass of the Grenadiers of the Imperial Guard, with music playing, and the great Napoleon at their head, came rolling onward from the farm of La Belle Alliance. With rapid pace they descended. Those spaces in our lines which death had opened and left vacant, were covered with bodies of cavalry. The point at which the enemy aimed was now evident; it was an angle formed by a brigade of Guards, and the light brigade of Lord Hill's corps. Lord Hill was there in person.

The French moved on with arms sloped, *au pas de charge*. They began to ascend the hill. In a few seconds they were within a hundred paces of us, and as yet not a shot had been fired. The awful moment was now at hand. A peal of ten thousand thunders burst at once on their devoted heads. The storm swept them down as a whirlwind which rushes over the ripe corn; they paused; their advance ceased; they commenced firing from the heads of their columns, and attempted to extend their front; but death had already caused too much confusion among them; they crowded instinctively behind each other to avoid a fire which was intolerably dreadful. Still they stood firm—*la garde meurt, et ne se rend pas*.

For half an hour this horrible butchery continued. At last, seeing all their efforts vain, all their courage useless, deserted by their emperor who was already flown, unsupported by their comrades who were already beaten, the hitherto Invincible Old Guard gave way, and fled in every direction. One spontaneous and almost painfully animated 'Hurrah!' burst from the victorious ranks of England. The line at once advanced, generals, officers, soldiers, all partaking in one common enthusiasm. The battle was over. Guns, prisoners, ammunition, waggons, baggage, horses, successively fell into our hands.

Night and fatigue compelled us to halt. We halted on each side of the Genappe road, and in a short time numerous columns of Prussians came pouring along in pursuit of the enemy. Each battalion cheered us in passing. The officers saluted, and many embraced us. Never was witnessed a more enthusiastic moment. We felt amply rewarded for the exertions of the day. The Prussians continued the pursuit without interruption. Lord Hill and staff retired to a small cottage where we now are. We have but one room between nine of us, including his Lordship. All but myself are asleep.

In reading the various accounts of this battle, it is curious to observe the discrepancies as to the time it commenced. Lord Hill has however settled this point. On arriving in London the autumn after the conflict, he passed his first evening at the house of his friend Lord Teignmouth.

"Can you tell me," said Lord Teignmouth, "at what time the action commenced?"

Lord Hill replied, "I took two watches into action with me. On consulting my stop watch after the battle was over, I found that the first gun was fired at ten minutes before twelve."

The day after the battle. Sir Noel Hill wrote thus:—

Brussels, June 19, 1815.

My dear Maria,

We are *all* well. Robert and Clement are wounded; but, thank God, not dangerously. Robert's wound is severe, and will confine him some time. I have seen the surgeon who attends him, who assures me there is *not the slightest chance of any bad consequences.* The ball—musket—has passed through the fleshy part of the right arm, and slightly grazed the breast.

Clement was *pinned* to his saddle by a fellow's sword through the fleshy part of the thigh, and his wound may confine him some time, and it must be painful, but there is no sort of danger attending it. Now for the pleasant part of my story.

We gained a complete victory yesterday, *Bony* in person commanding the French. He has retreated, leaving most of his artillery, and immense numbers of prisoners, in our hands.

Our army has advanced this morning.

Yours ever most affectionately,

T. N. H.

To this letter Colonel Clement Hill would add a postscript:

> To convince you all there is not much amiss with me, I add a line to Tom's account of me. My wound may confine me for a short time, but I have scarcely any pain, and we are all in high spirits at the complete drubbing Bony has had, towards which I hope the Blues did their share.

As this brave officer, who made thus light of a severe wound, was being conveyed to Brussels, he came up to one not quite so gallant as himself, who he had reason to think was frightened out of the field. He was trudging along at quick march.

"Eh, my good fellow," cried the colonel, "I thought you were wounded: were you not?"

"No, no!" said he, "but *I had some very narrow escapes!*" Lord Hill himself soon recovered his bruises, and begged Sir Noel to go to the field and look for the horse that was shot under him, and if dead to have the poor animal buried; if not, to put him out of his misery. He was found quite dead, and on examination it was discovered that he had been shot in several places.

His Lordship now passed on with the army into France. Sir Noel Hill's letter shows they were in high spirits:—

Cateau, June 23. 1815.

My dear Maria,

Robert and Clement are going on as well as possible; but I dare say you will get later accounts from them than this. Rowland and myself are quite well, and have only to regret that our brothers cannot witness the finishing stroke of Master *Bony*. He cannot surely withstand the storm that is brewing all around him, after what he suffered on the 18th. He brought against us one half of his army, and by far the best troops he had; so that *we*—even this army—need not be much alarmed at the other half, without the assistance of the Russians, Austrians, &c., who, it is understood, are well advanced; and perhaps our having halted today is to allow their armies to come up.

Bonaparte's orders to the peasantry and people in general, to defend the country, have not so far been attended to; but, on the contrary, we have been well received, particularly in this place. Rowland and his staff came into the town without a single soldier. The white flag was immediately hoisted, and a band of music with most of the inhabitants came out to welcome our arrival, singing and playing *Vive Henri Quatre*. Bavay, the first town we entered in France, had still the eagle standing in the market-place, and the people did not seem very happy to see us, so that one cannot judge exactly of the sentiments of all; but I should think our late successes would determine most of those who were wavering, in favour of the good cause.

Rowland is gone with the Duke of Wellington to pay a visit to old Blücher, who is within a few miles of us. The poor old fellow was terribly maltreated in one of his affairs with the enemy. His horse was shot, and they rode over him; but he takes a deal of killing. His head being tolerably thick, he received but little harm.

Kind love to all.

Yours ever most affectionately.

Lord Hill's letter describes his visit to Blücher:—

Cateau, June 24. 1815.

My dear Sister,

Before this time you will have heard, in various ways, of the glorious result of our Battle of Waterloo, on which occasion I am really inclined to think that the fate of Europe was decided. Bonaparte is still retreating, and we are following him. It is possible he may endeavour to collect at Laon, where there is a position; but in my mind he cannot again make any serious stand against us. The Prussians are close to us; but the Russians and Austrians are at a considerable distance, as it was not intended to commence operations till the 24th—this day. As soon, however, as they hear of what has taken place on this side, I have no doubt they will press forward.

Yesterday I rode with the Duke of Wellington to see Blücher. We found the old marshal amusing himself with Bonaparte's hat, stars, and personal baggage, which with his carriage was taken by some Prussian cavalry. I verily believe there never was so tremendous a battle fought as that at Waterloo; and it is astonishing how any one could escape. I have seen several who have seen Robert and Clement, and I feel perfectly easy on their account. The particulars of their wounds will have been described to you. The King of France is coming to this town today: the people seem rejoiced at the event. Let us be thankful for all mercies; and never forget that Providence which has protected us, and brought to pass the happy prospect of affairs. Alas, poor Currie! [5] Bridgeman is doing quite well. Kind remembrance to Sir John, and all dear friends.

Yours ever most affectionately,
H.

The Duke of Wellington's despatch from Waterloo contained the following paragraph relative to the services of Lord Hill:

I am also particularly indebted to General Lord Hill, for his assistance and conduct upon this as upon all other occasions.

He received, in a most complimentary manner, from the Prince Regent, the Guelphic Order for his distinguished exertions in leading the Hanoverian troops in the battle of the 18th. It was moreover soon afterwards announced to him by the Duke of York, that he was to wear a gold clasp in commemoration of the Battle of Orthez.

The beginning of July, when the posts at Paris evacuated by agreement were given up. Lord Hill marched to take possession of them. They were surrendered on three successive days; and the evening of the first he held a conference at the Barrier of St. Denis, accompanied by his staff. The French General awaited his arrival, attended only by a single *aide-de-camp*. In the distance a French column was perceived retiring as the British troops approached; but a French soldier stood on duty near the barrier.

Just as Lord Hill and his staff approached close to him, this fellow actually levelled and discharged his musket at the English party, but providentially the shot proved harmless. A French *aide-de-camp* instantly galloped up and apologised, making the excuse that the soldier was intoxicated; but a similar outrage had well nigh proved fatal to the

---

5. Lord Hill thus mentions Colonel Currie in a letter to the Duke of Wellington:—
"Lieutenant Colonel Currie had been in the army I believe, about twenty years, and on my staff upwards of nine years, during which latter period he has rendered most essential services to me and to his country."

officer sent into Paris by the Duke of Wellington with a flag of truce, for he was shot through the body. Lord Hill, however, took no further notice of the circumstance.

At Paris Lord Hill occupied the Hôtel de Montesquieu, where he entertained some of his Shropshire friends whom the stirring events of the period attracted to Paris. He also participated in the brilliant *fêtes* and reunions, and himself gave a very splendid entertainment. Then came the grand reviews. Whenever he could, he escaped from Paris into the open country, near the Bois de Boulogne, enjoying the quietude of its groves more than all the magnificence of the saloons of Paris. From this place he wrote to his sister:

> I have every reason to think that I shall not be prevented having the pleasure of seeing you in Shropshire about the 17th or 18th of next month. I have spoken to the Duke of Wellington on the subject, and find there is no objection whatever to my returning to England for a short time. I should have wished to have been at home for a few days before the 19th, but I fear I cannot well leave Paris before the 12th, chiefly on account of a grand review of the Russian Army, which is to take place on the 10th or 11th. That is also the period about which the British Army may expect to be moved from the neighbourhood of Paris, for the purpose of being cantoned in the towns and villages towards Amiens, &c.

He then expressed his opinion on graver matters, thus:—

> With respect to the state of public affairs, it is difficult for me to say what it is. I fear, however, that the Bourbons are not very popular, and that the Jacobins and other parties are kept in order entirely by the great armies which are in this country. One thing I am quite clear should be done, which is, that the allies ought not to leave without so completely clipping the wings of France as to render its government, be it what it may, totally incapable of disturbing the peace of Europe again: the only way of doing which is to disband all the present forces, and to occupy with foreign troops, for some time to come, all the strong towns on the frontiers of France. I am also of opinion that all Napoleon's trophies ought to be removed, and all the plunder taken by him restored to its proper owners. I have been living in the country some days, but return to Paris today. I expect to meet Lord Castlereagh at dinner at Prince Frederick's.

We have now traced the career of Lord Hill through the most stirring periods of his active military life, passed without failing in any undertaking, or having made one personal enemy. Conscious of his own powers, he veiled them with an unequalled modesty, so that jealousy was disarmed. Whatever opportunities were placed in his way, he never used them to enrich himself, and his nature was too noble to make the character of another a stepping-stone to his own fame. With powers of mind adequate to the most original military conceptions, he was, as to orders from his principal, most punctiliously obedient; and if ever he did take a step not prescribed, it was always in accordance with instructions, and led to some brilliant achievement without the precedent of infringing any rule.

Lord Hill: A Short Biography

1

Among his lieutenants in the Peninsula there was none in whom Wellington reposed more absolute confidence than Rowland, Lord Viscount Hill. He was assured of his cool judgment, his imperturbable self-possession, his intuitive grasp of his superior's far-reaching plans, and of a self-abnegation altogether untainted by personal ambitions. In strong contrast to Craufurd, who was all fire and passionate impulse, though he could dare much on occasion he was never betrayed into imprudence; and unlike Picton and other warriors of a hard-swearing generation, he was so temperate of speech that a single occasion is recorded as noteworthy, when he was tempted to an ejaculation resembling an oath. Perhaps there was little merit in curbing a temper so absolutely under command.

With his squire-like seat on horseback and his phlegmatic face, he was familiarly known by the *sobriquet* of "Farmer Hill"; but the soldiers, who appreciated his kindly care for their comforts, affectionately translated "Farmer" into "Father." Wellington said, indeed, in the conversation with Lord Stanhope, that, like all his lieutenants, Hill shrank from responsibility, but when he said so, he must have forgotten Arroyos Molinos and Almarez. Hill was the only one of his generals to whom be confided independent and most important commands; undoubtedly, of all his comrades-in-arms, Hill was the man to whom he was most tenderly attached; and he gave proofs of his firm faith in his capacity and organising power, when he handed over to him the command of the army, with the title of General-Commander-in-Chief.

Rowland was the second son in a prolific household of sixteen. He was the scion of an ancient family, and his father was heir-presumptive to the Shropshire baronetcy, to which he succeeded. Those Hawkstone Hills were a martial race, and when England had caught fire at the French conflagration, five of the brothers went into the army. Moreover, there was variety of talent in the family, for his uncle and namesake was the Whitefield and famous field preacher of the Anglican Communion. Young Rowland gave no indication of the manner of the distinction he was to attain. He is said to have been a gentle, good-humoured, and almost stupid boy, who, like the "old madman" in *Tom Brown*, amused himself with hedge botany and the study of eccentric animals. As he shirked cricket and other boyish pursuits, it was only that good-nature of his which saved him from being sent to Coventry.

Certainly no one could have suspected that soldiering was his vocation. A girl playmate said that his sensibility was almost feminine. He shrank from the very sight of blood, and once fainted over a companion's cut finger. The incident was recalled to his recollection when he had come home after one of the bloodiest battles in the Peninsula, and was asked how he could support the sight of such horrible carnage. The answer was eminently suggestive of the man. "I have still," he replied, "the same feelings; but in the excitement of battle all individual sensation is lost sight of." It was a surprise to his parents, who had intended him for the law, when he insisted on following his elder brother into the army.

In 1790, at the age of eighteen, he was gazetted to the 38th Regiment. In those days the French were our acknowledged masters in everything military. Generations of discredit and decadence had gone by since the victories of Malplaquet and Blenheim. As Wellington studied the art of war at Brienne, Rowland obtained leave to study at Strasburg. A year afterwards, on his return, he was promoted to a lieutenancy in the 53rd, joining his new regiment, like Waverley, with a dozen stalwart recruits, enlisted on the ancestral estates. He had found his vocation, unlikely as it had seemed, and was set upon the determination of achieving success. Getting leave again, he went back to Strasburg, but this time his sojourn was cut short by storm-warnings. In the beginning of 1792 it became clear that Europe was verging towards a cataclysm.

But, though Hill was to play so conspicuous a part in the impending war, for years he was condemned to comparative inactivity; yet, reading between the lines of his life, we can see the evidences of latent ambition. When the war broke out in 1793, the young lieutenant had raised an independent company, and was rewarded with his captain's commission. His company, when handed over to the authorities at Chatham, was ordered to Cork, whence it was marched to Belfast, to be embodied in the 38th Regiment. He used to recall one amusing incident of his short stay in Ireland. He had gone on a visit to a brilliant literary man, distinguished for originality and eccentricity as for talent. Shown to his room, before dinner, he looked in vain for any washing apparatus. When his hand was on the bell, the floor opened, and a wash-hand stand, with everything from towels to hot water, rose into its place.

It was an adaptation of the *tables volantes* of the French *petites maisons*. He used to say he never was so much surprised, save when he saw an anticipation of the modern invention of a tramway bringing dishes from the kitchen to the dining-room. His stay in Ireland was short, for the ardent youth of deceptively apathetic aspect, had no mind to fritter away his opportunities in country quarters. He had made some mark at the Horse Guards, and, moreover, he had found a friend in Mr. Drake, who in July was appointed Minister-Plenipotentiary to the republic of Genoa, then trembling for its future between the French hammer and the Austrian anvil. Drake had instructions, besides, to accompany the English expedition to Toulon, and he nominated Hill his assistant secretary.

There is nothing more luridly dramatic in the annals of the long war than the tragedy of Toulon. For the horrors of the Moscow retreat fell in the way of professional work, on an army that had provoked ruthless reprisals. In the revolt of Southern France against the Terror, when the Girondists had fallen under the axes they had sharpened themselves, Toulon hoisted the white flag, and invited British protection. It was given in that grudging and inefficient fashion which marked every initiative of our operations. We had the chance of capturing the Mediterranean fleet of the French—thirty of their line-of-battle ships were lying in the harbour—and of seizing and holding their Mediterranean arsenal.

There were men of sense who saw that it was a golden opportunity, and there were experts who said that 40,000 or 50,000 men was the smallest strength with which Toulon could be defended. We landed a paltry force of 2000 Britons to stiffen foreign contingents, many of which were worthless. The admiral did all that could have been asked of his means, but matters were complicated further by the arrival of our Spanish allies, with their eternal *mañana* and their inflated pretensions.

Lord Hill

On land, among the British troops, all the talent was with the obscure subalterns, for among them were Hill and Beresford and the future Lord Lynedoch. Among the ships of the fleet was Nelson with the *Agamemnon*. But behind the French batteries, which were being pushed forward to the brows of the encircling heights, was the aspiring Corsican gunner, then barely twenty-five, who made the siege of Toulon his spring-board. Young Hill had his chances too, though poor in comparison, nor did he fail to make the most of them. He seems to have had no special interest, save the backing of the civilian Drake, and with the example of French Commissioners from the Convention before their eyes, civilians were regarded by our fighting men with somewhat contemptuous jealousy. But Hill acted as *aide-de-camp* successively to Lord Mulgrave, O'Hara, and Dundas. O'Hara was a brave and hot-headed Irishman, who had come from Gibraltar to assume command of the garrison.

On "the Rock" he has left his record behind him, in a grand reputation for hospitality, and a watch-tower which bore the name of "O'Hara's Folly." At Toulon, where skill and science had rare opportunities, his one idea was to repel force by force. Whenever the enemy broke ground he hurried forward to fight them, and to carry their advanced batteries by frontal attack. He was fast using up his gallant Britons, who, as Kinglake said of the Crimean *Zouaves*, were the sharpened point of his lance. These Britons never showed to more advantage than when they stormed the battery on the heights of the Arenas. They hunted the broken enemy before them in hot pursuit, to be involved in the laps of the rugged ground, and assailed on all sides by overwhelming numbers. Many were cut down, more were made prisoners, and among the rest O'Hara himself, who was, as always, well to the front.

His *aide-de-camp* was more fortunate, for he came out of the fray safe and with honour. It was owing to the coolness with which he conducted the retreat that he was selected to go home with despatches. In the sanguinary action he had a remarkable escape. He had climbed a tree to take observations of the enemy, when O'Hara called him down. Another *aide-de-camp*, who mounted to his place, was immediately killed. In after days, when the tide of naval and Peninsular victories had set in, the fortunate messenger from a Trafalgar or a Vittoria was the hero of the hour. He carried all the barriers of etiquette that guarded the convivial privacy of the Regent; his arrival was the signal for decorating London with flags and laurel, for kindling bonfires and letting off fireworks from Dover to Cape Wrath. He was sure of an immediate step, with fair prospects of future promotion. Hill's mission, though flattering, was a less agreeable one. His despatches announced that Toulon was untenable, and prepared the Government to break the news of an evacuation to the country.

The evacuation followed his departure in a few days, and he was spared those almost unexampled scenes of terror, in which the naval officers necessarily took the lead. The harbour of the port was the stage of an amphitheatre, which the French batteries were illuminating with incessant discharges from the surrounding heights. Shot, shell, and shrapnel tore through rigging and planks, lashing the surface of the harbour into showers of foam and spray. And all the time the miserable population, warned from their homes at a moment's notice, were very literally between the devil and the deep sea.

They had no mercy to expect from the Terrorists who superintended executions; their sole hope of refuge was the British fleet, and, in panic and desperation, women and children were scrambling for places in the overcrowded boats that were to convey them across the zone of fire. Nor were all the boats at their disposal by any means, for belated business had to be attended to. A naval contingent, under Sidney Smith, was doing its best to fire the French ships which should have strengthened the British navy, and the fall of blazing spars, with frequent explosions of magazines, added to the perils and horrors of the night.

At Toulon Captain Hill had attracted the notice of the future Lord Lynedoch, then simply known as the Laird of Balgowan, and serving as a volunteer—in the following year, 1794, "Colonel" Graham—who was raising his corps of Perthshire volunteers, afterwards the 90th Regiment. Graham, who was an excellent judge of soldierly qualities, remembered his Toulon acquaintance, and offered him the majority. It was gladly accepted, and three months afterwards Hill bought his step as lieutenant-colonel. Thus at three-and-twenty he was in command of a regiment; and of a regiment which, thanks to him, was destined to crown itself with glory in Egypt. Meantime, in common with other corps, it was the plaything of circumstances, and of a War Office that never knew its own mind from one month to another.

As our sailors made sure of victory, our soldiers expected to be baffled and were seldom disappointed. There were endless orders and counter-orders; marching and counter-marching; sailing away and sailing back. In the autumn of 1795 the 90th was with the expedition under General Doyle to Isle Dieu, off the coast of Poitou. The regiment remained in occupation of the island, when Hill, who was always devoted to field sports, and who used to supply Lord Lynedoch after his retirement with pointers from Shropshire, imported greyhounds for the use of the mess, and amused their leisure with coursing.

Brought back to Southampton, it was ordered to St. Domingo. Then it was counter-ordered to Gibraltar, where the colonel had warm welcome from his old chief O'Hara. For two years he was on garrison duty there, and with his regiment was at the descent on Minorca in 1798. From Minorca he obtained leave of absence, and while on leave, on New Year's Day, 1800, was gazetted brevet lieutenant-colonel At that time things were quiet in the West Mediterranean; he had left a capable substitute in command of the 90th, and, at the request of his old patron Drake, he applied for leave to accompany him on a diplomatic mission to Switzerland, intending to rejoin at Minorca after a tour in Italy.

Leave was readily granted, but he changed his plans when he heard that the regiment was to be sent on active service. He took passage on a troopship to Gibraltar, narrowly escaping a French fleet which had suddenly put to sea. Thence he sailed with a large convoy, sent in search of Sir Ralph Abercromby. The convoy missed Sir Ralph, who had gone over to Malta, but Hill found his regiment at Leghorn and returned with it to Minorca. He commanded it on the mismanaged descent on Cadiz, where neither the admiral nor the general, nor Moore, who was second in command, gained any credit by the ineffective demonstration. Hill, who was always of a weakly constitution, had a serious attack of illness, and when he returned to Gibraltar, was forbidden to eat anything but fresh meat. He complained afterwards that it was a costly regimen, for victualling the fleet for the Cadiz voyage had run up provisions to famine prices. Even in the memorable siege three guineas and a half for a turkey would have been considered extravagant. Fortunately he had the warm sympathy of his friend the Governor, whose habit was to keep open house for all comers.

These aimless expeditions and idle alarms were bad training for the troops. But the day was at hand when British soldiers were to be pitted in a fair field against the veteran French, and Abercromby's Egyptian campaign was to restore the *morale* of the army. The Government had entered on it with a light heart, but on the strength of information apparently reliable. The despatches of the French general had been intercepted; they had been written in the darkest pessimism, and if Kleber had intended to deceive he could not have done it more successfully. He described his forces as sick, disgusted, and demoralised, and he reduced their numbers by exactly a half. Abercromby had sailed with 16,000 men, expecting to deal with the same number of fever-stricken Frenchmen. He found himself confronting over 30,000 veterans, as fit to take the field as when Buonaparte deserted them, and holding the fortified harbours which forbade access to the interior.

How he effected his landing on the open beach, in face of a watchful foe and beneath a semicircle of armed batteries, is matter of history. Hill kept a diary which is brief as may be. The entry for 12th March 1801 is:

> Attacked the French, defeated them and gained a glorious victory, was wounded and went on board the fleet.

As matter of fact, he and his regiment had the honours of the day. Abercromby was advancing on Alexandria and the French positions along a natural causeway—a mile and a half in breadth—between the sea and the lake. The 90th, in line, led the advance. General Brou with his *chasseurs-à-cheval* charged them furiously. There was no time to throw the regiment into square, and had it closed up to meet the cavalry shock, the passage would have been left open. Hill calmly halted his raw infantry, in the same thin red line that stemmed the Russian onset at Balaclava. Ordered to reserve their fire, they stood the impact like seasoned veterans. The *chasseurs* were met with a point-blank volley, which emptied saddles by the score, and the shattered ranks were received at the point of the bayonet.

The survivors of the crack corps rode back in dire confusion, and the 90th resumed its march. But their colonel saw no more of the fighting. Struck on the head by a ball—fortunately it did not come from a Lee-Metford carbine—he was partially saved by the peak of his helmet. He revived when borne back to the field-hospital, and there, a couple of days afterwards, he was cheered by a note from Lord Keith, dated from the flagship:—

> Dear Hill,—I am happy to hear you are so well, and I think you will be more at ease here than where you are. . . . I will do all I can to make the ship comfortable to you.

Five days afterwards, as he lay in the *Foudroyant*, Abercromby was carried into the same cabin. There the old chief lingered for a week in agony, with intervals of delirium, knowing well that the end was near. Like Craufurd, he had a soldier's burial on the bastion of Fort St.

Elmo at Valetta.

While still confined to his berth Hill had a visit from the Capitan Pacha, who presented him with a sabre, a gold box, and a shawl, in recognition of the gallantry with which he had led his regiment. Very gratifying was the kind hospitality of the admiral, though Hill was used to friendly acts and kindly offices—perhaps there was a vein of undue gentleness in his martial temperament, for he is said seldom to have made an enemy, and never to have quarrelled with any man. But still more touching was the conduct of his servant whom he had left at Hawkstone. When the man heard his master was wounded, he insisted on starting for Egypt to join him, and at that time the Channel and Mediterranean were swarming with hostile cruisers and privateers.

The letters he brought from Hill's uncle and sisters are pleasantly suggestive. They are full of the little home-like details which the writers knew would cheer the invalid. There are messages from old servants, and mention of humble friends, and notably of the pheasants in the Hawkstone covers, and of the colonel's pet poultry. But long ere the letters had been delivered he was in the field again. In the middle of April 1802 he was in command of the camp at Hamed, and in the subsequent operations he played a conspicuous though subordinate part. Perhaps they have never received the attention they deserved, for they fired the martial spirit of the British linesman, depressed by a succession of disasters. The army had lost faith in its leaders, and it was the sullen determination of Hutchinson, supported by an iron will, which paved the way for the victories of Wellington.

He had succeeded to Abercromby; he had barely 11,000 soldiers at his disposal, supported by a horde of undisciplined Turks; there was no news of Baird, who was on his way from India; but what he knew was that the French in superior strength, with ample artillery, held the positions which were the keys of Lower Egypt. When he had left Coote with 6000 men to blockade Menou in Alexandria, he had only 5000 at his disposal for the advance upon Cairo, where Kleber with double that number had his headquarters. When the silent man, who had neither confidants on his staff nor friends among his officers, issued his orders for the march, there was something like a mutiny in the higher ranks.

It seemed to them as if a captain, either drunk or mad, was steering his ship upon reefs and breakers. For once British regimental officers signed a round robin, inviting the chief's lieutenants to assume the command. Happily Moore and Coote, whatever their private opinions, had sounder ideas of discipline, and Hill with the other generals of brigade lent them loyal support. The venture was rash, but the results, which were astounding, justified the general's self-confidence. There was a striking example of the unexpected in war, when 5000 French veterans were broken before the rush of the Turks. Cairo capitulated, Alexandria followed suit, and then was seen the inconceivable spectacle of 8000 Frenchmen, retaining their arms and followed by their batteries, marching in peaceful submission to the coast, under the escort of half their number of Britons.

The memory of those days of glory and triumph had far-reaching results. The regiment returned home and was ordered to Fort George to be disbanded. But with the *coup d'état* of Brumaire the hopes of an enduring peace were doomed to disappointment. With Buonaparte wearing the purple of the Consulate, it was no time to reduce our military strength, and the 90th, having replenished its ranks, was despatched to Ireland. Ireland was the object of immediate interest, alike to Buonaparte and to the British Cabinet. Three-fourths of the island was seething with disaffection, and the French believed that if they once established a footing there, a revolted province might be their base of operations against England.

French squadrons which had eluded our blockades were continually on the Irish seas, and our frigates were keeping a watchful guard to intimate the landing of some flying expedition. It was in these circumstances, and in August 1803, that Colonel Hill was appointed a Brigadier-General on the Staff. He parted from his comrades-in-arms with great mutual regret. The officers issued an address, saying that the renown so rapidly acquired in the brief regimental existence was entirely due to the discipline the colonel had established and maintained. They added that the discipline had been so tempered with mildness as to endear him to every individual in the regiment.

The Bay of Galway was as likely a place as the Bay of Bantry for a descent. The new brigadier-general was stationed at Loughrea, in command of some light infantry of the Irish militia, and with supervision of all the western coast. There was the same false economy which nearly proved fatal in Spain. Irish affairs were miserably mismanaged by the Horse Guards. The Galway volunteers broke into mutiny, simply because their pay was long in arrear. It was a reason with which Hill could sympathise, for he had the utmost difficulty in wringing money from headquarters, not only for his own pay and allowances, but for each extra piece of service which was ordered or urgent. He settled the matter with his characteristic blending of the mild with the firm.

He had the mutineers tried by a Court of Yeomanry Captains, who were instructed to investigate the justice of the complaints. In forwarding the report to Sir Eyre Coote, while acknowledging that the men had undeniable grievances, he said their conduct was none the less reprehensible, and added that though he believed in their penitence he hesitated to restore their arms. Sir Eyre took a merciful view of the case, and the ringleaders who had been in temporary confinement were released; but Hill had established his reputation as a disciplinarian. Shortly afterwards he was able to report that all the militiamen and volunteers under his command were animated by a loyal and soldierlike spirit.

He studied the possible *kriegspiel* from all the points of view of a general who might have to face an enemy landing anywhere. He visited all the places where a descent could be conceivably effected. He surveyed all the passes leading inland, decided on the positions where an advance could be most effectively opposed, and arranged for the prompt destruction of the bridges on the roads that were practicable for the passage of artillery in that wild country. With a disaffected peasantry an enemy might have landed and marched far into the bowels of the land, without intimation reaching Loughrea or any quarter of the British garrison.

Consequently he arranged a system of signalling which, as he wrote to Sir Eyre Coote, could communicate minute information with profound secrecy. Between Loughrea and Galway he established a line of semaphores, and no little trouble he had—strange as it may appear—in persuading the landowners to consent to the erection of those telegraphs. For the squires and even the "Shoneens" were Protestant for the most part and had no sympathy with the French. There is a curious letter of his to "Dick Martin" of Ballynahinch, who owned half Connemara. It shows that Hill had surveyed those unexplored wastes more carefully than any land surveyor, and gives the most detailed instructions as to what ought to be done in the event of a French column marching upon Oughterard.

During the first period of his Irish duties he was incessantly haunted by the reasonable expectation of invasion. During the second, he could dismiss that apprehension, for, though Austerlitz had been lost, Trafalgar had been won. In the interval came the interlude to which we have alluded, when in command of a brigade he sailed from Cork to take part in another of our luckless continental expeditions. The troops reached the Weser, only to re-embark when they heard that Buonaparte was carrying all before him. Luckless the expedition was from the first, for Hill wrote home, when he was keeping a cold Christmas, that when he reached the river the headquarters ship of each regiment attached to him was missing: "some were wrecked on the Dutch coast, and many souls perished on the Goodwin Sands." But that hopeless expedition was fortunate for him, for it was then he made the acquaintance and won the appreciation of Sir Arthur Wellesley. They had met first at Deal, when the Cork transports touched there: for Sir Arthur was in command of another of the brigades.

2

In June 1808 came a note from Sir Arthur:—

My dear Hill,—I rejoice exceedingly at the prospect I have before me of serving again with you, and I hope we shall have more to do than we had on the last occasion on which we were together.

The hope was fulfilled. Ministers had at last decided to strike at Napoleon through Portugal, and Sir Arthur—he had scarcely sailed before he was superseded—was selected as the fitting man for command. But vacillation and the policy of penny-wisdom were still in the ascendant. The 30,000 men destined for the army of Portugal were scattered for the most part in camps on the Channel and in the eastern counties, or in fleets between Cherbourg and Cadiz. As Napier says, the only force available for immediate operations was the 9000 in Irish garrisons who mustered at Cork under Hill. Even at Cork there were delays which tried Sir Arthur's patience: but till his arrival Hill took the utmost care of his men, landing them regularly for service and supplying them with fresh provisions.

By the way, among the 9000 there were no fewer than 227 drummers, reminding us of Ayton's metrical romance of the Fairshon's feud with the M'Tavish. They sailed at last on July 12, but next day Sir Arthur quitted the convoy in a fast-sailing frigate for Corunna, whither he went to consult with the Asturian deputies, whose importunity had set our slow machinery in motion. General Hill reported good progress to Lord Castlereagh from the *Donegal* at sea; for a marvel, none of the transports were missing and the troops were in perfect health. When Sir Arthur came on board the *Donegal* at the appointed place of meeting, he had settled his plans. Junot held the south. Bessières was threatening the northern provinces; but he decided on disembarking at the mouth of the Mondego and marching straight upon Lisbon.

While off the river he had the unwelcome news of his being superseded: it only excited him to more strenuous effort, for it was everything to take the enemy by surprise. On August 1 he began landing his 9000, and on the 5th, before the disembarkation was completed, he was happily reinforced by General Spencer from Cadiz, bringing 3000 more. With these feeble means, with the Atlantic rollers behind, breaking on a rock-bound and harbourless coast, the first campaign in Portugal was begun.

In their first meeting with the French the British had the best, for though Junot had early information he had to concentrate his scattered troops. Yet his able lieutenant, Laborde, though inferior in strength by a third, had the advantage of formidable positions. On August 16 he occupied the lofty plateau which took its name from the village of Roliça, and commanded the steep and narrow valley through which the main road led to the south. He had covered the heights with detachments, and in case of reverse he had a second line of hills to fall back upon.

On the morning of the 19th he was assailed in three columns. Hill, supported by cavalry and covered by the spluttering fire of a cloud of skirmishers, led the attack to the right of the road and pushed it fiercely. Hard pressed at all points and with both his flanks menaced, Laborde extricated himself with admirable skill, and, covered by his cavalry, retired on his second position. That involved new dispositions on the part of the British. Generals Hill and Nightingale were ordered to a full frontal attack on those frowning heights of Zambugeera. It was a trying experience for entering young troops who had never before fired a shot in anger.

The only approaches to the precipitous faces were by foot tracks through rugged gullies. The columns, preceded by the skirmishers, involuntarily deployed, in inevitable disorder, as they worked their way through the tangled shrubbery that clothed the bottom of the rocks. Neither general spared himself: the defence was as obstinate as the assault was determined, but Laborde saw his left and centre forced back by irresistible pressure. Looking vainly for Loison, who should have been coming up from the east, he held tenaciously on to his right, till there too he was compelled to retreat. After an obstinate defence that did him as much honour as a victory, he left the road to Torres Vedras open, abandoning three of his guns. Rifleman Harris, from the private's point of view, gives a graphic account of the fierce fighting on the 17th, and of Hill's composure at the critical moment.

> The 29th Regiment received so terrible a fire that I saw the right wing almost annihilated, and the colonel (I think his name was Lennox) lay sprawling among the rest We had ourselves caught it pretty handsomely, for there was no cover for us and we were rather too near. The living skirmishers were lying beside heaps of their own dead, but still we held our own till the battalion regiments came up. 'Fire and retire!' is a very good sound, but the Rifles were not fond of such notes. . . . At the moment a little confusion appeared in the ranks, I thought. Lord Hill was near at hand and saw it, and I observed him come galloping up. He put himself at the head of the regiment and restored it to order in a moment. Pouring a regular and sharp fire upon the enemy, he galled them in return, and remaining with the 29th till he brought them to the charge, quickly sent the foe to the right about. It seemed to me that few men could have conducted the business with more coolness and quickness of manner under such a storm of balls as he was exposed to. Indeed I have never forgotten him from that day.

It was not his first meeting with the general. The day before the battle he says:—

> We were pelting along through the streets of a village, the name of which I do not think I ever knew. I was in the front and had just cleared the village when I recollect observing General Hill (afterwards Lord Hill) and another officer ride up to a house and give their horses to some of the soldiery to hold. . . I stood leaning upon my rifle, near the door, when the officer who had entered with Lord Hill came and called to me. 'Rifleman,' handing me a dollar, 'go and try if you can get some wine, for we are devilish thirsty here.

Harris hurried off for the wine, and when he brought it, found General Hill loosening his sword belt "'Drink first, rifleman,' said he, and I took a good pull at the pipkin and held it to him again. He looked at it and told me I might drink it all, for it appeared rather greasy." Harris honestly handed back the dollar, for in his haste and the bustle he had not paid for the wine. "Keep the money, my man," said

Hill, giving a second dollar. "Go back and try if you cannot get me another draught." That was "Father Hill" all over, with the consideration, affability, and free-handedness that won the hearts of his men.

On the 19th the army fought again at Vimiero, but there Hill was merely a spectator. The village was in a valley, overlooked by a mountain dominating a little eminence to the south-east which was the key of the British defence. For it was Junot who took the initiative and advanced to the attack. Again it was a battlefield of wood and rock and of the vineyard enclosures surrounding Vimiero. The French assault was delivered in three columns. Hill's brigade remained on the slope of the mountain: in immediate support of the centre and a reserve for the whole army. It was never called into action. The central attack failed; the battle was over early in the afternoon, and Wellesley, when assured that the enemy had made his last effort, had all in readiness for changing defeat into disaster.

General Ferguson, having repelled a bold flanking movement on our right, was driving Solignac's broken column before him. Wellesley, who with half his forces had beaten Junot, meant to follow with that half in hot pursuit: while Hill, Fane, and Anstruther with the other, taking the road by the sea to Torres Vedras, were to turn the mountain ranges and cut the French retreat upon Lisbon. But Ferguson was recalled, to his intense disgust, which meant that the impending change of command had been accomplished. Burrard had come up in time to see a part of the action, but had generously left the finishing of the work to Sir Arthur. Now he had taken over the reins, and decided that it would be prudent to remain on the defensive, awaiting Moore with the reinforcements which were known to be off the coast. Then followed the convention, miscalled, of Cintra, which provoked a storm of indignation. The three commanders—for Sir Hew Dalrymple within twenty-four hours had in turn superseded Burrard—were recalled to England to give evidence before the Court of Inquiry.

Moore succeeded to the command of a nominal force of 30,000 foot and 4000 horse. For the calculations were on the imaginary strength of depleted battalions in Portugal, and the contingent of 10,000 under Baird was still at sea. His instructions were to make a diversion in Spain, in favour of the Spanish armies, when the Emperor was in the Peninsula in person, with 180,000 foot and 40,000 horsemen, all disposable, without drawing upon his fortresses or endangering communications. Nevertheless, Moore proceeded to obey orders, and there is no reproaching him with lack of audacity. The rather that he was not of a hopeful spirit, and fully realised the difficulties.

For sound reasons he decided to march towards Madrid by way of Almeida and Ciudad Rodrigo. The direct road from Lisbon lay through mountainous country, and he was informed that it was impracticable for guns. He discovered to his regret that the information was false; meantime he had reluctantly violated a fundamental rule of war, and separated from his field batteries. They were committed to the charge of Sir John Hope, who was to follow the easier and more southerly route to Talavera, and thence crossing the Guadarama Sierra, to rejoin his commander at Salamanca. Hill with the 1st Brigade was a part of Hope's column. They had no fighting, but much hardship and infinite anxiety. From want of supplies and of money to buy them, the small force was broken up in six divisions, each separated by a long day's march.

Hope concentrated at the Escorial beneath the Guadarama, but, having gone to Madrid to interview the Spanish statesmen, he came back with the conviction that nothing was to be hoped from them and that he most look to his own safety. It was high time—he was enveloped by the French, and the 4th Corps in particular seemed to be omnipresent. He dragged his guns and waggons over the mountain, saving them on the northern side by the skin of his teeth. Moore had the guns and ammunition again, of which he had well nigh despaired, and Hope and his generals of brigade had saved the army.

For Hope had reached Salamanca on the eve of the retreat, inevitable after the disaster of Tudela, when Lannes scattered the levies of Castaños and Palafox. We hear little of Hill between Salamanca and Corunna. He played no such sensational part as Paget or Craufurd, who held the pursuers in check and broke down the bridges. But at Corunna he had his share of the glory. Napier, who is not given to exaggeration, describes the situation as dangerous but not desperate. The problem was to win a battle under every disadvantage, and to embark the victors in a crowded harbour, in face of an enemy formidably superior in numbers and covering the heights with heavy artillery. The fighting was very fairly distributed among the 14,000 march-worn soldiers who held the inner amphitheatre of hills.

Hope's division was on the extreme left, resting on the tidal estuary of the Mero, and taking the offensive when Foy's successive attacks had failed, it flung him back in hopeless disorder. The fall of night put an end to the action, but enough had been done for honour and safety. Moore had been laid in a rough coffin, awaiting burial at daybreak: torches were flitting about the field, where ambulance men were seeking to succour the wounded: and a circle of picket fires marked the sweep of the British lines. Soult could believe that he would have another opportunity on the morrow. Then Hope, who had succeeded to the command, set about the embarkation. The great powder magazines had been exploded in the morning: the jaded and foundered cavalry horses had been shot: the heavy guns had been sent on board the transports.

Now shipping the men went swiftly and silently forward, and with the dawn, when the French realised that our pickets had been withdrawn, the only English left on shore were Hill's brigade, who, having covered the embarkation from beneath the ramparts, were in occupation of the citadel. The brigade was quickly embarked in turn, when the bulk of the transports had cleared out of the harbour, though the French had pushed forward a battery which caused considerable confusion in the fleet. Nevertheless Beresford, with the rear-guard, kept possession of the citadel till the last of the wounded were placed in safety.

3

Napoleon's marshals had carried out his orders. They had driven the English into the sea, victorious but discomfited. His admirably devised plan of garrisoning Spain was in full operation; with Madrid for a centre, his disciplined legions in their irresistible superiority were everywhere scientifically disposed so as to crush any serious efforts at resistance. In every engagement the Spaniards had been routed and their levies dispersed. The fall of Saragossa, after a heroic defence, had set Lannes with his 25,000 at liberty. The final subjugation of Portugal seemed assured. Victor in Estremadura was menacing Badajoz; Lapisse in Castile was threatening Ciudad Rodrigo; Soult had peremptory orders to bear down upon the north and seize the great commercial capital of Oporto. The only adverse circumstances were the invincible jealousies of the generals and the condition of Soult's army.

It had been worn out, in strength and spirit, shoes, arms, and clothing, in the hot pursuit of Moore through the highlands of Gallicia. Cradock had been left at Lisbon, in command of the feeble rearguard, and his position was well nigh desperate. He had barely 10,000 British troops, and in the reasonable fear of being abandoned to their fate the violence of Portuguese factions had come to a head. He had so little hope of help from home that there were secret instructions to embark his men in case of necessity, bringing the Portuguese fleet and the contents of the arsenals away with him. Insufficient justice has been done to his constancy, coolness, and military skill. He held tenaciously to his forlorn charge, while taking every precaution against the worst, and his masterly preparations for the defence of Lisbon had anticipated Torres Vedras on a smaller scale. But, at the moment when evacuation seemed imminent, events took a sudden turn.

In the English Cabinet a hot fit had succeeded to the cold, and it was decided that Portugal was not to be abandoned. The immediate despatch of strong reinforcements was commenced: the good news brought a revulsion of feeling with the Portuguese; they volunteered to call out all their levies—ban and *arrière-ban*—and offered the command to an Englishman. Beresford landed at Lisbon, to be gazetted a Portuguese marshal, and proceeded to lick his excellent raw material into shape. But a greater actor was to appear on the scene, for Wellesley superseded Cradock.

Cradock had cause to complain, yet the wisdom of the choice was abundantly justified. Sir Arthur came with the prestige of his former victories, and the patriotism of the desponding Portuguese was warmed to fever heat. They hopefully worshipped the rising star, and prepared themselves for hard times and heavy sacrifices. Moreover, the new general had come with solid pledges of support, for with other troops he brought four regiments of cavalry, and hitherto in cavalry we had been lamentably deficient. Nor did he come a day too soon, for the outlook on all sides had become darker than ever. The Spaniards, thoroughly beaten before, had rashly provoked fresh disasters. Cuesta had been routed at Medellin, and the army of La Mancha had been scattered at Ciudad Beal.

Soult was not only established at Oporto, but by a liberal policy he was said to be conciliating influential *fidalgos* and citizens. Now that Victor had for the time disposed of Cuesta, the road to Lisbon lay comparatively open. But Victor was still obstructed by the frontier fortresses and the barrier of the flooded Tagus. Sir Arthur was in a strait between two decisions, with a confusion of interested counsellors; but he never made more conspicuous display of the daring strategy and imperturbable self-confidence which were invariably tempered by prescience. He came to the conclusion that the more pressing necessity was to rid the northern provinces of the French, which would at the same time liberate Gallicia. There was peril either way, but he decided that there was time to deal with Soult without serious danger from Victor.

Soult, dazzled by visions of a Portuguese crown, had cast longing looks at Lisbon. He commanded all the passages of the Douro; his light cavalry held the fords and bridges of the Vouga; but his further march had been arrested by the prospect of flooded rivers and formidable defiles. Sir Arthur's advance would be so far without military impediment, but when he had negotiated the floods and dragged his guns through the nearer gorges, he would find the enemy on the line of the Vouga, and in occupation of the farther passes. Beyond these was a virtually impregnable position, girdled by the broad and rapid Douro.

Soult might well, to all appearance, have deemed himself secure, and the English general seemed to be courting disaster. But Soult, though fearing nothing from surprise or direct assault, had realised that his position was untenable, and was contemplating retreat on Salamanca. He was being threatened from behind by Spanish and Portuguese partisans; his line of retreat was being menaced by Silviera; and, as Wellesley learned, when concentrating at Coimbra, the marshal was the object of a formidable conspiracy and was being betrayed by the men he most implicitly trusted. Both knew that the evacuation of Oporto was a foregone conclusion; and had Wellesley waited, as the more cautious Cradock would have done, we should never have heard of the "Passage of the Douro."

But time was still of supreme importance. If Wellesley struck fast and hard, Soult's precipitate retreat would result in an immense disaster, and the moral effect would be great. Moreover, if Soult, a master of orderly retiring, took men and guns and military train safe to Salamanca, he would be more formidable than at Oporto: if he were driven over the mountains into Gallicia, he need not be counted with for many weeks to come. And when the plan of operation had once been settled, and when Beresford in relatively slender strength was to be thrown across the Salamanca route, accelerated action became imperative.

The army moved forward from Coimbra in three lines. The main advance took the direct road to Oporto. On the right Beresford's Portuguese, stiffened by two British battalions, marched upon Lamego. The 3rd Division under Hill was to follow the coast road and turn the extreme right of the French, which rested on the Lake of Ovar. Sir Arthur had learned that that long sheet of water—open to the flow and ebb of the tides—had been left unguarded. Accordingly he had arranged an unpleasant surprise for Franceschi, the Craufurd of the French outposts, the dashing leader of light cavalry; and a letter written to Hill on the 8th shows his minute attention to details he might well have confided to subordinates. He tells Hill that he will find a flotilla of boats awaiting him at the foot of the lake, that Colonel Douglas had orders to look up the boatmen, and he recommends the general to cook a day's provisions at Aveiro, and to see that the men had a full meal at Ovar.

As such careful foresight deserved, all went well to Ovar. The Portuguese fishermen toiled at the oars with zealous patriotism, scaring clouds of waterfowl and sea-birds from solitudes within sound of the ocean surf; and the flotilla, timed to reach Ovar at daybreak, had to lie off in the dusk before disembarking. Hill had turned the right of the French, as Beresford by that time had turned the left, and it was only owing to one of the accidents of war that Franceschi with his horse and Mermet with the supporting infantry were not caught in the toils so carefully spread for them. But Franceschi proved himself an apt pupil of Soult in the art of extricating himself from situations threatening destruction.

As it was, he probably owed his safety to Sir Arthur's peremptory orders and Hill's too docile obedience. On the 10th, surrounded as he was by the English forces, he led his horsemen across Hill's front, and led them with impunity. The impetuous Craufurd would certainly have attacked, and if a Nelson had been in command of the division he would assuredly have disobeyed orders. But Hill with sublime self-restraint let the enemy and the opportunity go by. In his implicit loyalty to his chief he refused by a personal success to risk upsetting a complex scheme of operations, and as he knew nothing of the strength of the French supports, even a victorious advance might have sacrificed his division. The decision is characteristic of his temperament: but, when the Duke of Wellington spoke of him afterwards as shirking responsibility, it would be interesting to know whether the inaction at Ovar was in his mind.

That he did not always shrink from responsibility was to be shown at Almarez, and no one ever charged him with lack of spirit. On the 12th, at the memorable passage of the Douro, he was to give his proofs, if fresh proofs were needed. Franceschi and Mermet had crossed the Douro in the night, breaking down the only bridge behind them. Soult believed he had secured every boat on his own side of the river. He had already been sending off his guns and baggage: but, knowing nothing of the rough handling of Loison by Beresford, he decided to delay his march for another day, that that general might draw in his detachments. He might well believe that there was no need to hurry. The broad river was rolling by in angry flood, and his absolute confidence in the impassable barrier was his undoing. His own quarters were in the west end of the city, and all his attention was given to the lower river, for he believed that Hill's division had come by sea and that the ships could be used for crossing at the estuary.

Above the bridge in the centre of the city the Douro makes a sharp bend, and the bend is commanded by the convent-crowned heights of Sarco. Behind those heights Sir Arthur had concentrated his main force, and it was effectually masked. He had detached General Murray to cross at Avintas, three miles higher up, and both Murray and Beresford were in danger if the river were not passed that morning. It is doubtful whether the problem would have been solved had it not been for a happy chance. A barber gave Oporto to Sir Arthur, as a pedlar saved Soult from capitulating. Eluding the vigilance of the sentinels, the barber had brought a skiff across.

Surveying the situation from the convent, Sir Arthur had seen that the sweep of the river was unguarded, though in the distance, through clouds of dust, columns in retreat were to be distinguished. Beneath him, on the opposite bank, was an unfinished building, which seemed designed by Providence for a *tête de pont*. It would offer shelter for a considerable force, and to the west was an open space which could be swept by musketry. If the head of a column were lodged there, the rest would be comparatively simple. There was the little skiff, and Colonel Waters, famed for many daring exploits, volunteered to go with the barber on a quest for boats. The Prior of Amaranta made a third in the party.

The adventurers, successful beyond hope, brought back some barges in tow. "Let the men embark" was the curt order when someone suggested difficulties. Some troops of Paget's and Hill's divisions were cautiously advanced to the bank. One officer and twenty-five men of the Buffs were the first to land. Boat-load after boat-load was ferried over before the garrison took the alarm. Then there was the roll of drums, beating to quarters, and a confused noise of shouting as regiments rushed to arms. A mixed multitude passed out of the city, and throwing out swarms of skirmishers, came surging up to the walls of the seminary. The fire swept the walls and searched the loopholes. Paget, who was among the first to cross, was one of the first to fall.

Hill took his place in directing the defence. By this time the enemy had brought cannon into play, but their fire was kept down by the British batteries on the height, and these swept the exposed *terre pleine* in such deadly fashion that the assault on the seminary was confined to a single side. Still the assault was so sustained, and the situation so critical, that, as Napier says, "Sir Arthur would himself have crossed, but for the earnest representations of those about him and the just confidence he had in General Hill."

Already, as he was hesitating, the crisis had gone by. The citizens were signalling from roofs and windows that the enemy had abandoned the lower town, and already they were bringing over many boats that the evacuation had released from embargo. Sherbrooke, near the broken bridge, was busy embarking his battalions. Murray's division was seen descending the opposite bank: and again, beyond the seminary through the clouds of dust, other columns were seen retreating. They were not suffered to pass unmolested, for Hill, pushing forward to the enclosure walls, kept pouring in a steady fire. He could not venture to quit his cover, for with him were only three regiments, and one of these was Portuguese. But all the time the army was crossing: Sherbrooke, with the guards, as he gathered additional strength, was pressing hard on the rear of the enemy, while shell and shot were being showered on them from the guns on the crest of Sarco. Confusion and panic would have been changed to utter rout had Murray's division been handled by Hill or Craufurd.

Hill kept up regular correspondence with a favourite sister. Nothing can be more modest than the descriptions of his own doings, and we may add that his letters of that period show that even generals of division were little in the confidence of the commander-in-chief. Sir Arthur kept his own counsel, and in the campaigns of the Douro and Talavera, Hill can only hazard surmises as to what may happen next. Modest as he was, he felt he owed it to his family that he should have his fair share of commendation. He resented Lord Castlereagh's public comments on Sir Arthur's hurried despatch on the passage of the Douro, and he wrote:

> No officer is more deserving of praise than General Paget; but he was wounded so very early in the business that he was not present when the serious attacks were made, which indeed did not take place till after the greater part of the 66th and 48th had come up, although Lord Castlereagh would wish it to be understood that General Paget and the Buffs resisted the whole

French army.

Hill, though generous, was only human: it may have been the undue credit attributed by Castlereagh to the Buffs which inspired a rather spiteful remark on the eve of Talavera.

The soldier still interested in his poultry and pheasantries at Hawkstone had not been parted from all his pets. As he asks anxiously after the kennels and the chicken coops, so even in the swing of rapid movements he reports on Dido, his spaniel bitch, which had been confined during the advance to the Douro, and his brother Clement, who was one of his *aides-de-camp*, writes:

> I must tell you how careful Dido is of her family. Two of them have been brought in a basket, and the other morning, when the baggage was going off, she went upstairs by herself, and brought the basket in her mouth for the puppies to be put in.

Marshal Beresford, a *connoisseur* in wines and *cuisine*, was noted for keeping the best table in the Peninsula. He had his French *chef* with a *batterie de cuisine* in his baggage. But if we may take Hill's own word for it, though hospitable to excess, he lived very frugally. He writes in one of his letters:

> Mr. Mackworth[1] is a fine young man: I wish I had it in my power to show him more civility. All I can do for him is occasionally to give him a very bad dinner.

Larpent, Judge-Advocate-General to the armies, once excused himself from dining at headquarters, as he was engaged to Hill. "Very well," said Wellington, "but I advise you to come to me nevertheless, for Hill gives the worst dinners in the army."

Soult had been driven out of Portugal and hunted back into Spain. By something like miracles of skill, coolness, and daring, he had saved the bulk of his army, but they were reduced to worse condition than when he was beaten at Corunna. He had lost his guns, his stores, and his baggage. Sir Arthur's calculations had been justified by events, and now he could turn his attention to Victor. On 17th June Hill was writing from Abrantes, where the victorious army was encamped, short of money, and shoes, and everything else, but full of spirit and eager to advance. He had his quarters in a small house in the town; his men were in temporary huts they had run up for themselves. He thought it probable they would tarry there for some time: but ten days later the camp was broken up.

In strange ignorance of the strength of the northern French armies, in reliance on the fallacious assurances of the Spaniards, Sir Arthur meant to move on Madrid by the valley of the Tagus. When he met Cuesta, their staffs intermingled to the thunder of the cannon, the beat of the drums, the music of the bands, and the shouts of the Spaniards. It was the meeting of mediaeval and modern war; of age, infirmity, and antiquated methods, with energy, stern simplicity, and prompt decision. Sir Arthur may have rued his advance and foreseen his retreat when he saw the unwieldy figure of the Spanish veteran in slashed doublet and trunk hose, with an *aide-de-camp* in superb accoutrements walking on either side of his saddle in readiness to lend support to the tottering horseman.

The interchange of courtesies did not reassure him, nor was he misled by the magniloquent vaunting of his vain-glorious colleague. Cuesta failed him on every occasion. The sullen old valetudinarian who went to "observe" the enemy in a coach and six had alternate fits of sluggishness and frenzy: one day nothing would induce him to move; on the next he would risk his men with the harebrained valour of a Don Quixote. Though the rich Vera of Placentia was near, the English were starving, and Hill wrote on 25th July:

> Instead of our having supplies to take on, the soldiers have not yet had meat or bread for *yesterday*.

In that letter he ventured on a rash prediction. Victor was in retreat, and he says:

> If we can get the French out of Spain without an action, which I do not think unlikely, I shall be satisfied.

Napoleon showed greater prescience. Dictating minute instructions to Soult from distant Germany, he had said: "Wellington will probably advance by the Tagus against Madrid; in that case, pass the mountains, fall on his flank and rear and crush him."

When Sir Arthur with barely 20,000 men was pressing forward to meet Victor, he little realised the danger impending from the north. Soult had 50,000 bayonets and sabres at Salamanca: the very day the British passed the Tietar he was threatening the defile of Baños in the *sierras*, and Cuesta, who had undertaken to guard it, had only sent a couple of weak battalions. Had Joseph had anything of the genius and energy of his brother, the avalanche must have fallen and the victors of Talavera must have been crushed. But the usurper was distracted by conflicting counsels and disposed to sacrifice everything to the safety of his capital.

Hill had no part in the operations when Victor was retiring and returning. The French marshal had fallen back on the central army led by Joseph and Jourdan, and it had been joined by the fourth corps from La Mancha under Sebastiani. The allies, who had taken positions at Talavera, found themselves confronting 50,000 veterans. In numbers the armies were not unequally matched, but the brunt of the battle impending was to be borne by 19,000 British. Sir Arthur had begun to understand the fighting worth of his allies, and made his dispositions accordingly. The Spaniards were in positions virtually impregnable, their right resting on the town and the Tagus. The field of operations was enclosed in a square, about two miles in diameter either way.

To the north lay the Alberche: to the east the Tagus: to the south the line of defence held by the allies. To the west was the ridge of a lofty *sierra*, which sunk at half distance into the plain. The British aligned to the west of the Spaniards had their left on a detached hill which proved to be the key of the positions and pivot of the fighting. For immediately in front of it was a dominating height, which when it fell into possession of the enemy searched the British lines with an oblique fire, and threatened to make the lower eminence untenable. Sir Arthur made at least one serious mistake. He neglected the deep ravine lying between those confronting heights and the loftier *sierra*, and had hastily to modify his arrangements when his left was menaced by a turning movement. It was broken ground, between the Alberche and the town, thickly covered by olives and oak trees, which masked the evolutions on either side, as it broke the order of the attacking columns. General Campbell's division stood next to the Spaniards; then came Sherbrooke, and Hill was to the extreme left, with the cavalry massed behind him.

At three in the afternoon the enemy crossed the Alberche in two columns, and stealing onward under cover of the trees, surprised our outposts at Casa Salinas. Indeed we narrowly escaped an irretrievable disaster, for Sir Arthur himself was nearly taken prisoner. But his presence restored order; he rallied the old 45th with some companies of the 60th, and brought them to the support of the younger battalions which had been thrown into confusion. Moreover the cavalry came to the rescue, and the British withdrew fighting, having sustained heavy loss. Mackenzie fell into line behind Sherbrooke; Donkin, with his brigade, took post on the lower hill on the left.

It seems to have been assumed by Sir Arthur that the approach of night would suspend the battle. For Hill was not called up to the support of Donkin, and nothing was done to secure possession of the dominating eminence in front of Donkin's position. But the French were blooded and full of fight, and Victor had no mind to restrain them. On our right the mere show of an attack had thrown the strongly entrenched Spaniards into a panic, and the panic would have ended in a rout had not the onset been checked by flanking movements of the English cavalry.

That onset was the mere impulse of a wild rush; scarcely even a feint: Victor never expected to storm those formidable positions. The serious attack was directed to our left, where, seeing the weakness of the force with which it was held, he hoped to seize the key of the positions. He came very near to succeeding. Leading Villatte's division across the plain, hurrying up all his field pieces and light cavalry, he established his guns on the isolated hill and concentrated a tremendous cannonade upon Donkin. Fortunately Donkin's hill was a natural redoubt Steep and rugged where it faced the French, it was skirted at bottom by a deep ravine. On the southern side, towards Hill and his division, the slope was comparatively gentle. Under cover of the vehement cannonade, Ruffin and Villatte rushed to the storm. Donkin forced back the frontal attack, but the assailants had swept round his left and seized the summit above him.

Hill had been dining in Talavera. No one had dreamed of an attack that evening, and he was riding quietly back with Major Fordyce when he heard the firing. He reached the encampment to meet an order to hurry up with supports. It was fast drawing towards dusk, and objects were barely distinguishable. He was hastily giving instructions to the colonel of the 48th, when, as he tells himself in a memorandum drawn up in 1827, for the satisfaction of an officer of high rank, he "observed some men on the hilltop fire a few shots at us. Not having an idea that the enemy were so near, I said at the moment I was sure it was the old Buffs as usual making some blunder."

When he rode up the hill to stop the firing, he discovered his mistake. He was in the midst of the French. "I turned to ride off, when they fired again and killed poor Fordyce and shot my mare through the body. She did not fall, but carried me to the 29th Regiment, which by my orders instantly charged the French and drove them from the hill." It was a narrow escape, for a Frenchman had seized his bridle, and only lost hold when Hill set spurs to his horse. Had he been captured then, it is certain he would never have been commander-in-chief of the British army.

His brief, blunt memorandum gives but a faint idea of what happened in that critical half-hour. The enemy had won the heights, and had no mind to abandon them. The other British divisions, looking anxiously to their left, saw the hill-crest illuminated with incessant flashes, now advancing and again receding. For half-an-hour the combatants had been exchanging volleys point blank, and ever and again came the clash of bayonets. But at length arose the British cheer of victory, when the assailing column, in shattered fragments, was hurled down into the depths below. It was a near thing at the best; the position had been well nigh lost, and it was fortunate that the supporting regiments of Baffin's division had gone far astray in the ravine to the left. But in the fighting of that half-hour nearly 2000 combatants had fallen.

Victor was piqued by a failure, where he had only been baffled by ill-luck. He proposed to renew the attack next morning: Jourdan opposed, but Joseph acceded. His reasoning was sound, but the favourable opportunity had gone by. During the night Sir Arthur had altered his dispositions. Now the flanking ravine was guarded by two regiments of horse, and the mountain beyond was watched by a Spanish brigade. Nevertheless the renewed attack on the key of the line was sufficiently formidable, and for a time the issue was in doubt. Victor had been as active through the night as Wellington. He had massed all the guns of the 1st Corps on the eminence commanding Hill's position. With the dawn they simultaneously opened fire, scattering death broadcast among the defenders of the British hill, and raking our entrenchments to the right, up to the great redoubt in their centre.

Simultaneously, too, the dim plain in front was darkened by Ruffin's division coming on, two regiments abreast, supported by heavy masses behind. The roar of the French guns lulled when their own attacking columns crossed the line of fire. But it was succeeded by sharp exchanges of musketry. Then the ranks were broken on either side, and it became a soldier's battle—a sort of Inkerman. And, as men fell fast, the ranks were replenished by the supports on one side and the reserves on the other. Hill, who was everywhere in the front—it was no time for the coolest general to spare himself—had his horse shot under him and was slightly wounded. But again British obstinacy carried the day, again the French were precipitated down the fatal hillside. Their retirement was covered by the fire of their cannon, to which there was nothing more than a half-dozen of field pieces to reply, but they had left 1500 of their comrades behind.

For a space after that sanguinary prelude, the opposing hosts rested on their arms. In that informal truce, the soldiers of both armies, parched with thirst under the burning sun, amicably intermingled on the banks of the brook which traversed the plain between the outposts. Meantime the French leaders were consulting. Jourdan gave the wise advice to retire on the Alberche and there await the operations of Soult, when Wellesley, unless he fell back from Talavera, must have been caught in a vice between two armies; but his counsels were rejected and the pertinacity of Victor prevailed. Thus the real "Talavera" began at noon. This time the battle raged furiously along the whole line, and there were no feigned attacks. To the right the British everywhere held their ground, till the impetuosity of Sherbrooke's Guards, scattering in hot pursuit, invited disaster, and they were swept back in confusion on the surge of a returning tide. The centre was broken: the onset was not to be stemmed, and for the moment victory inclined to the French. Sir Arthur had taken his station on the height held by Hill, and thence he was surveying the scene.

On that hill the attack had been fierce as before, and it was menaced besides by a formidable flanking movement along the ravine to the left. But it was so firmly held that at that supreme crisis Sir Arthur could spare the 48th to support his centre, and in the centre the 48th restored the battle. To the left, in the great ravine, the brilliant though reckless courage of the cavalry had amazed Villatte's division and checked its advance. To the right ten of the guns of the 4th Corps had been captured, and the fall of Lapisse had disheartened the soldiers he had so gallantly led. The musketry fire slackened, sputtered, and died out.

The Frenchmen limbered up and withdrew their guns. Joseph decided to fall back to make sure of Madrid, and Wellesley was in no condition to pursue him. More than a third of his soldiers were *hors de combat*, and the others, who had fought the battle with empty stomachs, were exhausted by hunger, thirst, and hard fighting. If Talavera was a bloody and barren victory, that was the fault of our allies. It gave Sir Arthur. Wellesley his peerage, and General Hill carried off the second honours. He was rewarded with the colonelcy of the 94th Regiment, and was gratified by the graceful compliments of the Premier, when the army received the thanks of the House of Commons.

Talavera proved a barren victory, yet Joseph and Victor had saved the Peninsula for Spain. Had Joseph listened to the counsels of Jourdan, or had Soult been left untrammelled in the direction of operations, the result would have been different. But Victor was hot-headed, and Ney was jealous, and Joseph was a reed shaken by the winds. Between the perversity of crabbed old Cuesta and his strange misapprehensions as to the strength Soult was bringing to bear upon him, Sir Arthur, with the effectives of his victorious army, was in a situation of the utmost peril.

But his genius was always inspired by emergency, and he was never more admirable than when apparently cornered. With a skill and swiftness which remind one of Montrose's eccentric campaigns in Scotland, he not only carried his own troops across the Tagus between the converging armies of Victor and Soult, but shepherded the recalcitrant Spaniards into strong positions. Of course they rushed on disaster immediately afterwards, but for that he was in no way to blame. When Soult had crossed the Vera of Placentia to the Tagus, he found the allies impregnably posted. He might pass the river with risk and loss; but only to find himself within the sweep of *sierras* whose scarped sides were practically inaccessible. Lord Wellington had proved the faithlessness of his allies.

With rare exceptions they were little to be trusted in battle, and Cuesta seemed to take pleasure in crossing his plans. He had decided to fall back upon Portugal, and was only induced to delay by the representations of his brother, who had replaced Mr. Frere as envoy to the Seville Junta. Meantime he had taken up the line of the Guadiana, and the retrograde movement had been accomplished with no little difficulty. Critics have attributed misfortunes in recent wars to a system which undoubtedly fell far short of perfection. Wellington had no regular transport at all; the Spaniards would neither lend nor sell either mules or horses: he could not carry away the guns captured at Talavera: he abandoned stores and ammunition waggons at Arzobispo. His men were always on short rations, and often starving. Craufurd's experiences, when his ravenous brigade bayoneted the swine in the Estremadura woodlands, were but a sample of what all had to suffer.

Headquarters were established at Merida. The battalions, billeted to right and left, enfeebled by the wear of war with semi-starvation, were exposed to the malarious influences of the Guadiana marshes. The mortality was frightful. Hill wrote that of an army of 23,000 they could not bring 13,000 into the field. The rest were buried or in hospital. He had neither the knowledge nor the foresight of his chief, and he showed himself no prophet. "The cause is *hopeless*"—so he emphatically expressed himself, for the Spaniards had proved worthless on the field, and the numbers of the English were lamentably inadequate.

And he might well have thought so, when the united French might have launched upon Portugal ten times the numbers of the effective English. It is clear that Wellington had only Job's comforters about him when the man whom he trusted the most was *hopelessly* despondent. But we must remark that the chief kept his own counsel so closely that he made no confidants among the generals who stood nearest him. Hill wrote in the same letter—it was dated 10th November—"I do not know whether our future plans are fixed upon." He knew as little as the Madrid Intelligence Department of the lines of Torres Vedras.

The soldiers on the Guadiana were sickening and dying like flies, but Hill had his divisional headquarters on the comparatively salubrious heights of Mondego. There, in his enforced leisure, he was the sporting Shropshire squire. His brother writes:

> We lead quite a country life, going out coursing three days a week, though I should not wonder if Buonaparte gave us a chase of another sort one of these mornings.

They seem to have got together a scratch pack of hounds, for the general wrote that they now and then indulged in a fox-hunt, sometimes attacking a boar or a deer. And he sent home a portrait of his Spanish huntsman, sketched by his brother, remarking that the Spaniard dispensed with the orthodox horn, preferring a sort of pipe-lute which animated both the dogs and the field. Clement Hill with his satirical talent might have caricatured the sheep, for, like Skye-terriers, their beauty seems to have been in their ugliness. Nevertheless, the general bought four of them to lead with the milk goats, with the idea of sending them to England "to improve the Shropshire breed." From which we gather that a taste for acclimation must be hereditary in the family, for the late Lord Hill imported elands from South Africa. While Hill was killing time and foxes at Mondego, he had the satisfaction of being gazetted lieutenant-general.

A more important charge was now to be confided to him. Wellington, after tarrying at Merida against his better judgment, carried out his original resolution of evacuating Spain. The final decision was precipitated by weighing probabilities and by reports of the enemy's menacing movements. There were various lines by which they might attack, and he had to take his precautions against many contingencies. Yet when he went into winter quarters with his main force in the valley of the Mondego, he was compelled to break it up for the sake of the commissariat. Himself took post at a commanding centre, whence concentration could be most easily effected. The rear of that widely scattered army must be guarded against the French, who were in great strength in the south. For the most part he employed secretaries, but with his own hand, and on the eve of the retirement, he wrote to Hill the following flattering letter. For the first time he gave a general of division an independent and most responsible command.

> Badajoz, December 18, 1809.
>
> My dear Hill,—In the arrangements for the defence of Portugal, I shall form two principal corps, both consisting of British and Portuguese troops, the largest of which will be to the north-west, and I shall command it myself; and the other will be for the present upon the Tagus, and hereafter it may be moved forward into Alemtego; and I will not make any arrangement as to the troops that are to compose it, or as to the officer who is to command it, without offering the command of it to you.
>
> At the same time, I will not separate you from the army, and from my own immediate command, without consulting your wishes, &c.

Needless to say, Hill accepted joyfully, and a letter to Hawkstone shows how deeply he was touched and gratified by the unexpected proof of confidence. He adds:

> I am aware of the importance of the situation I am placed in, and trust I shall be attended with the same good fortune I have hitherto experienced.

It was a post demanding vigilant generalship. Regnier in Estremadura was a dangerous enemy, fertile in expedients, swift in evolution, and of the impetuous temperament that lost him the battle of Maida; and between Regnier and Hill nothing was interposed but the bands of Romana, who dared not face the French in the field, but was waging a partisan war in the sierras. Hill took post at Abrantes, on the southern bank of the Tagus, at its junction with the Zezere, where the broader river was spanned by a bridge of boats. His own division mustered 5000 men, and he had as many of the Portuguese. He set to work to strengthen the fortifications, and his engineers were busied over new works, a part of Wellington's general schemes for the defence of Portugal.

When Mertier from Andalusia, joining his division to that of Regnier, was threatening Badajoz, the appeals of Romana induced Hill to move to his support: but, id strict conformity to Wellington's intentions, he declined to entangle himself in the Spanish operations. With Regnier there was an amicable interchange of courtesies, though the French general in somewhat sarcastic letters taunted the Englishman with keeping his distance. But Hill, like his commander when facing Marmont on the Coa, was not to be provoked into fighting against his judgment

Wellington after long correspondence had obtained the assurances which decided him to maintain the defence of Portugal. Masséna, having superseded Marmont, was at the head of nearly 70,000 men of all arms, and had completed his dilatory preparations for an advance. Wellington had had ample time to think out everything, and had decided on his counter dispositions. When Masséna crossed the frontier, the allied positions extended from Almeida to Castel Branco, on the royal road from Spain to Lisbon, running north of the Tagus and parallel to it. The orders were that, if there was a serious attack on any point, the line was to bend back and not let itself be broken. There was to be a general retirement, converging towards Torres Vedras, though the army generally was contemplating the possibility of an embarkation.

Hill, with his independent command, had to act on his own judgment. It was to be apprehended that the enemy might seek to sever the communications between the two armies of the allies, but his line of retreat was marked out from Sazedas to Abrantes, whence he could cross the mountains and meet Wellington in the Mondego valley. He wrote on the 12th September that as Regnier seemed to have moved to the north, to unite with Masséna, he had prepared to pass the Zezere. Should the news prove false, he would be still in a position as effective. Masséna's whole army was on the Mondego by the 17th. Giving each man fourteen days' rations to carry, he was pressing forward by forced marches. Hill was ordered to Espinhal, there to await further orders. On the 24th Wellington had taken his stand at Busaco, willing on political grounds to blood his Portuguese and confident of victory, if his challenge were accepted. Again was his military sagacity justified, for Napoleon in urging Masséna on had virtually ignored the Portuguese in his calculations.

At the battle which covered some of the lieutenants with laurels,

Hill looked on as a spectator, though neither an idle nor a useless one. On the 25th, having been disappointed of an interview with Wellington, for which both generals were equally anxious, he was over the Mondego; and on the following day, he had taken his stand where the sierra sloped to the river. Masséna made a direct frontal attack on the allied right, and Hill's corps never came into action.

When the battle was raging, the corps was shifted to its left, behind the screen of the mountain ridge. At what Masséna believed to be the extreme of the allied right, the 74th had repulsed an attack of the enemy, and were retiring in perfect order to this crest Wellington had galloped up, expecting the attack to be renewed. "Hill," he said, "should attempt this point again. Give them a volley and charge bayonets." But the presence of this fresh reinforcement was enough, and the French had no stomach for further fighting. With such a position against them, held by such men, they had done as much as might be expected of mortal soldiers.

Hill's unbroken division recrossed the Mondego to observe the enemy. Wellington wrote that if Massena also passed that river a special message was to be sent at once, and "you may depend on my being with you in a few hours." But the marshal turned the northern extremity of the *sierra*, to make his flank march between the mountains and the sea.

Ten days afterwards the allied army was behind the lines of Torres Vedras. Hill had his post at Alhandra, on the right front, a formidable position washed by the Tagus and pronounced impregnable by the engineers; yet it is characteristic, that he remarked, with his habitual caution, "It is too extensive for my numbers." At Alhandra he was in clover. His brother wrote in high spirits: "We get all good things from Lisbon, and are living in a palace." He added in another letter:

> The people in Lisbon have quite got rid of their alarm, and the ladies come up by water to look at the French. Rowland is just gone down to do the civil to the admiral's family, who are come up on a party of pleasure.

"Rowland" was once more opposed to his old antagonist Regnier, who, after reconnoitring the position, resigned himself to sullen observation. Supplies were abundant with the British, but the French were in evil case. Sometimes they were indebted to our soldiers for little luxuries. A trace had been virtually proclaimed, and, as on the Coa and elsewhere, the men met on a friendly footing. Sir Rowland wrote:

> We are perfectly good neighbours and never think of molesting each other. On the contrary, I have been obliged to put a stop to the intimacy that was going on. It was by no means uncommon to see the soldiers of each army getting grapes out of the same vineyard, water from the same well, and asking each other to drink wine. Indeed I know of some instances, though not quite correct, of our officers sending to Lisbon for boots and shirts for some of their friends at outposts.

When Masséna had been starved into a retreat, at Santarem the tables were turned. The allies remained inactive in their encampments before frowning heights bristling with cannon, and an enemy too formidable in numbers to be outflanked. Sickness spread in the encampments skirting the Tagus, and Hill was prostrated by an attack of the country fever. A change to sea air failed to cure him, and the illness was complicated by an attack of jaundice. Letters from Wellington were full of sympathy and regret, but begged him not to return till his health was re-established. And it was only at Wellington's pressing entreaties that he consented to take orders from the doctors and sail for England on furlough.

4

A year was passed at home, and he was welcomed back by Wellington in a letter written ten days after Albuera, the bloodiest and most fruitless battle of the war:

> You will have heard of events here, which I hope will enable us to obtain possession of Badajoz.

The hope was frustrated, and indeed the attempt seemed a desperate one. When Wellington made a snatch at the fortress, with an inadequate battering train, the armies of Soult and Marmont were within easy relieving distance. He was forced to raise the siege, for he was in no condition to risk a battle on the plain with their united forces. Hill had been again placed in command of the covering army, which held the country from Albuera to Merida. Wellington fell back to positions on the Caya River, where he could venture to await a battle, if the enemy chose to challenge it. He had no desire to hazard an engagement where defeat must have had far-reaching consequences and where the odds were terribly against him.

But, as at Busaco, he made the stand from political considerations.

Fortunately the French were deceived as to his strength and disheartened by recent reverses Moreover, as they had been concentrating on the frontiers of Portugal, they were uneasy about their communications and their garrisons. The great combination was broken up when it had the fairest opportunity of crushing the allies. Soult was recalled by troubles in Andalusia: Marmont had evil tidings from the north. But Phillipon was given time to revictual his fortress, and Drouet was left with the 5th Division to mount guard in Spanish Estremadura.

The deadly repute of the valley of the Guadiana played no little part in all the operations. Both the combatants avoided it when possible; the ravages of fever and dysentery among British and Portuguese had been frightful, and now Wellington gladly withdrew to healthy stations in the interior. Hill was again charged with the duty of observing Drouet. As the frontier had been cleared of enemies, he could choose his positions, but his strategy was always influenced by regard for the health of his troops. He had 10,000 infantry, a division of cavalry, and four brigades of artillery—a force strong enough, not only for defence, but for demonstrations.

Napier writes that "that bold and vigilant commander, having 10,000 excellent troops, was a dangerous neighbour to Drouet." His information was good, for Morillo and his Spaniards were perpetually harassing the French general, and his movements were marked by extreme elasticity. When Drouet advanced, he withdrew his outposts; when Drouet fell back, he concentrated to follow him. Till the beginning of September his headquarters were at Villa Viciosa, a sylvan hunting palace of the Portuguese Royal Family, surrounded by extensive preserves. There he indulged in his favourite amusement of the chase, and the excellent discipline he enforced was rewarded by the abundant supplies brought in by the peasantry.

Meantime Wellington, who had been menacing Ciudad Rodrigo, had borrowed several of his battalions. They were returned when there were rumours that Napoleon, pending negotiations with Russia which were tending towards peace, intended to torn his whole attention to the Peninsula. Drouet had become more active, General Girard was occupying Zafra with several thousands of horse and foot: Soult had returned from Eastern Andalusia to Seville, and Hill, when he had his soldiers back, was ordered forward to Portalegre. It was in the middle of October that he had the opportunity of showing that, with all his coolness and caution, he had something of the dash of Craufurd and the fighting lust of Picton.

Girard had passed the Guadiana at Merida and was ravaging Northern Estremadura. Hill advanced to repel the invaders in conjunction with the Spaniards under Castaños. He knew that Girard was supported by Drouet, but he resolved nevertheless to endeavour to make him pay for his temerity by the capture of a part or the whole of his forces. He was fettered to a certain extent, for he had been ordered not to pass Caceres, where Girard was now established. But notwithstanding Wellington's *dictum*, then as afterwards at Almarez, he accepted responsibility and used his discretion.

On his approach upon the 26th, Girard abandoned Caceres, but the weather was terrific, and Hill, knowing nothing of the route the enemy had taken, halted his exhausted troops for the night at Malpartida. He knew next morning, and when taking a shorter hill road to cut them off learned that Girard was at Arroyo de Molinos, and in absolute ignorance of his movements. Indeed the French general believed the British were following him on the Caceres road.

Hill pressed onwards through the mountains, and the march was made doubly difficult by the weather, for the rain was still descending in torrents; but when the men bivouacked that night they were within four miles of Arroyo. Every precaution was taken to avoid discovery. Companies of light infantry occupied the adjacent villages, and kept the villagers under surveillance. All fires were forbidden, though the gusts of the storm blew down the tents and the men had to shiver under soaking canvas. There was no sound of bugle when in the darkness and in perfect silence they fell into their ranks.

In silence they marched down the long village street, crossed the valley, scaled another mountain, and at daybreak were looking down on Arroyo, where the French were resting in fancied security. Then the weather, that had tried them sorely, turned in their favour, for a blinding hail-storm coming from behind drove full in the faces of the French pickets. They had formed, under a sheltering eminence, in three columns. The left column plunged down into the steep main street of the village: the right marched eastwards to the spur of the *sierra*, where it was turned by the Truxillo road: the cavalry kept touch between both.

The surprise was complete; yet Girard's veterans, suddenly aroused, though scarcely startled, maintained their high reputation. If the onset was furious, the resistance was stubborn. It was a battle where the game was being driven by the beaters to the guns. But it was no helpless victims that were caught in the toils. With the hailstones driving through the street, with a dense mist rolling down from the crags of the sierra, as two British regiments came charging with fixed bayonets, the French were already standing to their arms. Their cavalry, hastily bridled, were covering the retreat of the foot, who were forming in squares beyond the village.

But the squares, suffering heavily from a galling musketry fire, were broken and forced back when our guns were brought up: the French cannon were captured and their horsemen cut to pieces or ridden down. Girard's nerve had never failed him: he sought valiantly to retrieve the disaster his carelessness had caused, and rallying his broken infantry into column, commenced his retreat on the road to Truxillo. But there the allies were already *a cheval*: the cavalry and artillery were closing up on his left, the captors of the village were coming up behind, and he had to choose between surrender and flight. Promptly he gave the word to disperse, and forthwith his soldiers, casting away weapons and knapsacks, were scrambling up the sides of the Sierra de Montanches—renowned for its swine and its hams.

The pursuit was hot and persevering, and many prisoners were made. But it was no even race between the fugitives and men weighted with arms and heavy packs; man after man succumbed to fatigue and breathlessness, yet the hunt was only ended on the crest of the mountain, where General Howard judiciously called a halt. Fifteen hundred prisoners were taken, in the village or on the hills, and among them sundry officers of rank, including the Prince d'Aremberg and General Brunn. Girard lost guns, small arms, and stores, with the contributions which had been the fruit of the foray, escaping himself by the skin of his teeth, with a handful of his men, by the bridge of Merida. Hill was the more gratified that his losses were of the slightest. Letters of congratulation poured in from brother generals, who appreciated the difficulties of the exploit and the glory it reflected on the British arms. Wellington immediately forwarded a despatch to the Prime Minister.

> It would be particularly agreeable to me if some mark of the favour of the Prince Regent were conferred upon General Hill: his services have always been meritorious and very distinguished in this country, and he is beloved by the whole army. . . . In recommending him, as I do most anxiously, I really feel that there is no officer to whom an act of grace and favour would be received by the army with more satisfaction than on General Hill (*sic*).

The answer was the conferring of the Knighthood of the Bath. Hill and his staff were invited to headquarters at Elvas, where he was invested by the commander with the insignia of the order, and the ceremony was celebrated with a grand military banquet.

The dignity had been bestowed with due pomp and ceremony, but Hill is said to have carried his characteristic modesty to excess. For months afterwards, according to a distinguished officer on his staff, the most good-humoured of men was obviously irritated if anyone ventured to address him as Sir Rowland, "and it was only very gradually that he could be driven to bear the honour."

While Wellington was occupied with the siege and storm of Ciudad Rodrigo, Hill had given the French another surprise in Estremadura. General Dombrouski had a narrow escape; he saved his men, but he lost his magazines. Ciudad fell, and Wellington was already meditating a more daring venture. On 28th January he sent Hill a letter, marked "secret and confidential." He said: "I am turning my mind seriously to Badajoz," and suggested that Hill should seize upon Almarez and hold the passage of the Tagus. That was the shortest route by which the army of Portugal could advance to the relief of the Spanish fortress. We say he " suggested," because everything was left to Hill's discretion, and at that time he deemed the attempt impracticable, a decision in which Wellington concurred. Nevertheless, no rescue reached the beleaguered stronghold. Badajoz fell like Ciudad; yet Wellington was compelled by the inaction of his allies to renounce his hopes of invading Andalusia, and move northward to make sure of the northern fortresses.

Badajoz had fallen, partly owing to the hesitations of Marmont, partly to the weakening of Soult by the withdrawal of troops for Russia. Divided counsels still prevailed. Marmont, cowed by his dangerous adversary, was holding back; and the Spaniards, always restless, though never reliable, were again finding Soult occupation. Wellington had dispersed his army into winter quarters on a line extending over four hundred miles. The impossibility of concentrating in a devastated country had compelled him to violate the first principles of war; but, as the enemy was likewise in evil case, he rightly counted on impunity. With the opening of a new campaign in the spring, he decided on the aggressive, for if the French were to be driven out of the Peninsula they must be beaten in pitched battles.

The question was whether his march should be into Castile or Andalusia, and he resolved on the former plan. Hill had been left to superintend the repairs of the Badajoz works, and to guard the place on the sides of Estremadura and Andalusia. But when Wellington marched into Castile the army of the centre would be left free to act and might strike at Hill by the bridge of Almarez. If the covering army met with disaster, Wellington's right flank would be imperilled. Wherefore the capture of Almarez was now of supreme importance, and with the altered circumstances it seemed feasible. On the 24th of April Wellington wrote urging Hill to make immediate and secret preparations, though he was not to march without further orders. The orders came a week later. But there had been an inevitable delay of twenty-four hours, in repairing the bridge over the Guadiana at Merida, and so nicely had the operations been planned that Wellington feared "Hill would be late."

Secrecy was indeed indispensable, for far superior forces were within striking distance. Foy's division was cantoned in the Tagus valley, and D'Armagnac was in Talavera with detachments from the army of the centre. Drouet was supposed to be watching Hill, and in a position to cut his retreat to Merida. It may be said that, notwithstanding the silence observed, the chances were in favour of failure, and failure might have meant annihilation. At that time, with the nervous apprehensions of the Government, a general, meeting a reverse falling far short of a catastrophe, might consider his career as ended. Yet Hill did not hesitate, and, taking all the precautions skill could suggest, he staked his future on the hazard.

On the 12th, passing his troops across the reconstructed bridge, he mustered 6000 men in Merida. By feigned demonstrations and false reports. General Foy had been deluded into the belief that with thrice his real force he was contemplating an invasion of Andalusia. There was no suspicion that his objective was Almarez, and his purpose was to carry it with a rush, before the enemy should be better informed. On the 16th he was at Jaraceigo, six miles from Almarez, where his operations were still effectually masked by the jumble of rough mountains with their intervening valleys. There he formed his troops into three columns, hoping to take the enemy at unawares after a long night march. Simultaneous attacks were to be delivered at daybreak.

The left column, advancing by side paths, was to assail the Castle of Mirabete; the centre was to force the pass, strongly fortified at the narrowest point, through which the royal road led northward; the right column, commanded by the general in person, following tracks only known to the goat-herds, was to assail the forts at the bridge. The difficulties, serious as they were known to be, were greatly underrated; the combinations failed, and surprise became impossible. For two days nothing could be done, and each day of delay increased the danger. Hill was seeking in vain for a passage by which he could move his guns.

On the third he came to a resolution which might have staggered the most daring leader of partisans. He left his cannon with the central column; he ordered Chowne with the left column to make a feigned attack on Mirabete; and for himself he led his right along the ledges of precipices to storm, with only the musket and bayonet, works defended by heavy guns. As Napier remarks: "A military career hitherto so glorious was likely enough to terminate in shame." But General Hill, being totally devoid of interested ambition, was unshaken by selfish considerations.

He led out his little force on the evening of the 18th, hoping to be in front of Fort Napoleon before daybreak. It gives some idea of the tracks along which he scrambled that the scaling ladders were sawn in sunder, to turn the angles of the cliffs. When day broke, the head of the column was near the bank of the river, but the body was still straggling behind in slow procession. Fortunately some low heights concealed the first arrivals, but there was no time to wait for the loiterers to close up. At that moment Chowne was menacing the Castle of Mirabete, and clouds of smoke from its batteries began to roll along the crest of the *sierra*.

The garrison of Fort Napoleon, aware by this time that the British were in their neighbourhood, crowded to the ramparts to gaze at the spectacle. They were startled to immediate attention by a shout beneath their walls. At sight of the smoke on the heights Hill had let his stormers loose; they came bounding over the nearest slopes, and rushed at the ramparts in open order. Before reaching them, they were welcomed with a heavy fire of cannon and small arms, while the guns of Fort Ragusa on the northern bank began to play on their flanks. Nothing stayed the rush. Headed by General Howard, they leaped down into the ditch and planted the sawn ladders, which proved too short. But the broad ledges projecting from the rampart were turned by an acrobatic feat: the ladders were dragged round them: and the parapet reached by a second escalade.

The garrison, overpowered, fled to the *tête de pont*, and there the pursuers entered with them in hand-to-hand fight. The chase was continued over the boat-bridge, but the pontoons on the farther side had been sunk by stray cannon-shot. Those of the fugitives who did not take to the water were slain or surrendered at discretion. The breaking of the bridge had left Fort Ragusa unapproachable, but, strange to say, the panic had gained its garrison. When it poured out upon the road to Naval Moral, the fire from Fort Napoleon hastened the retreat. Some of the soldiers plunged into the Tagus, breasted the current, and brought back some boats.

Hill, standing on the bank, in great jubilation, paid them handsomely with praises and gold. The bridge was restored, the river was passed, and, without losing a moment, the stores were burned and the works blown up. Finally, the bridge itself was destroyed. No more brilliant feat of arms was performed in the war. It raised Hill's reputation to the highest point, and no one could reproach him afterwards with excess of caution. The decision with which it was planned was equal to the daring with which it was carried out. When baffled by unexpected obstacles which would have driven a weaker man to renounce the enterprise in despair, he was only nerved to new exertions, and where one less fearless of responsibility would have lost his head, his brain was never brighter or more active.

Thenceforth, had he cared for disparaging and ignorant censure, he would have a freer hand in sparing his soldiers, for it was his habit to weigh the death losses against the gains. That the work was not completed as he would have desired was no fault of his. The fortifications at Mirabete were now at his mercy; it only needed a brief time to reduce them, and he was bringing his guns into position when a well-authenticated report was forwarded from Erskine, that Soult had broken into Estremadura, and then, in accordance with his instructions, he fell back promptly upon Merida. The surprise had set all the French in motion. Foy, in self-reproach, was stirred into activity. He passed the Tagus at Arzobispo, and, threading the mountain defiles, threw succours into Mirabete.

Soult was moving on Andalusia, and it was from Soult that Wellington apprehended danger. But there, as ever, French combinations were deranged by the inveterate jealousies. Foy, after his advance, had withdrawn, but Drouet, who had conflicting orders from Soult and Marmont, was still in a threatening position which demanded the utmost vigilance. Not that Hill had any fear of Drouet; on the contrary, he would have willingly offered him battle; but he was doubtful as to the intentions of Soult.

On 3rd June he wrote to Wellington:

If Drouet is not supported, it will not be difficult for me to disturb him in his present position.... On the other hand, if Soult keeps within reach of him, it will not probably be advisable for me to adventure farther.

Believing that Soult was contemplating an inbreak in force, Wellington hastened to send reinforcements. But Soult, with distractions on his flanks and rear, was content to send assistance to Drouet, whereupon Hill fell back. He found further supports at Albuera, and on those formidable heights, still strewn with the bones of the brave who had fallen in the battle, he confidently faced with superior numbers the antagonist who had followed him. Wellington had left him full discretion. He had not only permission, but every personal inducement to fight. The glory of a victory gained on that spot and in the circumstances would, as Napier says, when magnified by malevolence, have placed his fame on a level with that of the commander-in-chief. But his patriotism and chivalrous loyalty rose superior to selfish considerations. He believed that even winning a battle would have interfered with his general's plans.

Hill, who had shown himself so daring at Arroyo Molinos and Almarez, now, with an uncommon mastery of ambition, refrained from an action which promised him unbounded fame.

In July the British forces were nominally 60,000. Of these, 35,000 were with Wellington, 13,000 with Hill, and the remainder in garrison or hospital. Hill could not be withdrawn from watching Drouet, till the victory of Salamanca compelled Soult to concentrate and ultimately to withdraw to the east. In July Hill had written:

It is a most glorious event, but appears to have had little effect on my immediate opponents.

All was changed when in mid-August Wellington made his triumphant entry into Madrid. Joseph had fled with a rabble of soldiers and camp-followers into La Mancha: Soult had gone to join him, having sacrificed his better judgment with his daring scheme of abandoning Madrid and making a new base for French operations in Andalusia. Hill could write to Wellington that he was finally relieved from Drouet, and that he had sure intelligence that not only Estremadura, but Andalusia was being evacuated. He added: "The joy of the people is great indeed"

But the joy of Madrid was damped by uncertainty, to be succeeded by tribulation. Wellington's great schemes were baffled for the time, and the expulsion of the enemy from the Peninsula was to be deferred for another year. It was owing partly to the backwardness of the Spaniards, and partly to the false economy of the British Government, which starved him both in money and reinforcements. Reluctantly he resolved on abandoning the capital. He marched back to the north, driving Clausel and the army of Portugal before him, and laying siege to the Castle of Burgos which blocked his way. Arrived at Burgos on the 17th September, he sent orders to Hill to march on Toledo, and Hill established himself in New Castile, with his headquarters at Aranjuez, the favourite rural retreat of the Bourbons, when the heat did not drive them to La Granja in the hill country.

Hill waited anxiously for the news which never came: Burgos still held out, and his letters show how uneasiness passed into despondency. The failure was due to an inadequate siege train and short ammunition; but it is remarkable that Sir Augustus Frazer, who commanded the horse artillery at Salamanca, attributes the miscarriage "to the want of will to employ sufficient artillery, with the amplest power of having done so." Be that as it may, when Dubreton's obstinacy of defence had brought Wellington to a standstill, by the fortunes of war Hill missed another chance of adding to his renown by a glorious victory. And, strange to say, the chance was missed by the fact that Wellington had at last consented to become the *generalissimo* of the Spanish armies that he might the better secure effective co-operation.

The English at Alicante with their allies found Suchet sufficient occupation, and were even strong enough to assume the aggressive. Joseph and Soult were marching westward, for the usurper's dominating idea was to regain his lost capital. Wellington, whose eye ranged over all the battleground, had ordered Ballasteros, commanding in Murcia, to unite himself to Maitland from Alicante and hang upon the flanks of the French advance. Hill was waiting confidently behind the Tagus with a fine fighting force. He had the Light and three other divisions, with several Portuguese regiments and a strong body of English and Spanish horse.

If the French attacked, as they were almost compelled to do, for when they had come so far they could hardly refuse without fatal loss of prestige, Maitland and Ballasteros should have been ready to fall on their rear. But Ballasteros, in jealous discontent, had refused to stir: he bitterly resented Wellington's being put over his head: and it was small satisfaction that he was summarily disgraced, when the Cortes made him prisoner in his own camp. But the upshot was that Joseph and

Soult came on unmolested, threatening Hill with forces nearly double his own. He had been in constant communication with Burgos. Wellington had sent directions providing for every contingency, but added: "I write, as I always do, to provide for every event, not believing those instructions are at all necessary." Both were agreed that no battle was to be risked, unless with the odds in favour of a victory.

On the 21st the siege of Burgos was raised and the retreat begun. The same day a courier was despatched to Hill, with orders to join at Salamanca. The orders were superfluous, for he was already making his preparations, and it was high time. The heads of the French columns had been seen on the opposite bank of the flooded Tagus. The bridge at Aranjuez had been mined, but he was delayed for a day by the failure of the first explosion. There was some sharp skirmishing with the last detachment of his rearguard. Nevertheless on the last day of the month his infantry were well on their way to the Escorial.

It was a picturesque scene when he looked back from the crest of the Guadarama on his regiments winding their upward way along the zigzags in a snake-like train. And there were dropping shots from the rear, showing that the French were close on his heels. Next day, when on the plains of Old Castile, his scouts reported that French battalions were already ascending the pass. What force was behind them he knew not. Wellington's answer to his report, for now they were in close communication, shows the sagacity with which he calculated on the temperaments of his adversaries. He did not believe Soult was following in force: he must be merely keeping cautious touch. Hill crossed the Tormes at Alba, the same day that Wellington was back at his old position on the heights of San Cristoval overlooking Salamanca. The great victory had proved the rebound of a boomerang. It had forced Soult to evacuate Andalusia, but it had compelled the scattered French armies to draw together, in accordance with Napoleon's principle of operating in masses.

The united armies of the south and the centre were too strong, and Souham, who had seized the passages of the Douro, was within some short marches of his rear. Even then he hesitated as to abandoning Salamanca, and leaving the citizens to their fate after their patriotic demonstrations. For he wrote to Hill, who was to descend the Tormes valley, ordering him to leave a garrison in Alba. In answering. Hill asked if he had ever seen the place: a weak garrison in the castle would not suffice to command the bridge. But Wellington had still a lingering hope that the French might assail the heights of San Cristoval.

Joseph was, in fact, disposed to gratify him, but was over- ruled by the more cautious Soult. That marshal had devised one of his ingenious pieces of strategy by which, by a wide cast of the net of the *retarius*, he might entangle the enemy in its meshes. For by sweeping round upon the road to Rodrigo he made retreat inevitable, and Wellington's escape or surrender became but a question of hours.

It was a repetition of Marmont's fatal flank march, but on an infinitely wider circuit: and if Marmont was too reckless, Soult was too wary. Moreover, the elements fought for Wellington. His movements were masked by dense fog, and in drenching rain his enemies were bogged to the knees and saddle-girths in the tenacious mire of the by-road. Soult missed his cast, and Wellington reached Rodrigo after one of the most miserable marches on record. There was little food for the men and less forage for the horses. The famished soldiers scrambled greedily for fallen acorns, and many lives were saved by their breaking the ranks and shooting or bayoneting the swine in the woodlands. There was no shelter from the unrelenting dampness, and no possibility of kindling fires.

So ended, in mortification to the general and misery to the men, a campaign that had opened so brilliantly and been crowned by splendid successes. Yet Wellington had only to possess himself in patience: the strength of the French occupation had been shaken to its foundations, and to his prescience the issue was only deferred.

5

The army had gone into winter quarters. Wellington's first business was to brace up the relaxation of discipline—always engendered in British soldiers by a mortifying retreat—by masterful edicts and salutary reprimands. He had little to fear from attacks on any formidable scale. He had again dispersed his troops in salubrious quarters, and with due regard to considerations of the commissariat in a country which had been so devastated by the war that Sir Augustus Frazer, when riding from Lisbon to Santarem, had not seen a soul at work in the fields. But he had now distributed them with a view to the campaign of the next summer, which was to sweep the Peninsula clear of invaders.

While the Anglo-Portuguese were in repose, affairs were going badly for the usurper. Wellington had so arranged that the allies in the east found active occupation for Suchet. Everywhere the partisans were numerous, and successful rivalry inspired them to the most audacious enterprises. The insurrection in the north was spreading to the Basque Provinces, where the guerrilla chiefs hung emulously upon the communications with France, and Napoleon considered it of such vital importance that he sent Joseph peremptory orders to crush it. That was more easy to order than to execute. The insurrection gained head and engaged the army of the north with good part of the army of Portugal, when Joseph stood in need of every available man to stem the torrent of war that went surging forward upon Vittoria. Above all, it was Hill who had puzzled the enemy, and who finally crippled their combinations at the critical moment in the spring.

Hill was covering the right flank of the scattered forces. He had his headquarters at Coria, whence he commanded the passes over the mountains to the north or could strike at will up the valley of the Tagus. His exploits at Arroyo Molinos and Almarez had made him a terror. Everything in the way of enterprise was to be feared from a leader at once so calculating and so deliberately audacious. He can hardly have been said to have been a thorn in the enemy's side, for he kept quiet in obedience to instructions. But Napier writes that "the slightest change of his quarters or even the appearance of an English uniform beyond the line of cantonments caused a concentration of French troops as expecting one of his sudden blows."

The demoralisation of the retreat had had grave results. The hospitals were overcrowded: in January there were 22,000 men on the sick list: few of the transport animals had struggled through to Rodrigo. But in March, with bracing air and better food, most of the invalids had rejoined the colours. Beresford's severe discipline had drilled the Portuguese into excellent form. Wellington had clothed, fed, and paid many of the Spanish battalions, so that they were in condition to do good service. In March he had 70,000 Anglo-Portuguese veterans under his hand, with 20,000 fairly efficient Spaniards. Joseph had little more than half the force with which to confront him when he began to develop the plans which were still inscrutable to the enemy.

To the last moment his officers in high command were profoundly ignorant of his intentions. Their letters home were full of speculations, often absurdly wide of the mark. Perhaps Graham, Hill, Beresford, and one or two of his staff were alone in his confidence. He had decided to strike at the north, where he could interpose between Joseph and Bayonne, coming into touch with the spreading northern insurrection and the guerrillas who were swarming on the slopes of the Pyrenees. Hill was employed to mislead the enemy, and to persuade them that the tremendous infall, as in the Talavera campaign, would follow the course of the Tagus.

If Wellington struck north, it seemed certain to military students of the topography that he would strive to turn the left of the French. In reality he was to direct his main attack on their right, which nature had made apparently unassailable by flooded torrents and impracticable ravines. According to the received rules of war, in advancing he would keep his columns in touch. He moved forward to his objective in three bodies, separated from co-operation by mountains, morasses, and rivers. Yet these delicate combinations of his were so nicely devised that the slight delay did not sensibly derange them.

In the middle of May, Graham with 40,000 men was over the Douro, threading the gorges to the eastward. No intelligence of that audacious turning movement reached the unsuspecting king, who in blissful ignorance was slowly concentrating, and meditating new measures of government amid conflicting military councils. He had only eyes for Wellington, who was advancing on the Tormes with the centre, and for Hill, who had at last broken up from Coria and was bringing round his right wing by the passes of the mountains.

Hill's officers delighted in sport, like their hard-riding commander. Many a couple of greyhounds accompanied the march, and many a hare started by the advancing columns was run down in crossing the plains between the *sierra* and the Tormes. A long halt at Galisteo, where the corps was concentrated, was enlivened by a romantic *al fresco* banquet. The 28th Regiment, which had distinguished itself at Albuera, entertained the general and his staff on the anniversary of the battle. The arrangements were original. There were neither chairs nor tables; regimental plate and crystal were conspicuous by their absence. Each guest, from Sir Rowland downwards, brought his own knife, fork, and plate. Trenches were cut for the accommodation of their legs, and smooth sods of fresh-cut turf were the covering of the banqueting board. There was such promiscuous foraging for the miscellaneous *menu* as Lever describes in his *Charles O'Malley*, and the cooking over the camp fires was of the roughest, but the dinner was a great success.

Hill and Wellington met at Salamanca, and Hill was left in temporary command, while Wellington hurried off to the Esla to relieve his anxiety as to Graham. On his return the united armies again moved forward, the French abandoning position after position, as they were outflanked on either side. Not even at Burgos did they make a stand.

Joseph had neglected his brother's repeated instructions to repair the works and revictual the fortress. Breaching batteries and scaling ladders were all in readiness this time, but there was no need to employ them. Clouds of smoke, with a report that shook the ground, were the visible and audible signs of evacuation: the castle had been so hurriedly blown up that 300 Frenchmen perished in the explosion. Hill commanded the column that had followed the royal road, and now on the 13th June filed, unobstructed, over the bridge into the town.

The French had seen the British advance, when they hastily fired the mines in the castle. Nor could they understand why the pursuit was not pressed, for it was two days before Wellington and Hill resumed the march, moving on parallel lines. They congratulated themselves on reaching Pancorbo without losing a gun or a waggon. They knew not that the day of reckoning was only delayed, to give Graham time to pass an impossible country before coming down on their communications with France, and making sure that their defeat should be a catastrophe. On the 13th Wellington's army was in motion by the left: two days afterwards the centre and the right had left Burgos: on the 20th the nets had been drawn around the French, and Joseph was at bay in the basin of Vittoria.

The basin is enclosed on two sides by the Zadora, which was spanned by seven bridges. Vittoria was the Cinque Bras of Spain—the meeting place of five highways. It was traversed by the northern road to Bayonne. On the east were the ways leading to Bilboa and Durango. Towards the north-west two others branched off to Pampeluna and Estella. Two of the bridges were on the western roads, where the river flows due south; three were on the southern lip of the basin, where the river bends to the east, almost at a right angle. The sixth was down stream to the east: it led across to the village of Puebla, beyond the pass of the same name. The narrow defile is shut in by parallel ranges of mountain.

Graham, always pushing his advance, was threatening the bridges on the Upper Zadora and Joseph's direct retreat to Bayonne. Wellington was directing the frontal attack by the three southern bridges. Hill's line of operations was on the extreme right: he passed at Puebla, beyond the eastern ridge, and was to wait in the meantime at the mouth of the defile. Morillo's Spaniards were to scale the mountain to the right of the road; it seemed rather like scrambling than walking. They gained the crest, to be fiercely opposed, and though supported by their second brigade. Hill had to succour them with the 71st Regiment and some light infantry under Colonel Cadogan. For a time the struggle raged with varying fortune: supports were harried up on either side, and then there was a relapse into expectant inactivity. In the rough *Journal of a Soldier* in the 71st, (published by Leonaur as *Bayonets, Bugles and Bonnets*), we have a vivid incident of that weary waiting. Beneath the blazing sun the soldiers were parched. There was one little spring on the *plateau* that was swept with shot and shell. A man more desperate than the rest broke from cover to quench his thirst.

A ball pierced his head—he fell in the well, which was discoloured with brains and blood. Thirsty as we were, we could not drink it.

Having won the heights, Hill had passed the rest of his corps over the river and proceeded to force the pass. It was done with no small expenditure of life, and the village which closed the northern outlet was carried by storm. The French troops on the mountain were outflanked, and then the battle, which for hours had been stationary, went ebbing backwards towards Vittoria. The central columns had passed the Zadora, and were driving the enemy before them. Far away to the north-west the smoke of the cannon showed that Graham was developing his attack. The French had made their last stand on a ridge in front of the town, whence eighty guns belched out death on the British advance through enclosed cornfields.

The old soldiers of Napoleon were still full of fight, but Joseph was panic-stricken and Jourdan in despair. They had good reason. The road to the Bidassoa was choked with carriages. Two convoys despatched the day before were heavily dragging through mud and ruts. Vittoria was a scene of mad confusion: in the general *sauve qui peut* the plunder of years was being abandoned, with the stores and equipment of three armies. Graham would already have swooped down on the line of flight had it not been for the stubborn and skilful opposition of Reille. The beaten army broke away to their left, along the narrow road to Pampeluna, skirted by marshes which protected their flight. All their guns, save one, had been left behind.

At Pampeluna Joseph made no long halt. The Governor, preparing for a siege and short of provisions, refused to admit the rabble. Wellington went in search of Clausel, who had been approaching the field of battle. Hill was charged with the blockade of Pampeluna, but when Joseph had sent Gazan with the army of the south to occupy the Spanish valley of Bastan, which abounded in defensible posts. Hill handed over the blockade to the Spaniards, and marched north to clear the Bastan. He never showed as a strategist to more advantage: with insignificant loss, he drove Gazan from position to position till he lined the crests of the Pyrenees with his pickets. His brother wrote:

> We have gone through a very interesting part of the campaign, having completely driven that part of the French army to which we were opposed over the Pyrenees. Great part of Rowland's corps being detached from him, his force has been greatly inferior to the enemy's, and they have always had the advantage of strong positions.

Soult had been hurried from Germany to supersede Joseph: with amazing rapidity he reorganised an army and in a measure restored its *morale*. Thenceforth between San Sebastian and Roncesvalles there was no rest for the allies. Their scattered forces were always exposed to combined attacks. Soult's strategy was directed to relieving Pampeluna, and in the battles of the Pyrenees which baffled it he lost 15,000 men. Hill, as a rule, held his own, gaining praise from his chief for skilful manoeuvring. Only once was he forced back by superior strength, when the French won for a brief space the passes of Maya and Roncesvalles. The difficulties of the defenders were increased by torrents of rain and by fogs which shrouded the enemy's movements. Impromptu earthworks were washed away, and guns could not be moved from point to point.

The nerves of responsible generals, striving vainly to pierce an impenetrable veil, were perpetually on the strain. The *Journal of a Soldier*, from the soldier's point of view, (published by Leonaur as *Bayonets, Bugles and Bonnets*), gives a graphic account of the surprise and the obstinate, stubborn resistance on the retreat from the Maya ridge.

> Our fatigue-parties were out for forage and we were busy cooking when the signal was given on the 20th of June. . . .
> The French were in great force, moving up in solid columns. We killed great numbers of them, but they still moved on. We killed great numbers of them, but were forced to give way, contesting every foot of ground . . . We had the mortification to see the French making merry in our camp, eating the dinner we had cooked for ourselves. What could we do? They were so superior in numbers.

The key of the pass was regained before nightfall, and Hill reported that his men had done their duty gallantly. Shortly afterwards he was shifted to Roncesvalles, on the extreme right, and as autumn passed into early winter the sufferings of the troops became intense. The *Soldier* says:

> The weather was dreadful. We had always either snow or hail. We were forced to put our knapsacks on our heads to protect us from its violence.

There are significant touches:

> The mules used to run crying, up and down, hurt by the hailstones.

The Highlanders had to betake themselves to breeches.

> They could not live in their kilts; the cold would have killed them. In bright weather they looked longingly down on the plains of France, and they blessed the day that brought orders for the descent, which was to bring their general an addition to his laurels.

On the morning of the 10th November the armies came down on the Nivelle by moonlight. Hill's troops had been moved back from Roncesvalles to the Bastan. His orders were to deliver a frontal attack on D'Erlon, while Beresford assailed his right. The French had busily employed themselves in fortifying positions which nature had already in many cases made almost impregnable. Two parallel ranges, the Great and the Little Rhune, were precipitous scarps with rocky bastions. Hill, after a long night march, came into touch with the enemy at seven in the morning. Fatigue was forgotten. Covering his flank with the Spaniards, he sent the 2nd Division against D'Armagnac and carried D'Erlon's first positions.

The 6th Division, with a Portuguese battalion, had passed the river lower down, and with left shoulders forward were threatening the bridge above them, defended by D'Erlon's second line of redoubts. Fighting their way through broken ground, the 2nd Division was before the bridge at eleven. The bridge was carried, the flanking ravines were turned, the redoubts were either stormed or evacuated: the French fired their entrenched camp, and beat a retreat with the 6th Division in hot pursuit D'Erlon might have made a more determined stand, but the battle elsewhere to the north of the Nivelle had gone sorely against the French.

Alten with the Light Division had literally rushed the Little Rhune. Nevertheless Clausel with two divisions still stood firm; but when Hill effected his junction with Beresford, and their united columns drove a wedge between Clausel and D'Erlon, the hostile line of battle was broken. Assailed fiercely in front, menaced on either flank, Clausel's men were forced back in disorder, after stubbornly disputing each foot of ground. That rout made the strong positions of Soult's right untenable. The whole French army retired on the ridges before Bayonne, and were followed by the allies in order of battle. Four days afterwards. Hill had established his quarters at St. Pé. In a letter he says: "I do not see any prospect of our having another fight. The glorious news from the north, I trust, will settle Napoleon." Again he was no true prophet: within the month he had fought and won the memorable Battle of St. Pierre.

That was the last of Soult's five days' fighting around Bayonne, and when he broke out on Hill on the 13th of December, it was with every reasonable assurance of victory. From his central position in the city and its entrenched camp he could assail with overwhelming superiority any section of the beleaguering forces. He had tried elsewhere and failed, but Hill's position was exceptionally hazardous. On the morning of the 13th he was cut off from the rest of the army, for the Nive had come down in flood and the pontoons had been swept away. With 14,000 men and fourteen guns he had to hold his own against seven divisions, while a cavalry and infantry division were hovering over his rear.

Strong bodies of horse and foot had been passed from the camp through the city in course of the night. In the early morning they passed out through the eastern gates and formed in columns. Their movements were at first shrouded in fog, but it lifted as they were distinguished by Hill's pickets, and the battle was fought in brilliant sunshine. The one advantage of the weaker was the character of the battle-ground The solid roadway was skirted by swamps and thickets, so that the enemy could only avail himself of his superiority by bringing up his inexhaustible reserves. Hill made the most of his advantages, but never was combat more fiercely contested. His dispositions were skilful. For himself he was omnipresent: he headed the most critical counter-attack in person.

But for once the obstinate resistance was compromised by the timidity of two colonels of English regiments. It is true that the indignation of the soldiers lent fuel to their fire when brought back to the battle; and that wavering was more than redeemed by the stubborn courage of the Portuguese, who nobly sustained the reputation they had first won on the *sierra* of Busaco. Almost every officer on the staffs of the generals was either killed or wounded. The gutters in the High Street of St. Pierre are said to have been flooded with blood. Wellington pronounced it the bloodiest engagement of the war—he made that same remark more than once—and declared he had never seen so narrow a space so thickly strewn with slain. For when he heard the firing he had hurried up, sending battalion after battalion over the pontoons, which by this time had been hastily replaced. He arrived at the supreme moment, but would not interfere.

Hill had won the battle, and Hill should have all the glory. Yet when he came up the moment was supreme, for Hill had thrown his last reserves into the action. He was unusually excited, and for the first and last time was heard to mutter an oath. "Damn it, this won't do."

Wellington smiled and turned to his staff: "Hill is beginning to swear; we had better get out of the way."

"Hill," he said afterwards, "this day is yours," and he wrote joyfully to Sir John Hope and Sir J. Kennedy that "Hill had given the enemy a terrible beating."

The battle was a turning-point in the campaign. Wellington had achieved his grand object of drawing Soult away from Bayonne: now he could strike in either direction, and his advance was only delayed by the rains and the flooding of the country. Hill held a firm grip on the Adour, obstructing the French communications by the river.

There, as when Craufurd was guarding the Coa, the hostile pickets, only parted by a narrow stream, came to a very friendly understanding. Not only was there no sharpshooting, but they carried civilities and a system of barter to such length that Wellington issued a general order on the subject. There was one amusing incident in Hill's corps, and a rather delicate case. On a stone in the middle of the stream a canteen was placed with a piece of money: the coin was removed in due course, and the canteen filled with cognac.

One evening Private Patten, who was standing sentry, found to his disgust that the money was gone and the canteen was empty. In righteous wrath he dashed across next morning, seized the French sentry, stripped him of his accoutrements and carried them over. The consequence was the appearance of a French captain with a flag of truce, who urged that if the accoutrements were not returned he would certainly be court-martialled and his sentry shot. Patten protested that he had the clothes in pawn for the brandy, and was not only induced to give them up under pressure, but was sentenced to three hundred lashes, which was more than he had bargained for.

Though the fault was flagrant, it would have been hard measure had he been punished, considering that his superiors had winked at the abuse. The denouement was the same as that in a very similar case under Craufurd, save that Craufurd acted on an impulse and Hill with benevolent deliberation. Patten was paraded to receive his punishment, when Hill addressed the troops and severely improved the occasion. Then he gave his discourse a more agreeable turn, expatiated on Patten's numerous deeds of gallantry, and to the delight of his audience remitted the sentence. After all, Wellington might have court-martialled himself for similar indiscretions.

Larpent tells us that when before Toulon he rode down to the Garonne, concealed his general's hat with an oilskin, got into conversation with the French *videttes*, looked quietly about him, saw all he wished to see, and then mounted and rode away. As he remarks, it was risking rather too much.

In the second week of February the general advance was resumed. The passages of the Gaves—the wild torrents which pour down from the mountains to swell the Adour—were forced in swift succession, Hill's corps always working round to the right, on the upper waters of the tributaries. There was much skirmishing and some sharp fighting; bridges were blown up; fords depending on the rise and fall of the rivers were found and passed under heavy fire, but Soult made his only serious stand at Orthez, on the Gave de Pau. This is not the place to sketch the battle, where Hill played but a subsidiary part; Beresford and Picton bore the brunt. Hill's charge was to menace the massive bridge, which, though its strength had defied the destructive skill of the French engineers, was so commanded and defended as to be pronounced impassable.

But when Wellington changed his plan of operations, and the scales were trembling, Hill had orders to pass the river at any cost. He was either to cover the flank of the assailing forces from Harispe's attack, or in the event of victory to cut Soult's retreat to Pau. He could not force the bridge, but he forded the Gave higher up. When the day was won and the French were retiring, his rapid advance changed orderly retreat into panic-stricken rout. As he saw the confusion spread he pressed the enemy harder, till it became a race between vanquished and victors for the Adour. Cotton coming up with the cavalry took the lead, his troopers taking fences and jumping water in their stride, while the fugitives flung away muskets and accoutrements.

The pursuit was only stopped when the horses gave in from exhaustion. The flight had been fast, the confusion great, and there were many desertions among the unwilling conscripts, yet Soult rallied his forces again with little show of demoralisation. He had charged Clausel with the defence of his magazines at Aire, on the southern bank of the Adour. Hill was detached to seize them on the 5th March, and mastered the place after some sharp fighting. The bloodshed was greater than need have been, had the assault been more deliberately scientific.

But Wellington was acting on Napoleon's maxim of always driving a beaten enemy, and Hill's orders were peremptory. He was to attack at once, though he had neither knowledge of the ground nor time to examine it. Then Soult was withdrawing sullenly on Toulouse, often facing round, and always defending any position of vantage. The strongest stand he made, and the sharpest affair in which Hill was concerned, was at Tarbes, where he led his centre column down the steep main street, forced the bridge, and charged victoriously up the slopes beyond, to be confronted with solid masses on a farther ridge. Dusk closed the combat, and in the night Soult had retired again, to reach Toulouse by forced marches.

In that great southern arsenal of France, with its massive walls, its circle of heavily armed redoubts and girdling rivers, he turned at bay. He would not believe in the collapse of the Empire: he still hoped that Suchet would respond to his reiterated appeals. His veterans were rather irritated than dejected by repeated discomfiture: he was seconded by such fighting generals as Taupin and Harispe. In the days that were left him he laboured indefatigably at strengthening his outworks. The delay on Wellington's part was unavoidable: his corps were divided by the swift Garonne, and he could not control its rise and fall.

Hill, who had passed it once, was constrained to recross: he had turned engineer for the nonce, and was preoccupied with pontoon bridging. It tested even his proverbial coolness, which, in the consciousness of doing its best, calmly resigned itself to the inevitable. Afterwards, when talking over the campaign, he often alluded to the trouble those bridges had caused him.

> For instance, at a point where all seemed most promising, I found we had not enough to cross by exactly *one* boat, and we had all our work to do over again.

Even when all the bridging was at last effected, Soult had the advantage of working upon the inner radius. He had his divisions under his hand, whereas Hill's headquarters were eleven miles from those of the commander-in-chief, and the only way of communication was by the pontoons of the Garonne. The purposeless battle might have been avoided by telegraphs or a good postal service, but every day was strengthening the defences, and Wellington had good reason for haste. It was fought on 10th April, and on an Easter Sunday.

Again Hill's role was a subsidiary one. Opposed to Soult's left, he hung over the suburb of St. Cyprian, "in order to draw a part of the enemy's force and attention to that side." There were desperate fluctuations in the battle elsewhere. At one time it seemed that repulse of the allies was certain: at another, Soult saw the veterans in whom he trusted hurled down in wild confusion from the heights their gallantry had won. But Hill had the quality of selfrestraint. Unlike Picton, who would always turn a feint into a real attack, he held fast to his instructions unless influenced by unforeseen circumstances. He drove the enemy out of the exterior works, forcing them behind the old city walls, but there he halted. He had been ordered not to assail the second line.

Still hot from the fluctuating fortunes of the combat, next morning Soult was ready to renew the battle. Wellington held back for another day; for one thing, he wished to discuss the situation with Hill. And that day brought wise reflection to the French marshal. Suchet had not come to his succour, and he could not afford to be shut up in Toulouse. With his usual decision he arranged one of his masterly retreats. The morning of the 12th saw Toulouse evacuated, and further bloodshed was happily spared on that side of the battle-ground.

6

The Peninsular War came to an end. The Irishman who had triumphantly carried the British colours from Torres Vedras to Toulouse was rewarded with a dukedom, and five of his chief captains were raised to the peerage. Sir Rowland became Lord Hill of Almarez and Hawkstone. Eager to see his family and Shropshire, he was in England before the end of May. The nation was wildly enthusiastic over the return of the Peninsular heroes, and Wellington's "right-hand man" was overwhelmed with honours and congratulations. Swords were presented to him and Beresford at a great gathering in the Guildhall. He was cheered by excited mobs whenever he was recognised in the streets. His journey to Shrewsbury was a triumphal progress, and at Shrewsbury all Shropshire seemed to have mustered. His modesty was sorely tried, for he was the most diffident of men, and he only forgot his shyness in the heat and bustle of battle.

He had a sad experience of hand-shaking at the London Guildhall, but it was nothing to what he went through when presented with the freedom of his county capital. He declared that he ran away for the first time in his life. "I never fled from the fury of my enemies, but now I have been obliged to do so from the kindness of my friends." His young nephew, who had been taken to breakfast with him on his return by his venerable and reverend uncle and namesake, has an interesting recollection of the conversation.

The spoils of Vittoria were mentioned, which, as he says, seemed odd, seeing that the general prided himself on a china drinking-cup being the only article of booty he had carried off. It appeared, however, that that was not quite the case, for after Vittoria his servant, jealously catering for him, had transferred an ample provision of hams and tongues from King Joseph's carriage to Sir Rowland's—a striking contrast between the conduct of the English general and that of Soult, whose acquaintance he made subsequently at the Queen's coronation.

On that occasion the French marshal had showed his ready wit by paying Wellington a graceful compliment. In the hall of Apsley House he was arrested by Canova's statue of Napoleon, and expressed his admiration. The Duke remarked that it always struck him that the globe in the Emperor's hand was too small for the figure. "*C'est voyez vous, Duc que L'Anglèterre n'y est pas comprise*," was the answer, worthy of Talleyrand. Soult was again at Apsley House during the Exhibition of 1851, when his host, who was always outspoken, hit him hard with a stinging and less courtly repartee. The marshal, who was being shown the collection of paintings, remarked on the absence of important Spanish paintings. By the way, the rich loot he had gathered in Spain must have made him fastidious. "*Ah, Monsieur*," said the Duke, "*Je vous ai suivi*"

A model squire and county magistrate was spoiled when Hill took to soldiering. Self-condemned to celibacy, no man was more inclined to domestic life, and except at the calls of duty and glory it was hard to tempt him from his family circle. Few soldiers of his rank and modest means have been so indifferent to lucrative promotion. On five occasions at least he declined high appointments. Once after the battle of Toulouse; now when he was offered the command in Scotland; again when he had the refusal of the command in India; and twice when the

Mastership of the Ordnance was pressed upon him.

Now, like a boy broken loose from school, he was set upon enjoying himself. He took his favourite sister to London in spring, intending to have a good time. *Dis aliter visum*. He had engaged a box for an evening at the opera. In the afternoon he had a summons to Downing Street. News had come that Napoleon was on the march for Brussels. On the frontier the Crown Prince of the Netherlands was on guard with a motley corps of Dutch and Belgians, English and Germans. It was feared that his youth and impetuosity might hurry him into premature action; nor were the apprehensions groundless, as was shown when he sacrificed a regiment at Waterloo. Hill was charged with the delicate mission of moderating his ardour, for the Prince was known to hold him in high regard.

In that mission he succeeded, but in three days he was superseded by Wellington, who had hurried to Brussels from Vienna. Then the Duke made rapid preparations to meet the impending attack. His mixed army was in two corps. The first, under the Prince of Orange, touched the Prussians on its left flank, extending westwards to Enghien. There Hill took up the line of defence, and his troops were stationed from Alt to Audenarde. He had his headquarters at Grammont. By remarkable coincidences he was again opposed to his old antagonist, Girard of Arroyo Molinos, and was within gunshot of the *château* of the Prince D'Aremberg, who had been taken in the action and sent a prisoner to Shrewsbury, to be made welcome by Hill's Shropshire neighbours.

Wellington was persuaded that Napoleon must assail him on the right, and his frequent and curt despatches to Hill indicate his grave preoccupation. Hence to Hill were assigned some of the staunchest battalions in an unreliable army. Consequently it was the other corps which was engaged at Quatre Bras, and bore the long and stubborn brunt at Waterloo, when the French directed the first of their indefatigable onsets on our left and centre. As the battle shifted towards the left, he gradually brought up his eager battalions and struck in at the crisis with crashing effect

The old chief, who had his quarters at Grammont, was not present at the Brussels ball. On the 16th he had orders from the Duke to move up towards the centre and to charge Prince Frederick of the Netherlands with guarding the extreme right. That night he passed in a little house on the road from Brussels to St. Jean. The evening found his corps posted to the right of the Nivelle road. He took his own stand on an eminence, whence he could command the movements on either side. He kept his station there amid showers of shot and shell, merely descending to restore the battle where any part of his line seemed to waver.

The moment came which he had foreseen, when the Emperor was to make his last desperate effort. He looked anxiously on the stately advance of the Old Guard in solid phalanx. As he saw the head of the column shattered by the fire of the allied guns, he galloped down to put himself at the head of his light Brigade, which had been sheltering behind the brow of a lower hill. That charge of his was decisive. It was such a *mêlée* as will seldom be seen again, in these days of smokeless powder and long ranges. "Volleys at half pistol-shot"—as a staff officer describes it—were followed by hand-to-hand fighting and heroic single combats. It was then that Napoleon dropped his glass, with the despairing exclamation, "*Mon Dieu, ils sont mêlés.*" Adams, the brigadier, was struck down, and Colonel Seaton, afterwards Lord Colborne, took his place. Hill had his horse shot under him—the charger had five bullets through the body.

It was so much a case of every man for himself that for half-an-hour the general was scarcely missed. He had not actually been ridden over, like Blücher; he escaped with severe bruises, and when he reappeared the survivors of his staff welcomed him with heartfelt joy. When he fell, he was riding alone: for all his staff had been killed, wounded, or scattered. Maitland's Guards and Seaton's Light Brigade bivouacked on the ground, when sheer exhaustion had compelled them to relinquish the pursuit, while the Prussians, swinging round on the enemy's flank and rear, were following up the chase, sabring relentlessly. Hill, kept awake by the pain of his bruises, passed a sleepless night in the cottage he had occupied on the previous evening, listening to the moans of the wounded who had been carried back, and to the shrieks of the sufferers under the knives of the surgeons.

Three of his brothers had been in the field, and two had been taken to Brussels badly hurt. Next day, with Wellington, he visited Blücher. Neither of the veterans seems to have been much shaken by their falls, for, as Hill wrote to his sister, they found "the old marshal amusing himself with Buonaparte's hat, star, and personal baggage, which with his carriage had been taken by the Prussian cavalry."

Waterloo saw the close of Hill's active career. He took over the French posts around Paris when they were surrendered. At the end of the year he shifted his command to Cambray, whence he was summoned to London on disagreeable business. When Wellington heard that his old friend had suffered serious pecuniary losses, he wrote immediately:

> I have a large sum of money entirely at my command, and I assure you that I could not apply it in a manner more satisfactory to me than in accommodating you, my dear Hill, to whom I am under so many obligations.

The generous offer was warmly acknowledged, but gratefully declined. On his return to Cambray he had a severe illness. "Nothing," he wrote, "could be kinder than the behaviour of the Duke," who begged him to come to his house in Paris for change of scene. While at Cambray he again kept hounds for the amusement of his officers, but his own favourite pursuit was boar-hunting, and he had one narrow escape. The boar charged home: the onlookers were in alarm, but the old sportsman's nerve was firm as ever. Armed only with a short spear, he calmly stood the rush. A thrust in the face turned the charge, and a second went home to the heart Wellington sent him another spear when he heard of the exploit.

On the evacuation of France he left the Continent for the last time. There was a remarkable family gathering at Hawkstone, where the patriarchal father of the household saw himself surrounded by six sons and four daughters. Four of the sons, as by miracles, had escaped the perils of the war. Only the eldest of the family was missing. In his quiet Shropshire home the old soldier passed twelve uneventful years, still walking out with his gun or following the hounds, and interesting himself in the farmyard and garden. His kindness to his poor neighbours was unfailing; he was munificent in unobtrnsive charity, and it is said that when he bestowed a kindness he was far more embarrassed than the recipient

Nor was he to be tempted away by the tenders of honourable and lucrative posts. It was then he declined the Indian command and the Master-Generalship of the Ordnance. The latter would have made a sojourn in London compulsory, and he hated city life. But circumstances alter resolutions, and in 1828 he could not resist the offer of the blue ribbon of the army, which Wellington had honoured in the wearing. In that year the Duke consented to charge himself with the destinies of the country, and as Prime Minister he invited Hill to replace him at the Horse Guards. He answered immediately, and with his habitual promptitude of action brought his own letter to London.

All I shall say at present is that I accept the flattering offer with pride and gratitude, and that it shall ever be my anxious study to fulfil your Grace's expectations and wishes, which I trust I shall be enabled to do by unremitting attention to my duties.

He kept his word: he renounced pleasures for duty: he made his home in town, and thenceforth his visits to Shropshire were few and far between, except when health made change of air imperative. The part of his duties he disliked the most was rejecting incessant applications. The widows of officers besieged his door; the ladies were voluble, and it was not in his nature to listen to them with anything but kindly sympathy. When asked how he managed to get rid of these supplicants, he answered with a twinkle in his eye that he received them in a room with a single chair, and insisted on their being seated.

"Then they are sorry to see me standing, so they do not stay very long."

Both George IV. and his brother were exceedingly gracious, but the old soldier had less hesitation in dealing with the monarchs when they hinted at patting pressure on his conscience. Twice with King William, though he had strong personal regard for him, he gave unmistakable proof of his independence and straightforwardness; and it is but fair to say that His Sailor Majesty respected him all the more. The first occasion was when the king said with his seamanlike bluntness that he was "positively decided" that a certain officer should be promoted. Hill, couching his refusal in respectful terms, was as positively decided he should not; and when the king gave way, he sent straight for the officer, to report the interview and explain his reasons.

The second was when he was urged to vote in the Lords for the Reform Bill being remitted to Committee. "I said that, if I were to act contrary to my conscientious feelings and my known declarations, I should so lower myself in the eyes of the world and the army that I should not be able to render service to His Majesty or the country. The king said he could understand my feelings, and that everyone had a right to have his own: he had his." A very amenable man he was, but no one stood more stiffly on his rights or on the dignity of the office he safeguarded for his successors. In his diaries there is one significant note.

Came to town to see the king on the subject of orders issued without my knowledge. The interview was satisfactory, and I am inclined to think nothing of the sort will in future occur.

Firm as he was where a principle was involved, he had the old chivalrous loyalty. After his death a purse was found, with a crown piece enclosed in paper. On the paper was written:

> This crown was won by Lord Hill from His Majesty, King William IV., at Windsor Castle. I will do my best to preserve *it* for him.—H.

He had an anxious time when political ferment ran high and rioters were abroad. He made his old military chief the confidant of his troubles and his counsellor. And Wellington wrote in his off-hand style:

> Never mind, Hill: you have enough to satisfy your conscience. Everybody knows the army under your charge has saved the country.

His old age was green, but strength was failing: Peel's accession to power gave him a fresh lease of encouragement, and perhaps he held to office too long. He kept on at the routine of work in spite of a growing sense of exhaustion, but nature would not be denied, and the end came in the summer of 1842, when he sent in his resignation. It was accepted with flattering expressions of reluctance, and he was touched and gratified by an autograph letter from the young Queen. He was created a viscount when he took leave of the Horse Guards, and compliments, condolences, or congratulations showered in upon him from many old comrades.

He only survived his resignation for a few months, and on the 10th December 1842 passed peacefully away. He had lost the years of quiet rustication he had looked forward to, and worn himself out in the service of his country. We read only half his character in the portrait that has been bequeathed us. The face is that of a benevolent divine, rather than of the general who had led armies in the field and never spared himself in the hottest of the battle. We see nothing of the firmness that never failed in emergency, of the iron determination that held to the hill at Talavera, or of the fiery dash that swept all before it on that wild autumn morning at Arroyo Molinos.

ALSO FROM LEONAUR
AVAILABLE IN SOFTCOVER OR HARDCOVER WITH DUST JACKET

OFFICERS & GENTLEMEN by *Peter Hawker & William Graham*—Two Accounts of British Officers During the Peninsula War: Officer of Light Dragoons by Peter Hawker & Campaign in Portugal and Spain by William Graham.

THE WALCHEREN EXPEDITION by *Anonymous*—The Experiences of a British Officer of the 81st Regt. During the Campaign in the Low Countries of 1809.

LADIES OF WATERLOO by *Charlotte A. Eaton, Magdalene de Lancey & Juana Smith*—The Experiences of Three Women During the Campaign of 1815: Waterloo Days by Charlotte A. Eaton, A Week at Waterloo by Magdalene de Lancey & Juana's Story by Juana Smith.

JOURNAL OF AN OFFICER IN THE KING'S GERMAN LEGION by *John Frederick Hering*—Recollections of Campaigning During the Napoleonic Wars.

JOURNAL OF AN ARMY SURGEON IN THE PENINSULAR WAR by *Charles Boutflower*—The Recollections of a British Army Medical Man on Campaign During the Napoleonic Wars.

ON CAMPAIGN WITH MOORE AND WELLINGTON by *Anthony Hamilton*—The Experiences of a Soldier of the 43rd Regiment During the Peninsular War.

THE ROAD TO AUSTERLITZ by *R. G. Burton*—Napoleon's Campaign of 1805.

SOLDIERS OF NAPOLEON by *A. J. Doisy De Villargennes & Arthur Chuquet*—The Experiences of the Men of the French First Empire: Under the Eagles by A. J. Doisy De Villargennes & Voices of 1812 by Arthur Chuquet.

INVASION OF FRANCE, 1814 by *F. W. O. Maycock*—The Final Battles of the Napoleonic First Empire.

LEIPZIG—A CONFLICT OF TITANS by *Frederic Shoberl*—A Personal Experience of the 'Battle of the Nations' During the Napoleonic Wars, October 14th-19th, 1813.

SLASHERS by *Charles Cadell*—The Campaigns of the 28th Regiment of Foot During the Napoleonic Wars by a Serving Officer.

BATTLE IMPERIAL by *Charles William Vane*—The Campaigns in Germany & France for the Defeat of Napoleon 1813-1814.

SWIFT & BOLD by *Gibbes Rigaud*—The 60th Rifles During the Peninsula War.

AVAILABLE ONLINE AT **www.leonaur.com**
AND FROM ALL GOOD BOOK STORES

ALSO FROM LEONAUR
AVAILABLE IN SOFTCOVER OR HARDCOVER WITH DUST JACKET

THE FALL OF THE MOGHUL EMPIRE OF HINDUSTAN by H. G. Keene—By the beginning of the nineteenth century, as British and Indian armies under Lake and Wellesley dominated the scene, a little over half a century of conflict brought the Moghul Empire to its knees.

LADY SALE'S AFGHANISTAN by Florentia Sale—An Indomitable Victorian Lady's Account of the Retreat from Kabul During the First Afghan War.

THE CAMPAIGN OF MAGENTA AND SOLFERINO 1859 by Harold Carmichael Wylly—The Decisive Conflict for the Unification of Italy.

FRENCH'S CAVALRY CAMPAIGN by J. G. Maydon—A Special Correspondent's View of British Army Mounted Troops During the Boer War.

CAVALRY AT WATERLOO by Sir Evelyn Wood—British Mounted Troops During the Campaign of 1815.

THE SUBALTERN by George Robert Gleig—The Experiences of an Officer of the 85th Light Infantry During the Peninsular War.

NAPOLEON AT BAY, 1814 by F. Loraine Petre—The Campaigns to the Fall of the First Empire.

NAPOLEON AND THE CAMPAIGN OF 1806 by Colonel Vachée—The Napoleonic Method of Organisation and Command to the Battles of Jena & Auerstädt.

THE COMPLETE ADVENTURES IN THE CONNAUGHT RANGERS by William Grattan—The 88th Regiment during the Napoleonic Wars by a Serving Officer.

BUGLER AND OFFICER OF THE RIFLES by William Green & Harry Smith—With the 95th (Rifles) during the Peninsular & Waterloo Campaigns of the Napoleonic Wars.

NAPOLEONIC WAR STORIES by Sir Arthur Quiller-Couch—Tales of soldiers, spies, battles & sieges from the Peninsular & Waterloo campaingns.

CAPTAIN OF THE 95TH (RIFLES) by Jonathan Leach—An officer of Wellington's sharpshooters during the Peninsular, South of France and Waterloo campaigns of the Napoleonic wars.

RIFLEMAN COSTELLO by Edward Costello—The adventures of a soldier of the 95th (Rifles) in the Peninsular & Waterloo Campaigns of the Napoleonic wars.

AVAILABLE ONLINE AT www.leonaur.com
AND FROM ALL GOOD BOOK STORES

www.ingramcontent.com/pod-product-compliance
Lightning Source LLC
Chambersburg PA
CBHW031616160426
43196CB00006B/154